MODERN
VOLLEYBALL

Modern Volleyball

For Teacher, Coach and Player

by

K. Nicholls, B.Ed., M.A.,

*(Staff Coach–English Volleyball Association; F.I.V.B. Coach
England & Great Britain international player 1967–)*

Henry Kimpton Publishers
London 1973

Keith Nicholls.

M.A. Physical Education Leeds University 1971
B.Ed (Hons) London 1969
Dip.P.E.St.Mary's College of Education 1968.

Staff Coach of the English Volleyball Association.
Tutor Loughborough Summer School 1971 & 1972.

Has staffed courses for teachers, youth leaders etc for the Central Council
of Physical Recreation, Local Authorities and other bodies.

Has played for Great Britain and England since 1967. Has lectured at
the National Volleyball Coaches Conference in 1970 and 1971. Was the
coach of St.Mary's College Volleyball Club from 1965-69 one of the top
three clubs in the country during that period. Four of the players he
introduced to the game at the college had trials for the England team and
three are current internationals. Four girls from the ladies team at the
college, also coached by him, were members of the National Squad.

Has been co-editor of Volleyball magazine since its foundation in 1969
and has written numerous articles on coaching and teaching volleyball since
that time. He has travelled extensively in Europe watching top teams and
playing in the major tournaments. He has maintained close links with
coaches in Eastern and Western Europe as well as in Japan. He has
lectured in Physical Education at St. Mary's College of Education, Twickenham, Middx., and is now lecturer in Physical Education at Bristol Polytechnic.

A/ 796.32

Typesetting by Print Origination, Liverpool, England
Printed and Bound by Biddles Ltd, Guildford, Surrey.

FOREWORD

Volleyball is the finest game in the world. It has great appeal to people of all ages, both sexes, all nationalities and of all physical abilities. It can be played indoors or out and the equipment required is simple and cheap. It can be enjoyed as a recreational activity on the beach and is played with fantastic skill, agility and courage in the Olympic Games.

There is an enormous amount in this book. There are sections for everyone, layman, pupil, teacher, player and coach. It will take beginners a long way towards top class volleyball and will make the experienced think again.

The enthusiast's mission is destined to succeed. It is only a matter of time before volleyball becomes the supreme game throughout the world. If Mr. Nicholl's book brings closer that day he will be delighted, for he is a real enthusiast. I am sure it will.

Mr. Nicholl's has already made a significant contribution to the development of volleyball in Britain as a Staff Coach and a senior member of the national team. This book is a further significant contribution. I am sure that many who read this book will be inspired to follow in his footsteps.

I have great pleasure in writing this foreword to a most valuable contribution to the literature of volleyball.

N.H.Dingle.
Chairman English Volleyball Association.

ACKNOWLEDGMENTS

The game of volleyball has been a special interest of mine since I was introduced to it whilst a student at St Mary's College of Education, Twickenham. I would like to pay a special tribute to all those who have helped me develop my interest in volleyball and in particular to the following members of St Mary's College Volleyball Club for their encouragement and assistance during my early years as a coach; Austin Atkinson, Pete Bibby, Kevin Clarke, Pete Evans, Mick Forth, Roy Groves, Mick Hibbert, Pete Hoare, Nick Keeley and Tommy Quayle.

I would like to thank the following persons who have all played a part in the preparation of this book;

*G Bell and Sons for permission to reproduce Fig 202 p 195 from Acquiring Ball Skill: a psychological interpretation, H T A Whiting (1970)

Czechoslovakian News Agency for supplying photographs

Yasutaka Matsudaira and the Japan Volleyball Association for supplying photographs and bulletins

Chief Petty Officer Terry Weeks of the Royal Navy Physical Training School Portsmouth for assistance with the photography

Dr H T A Whiting of Leeds University Physical Education Department for guidance and assistance throughout the whole project

and last but certainly not least my wife Judith without whose encouragement, patience and considerable assistance the book would not have been completed.

K. NICHOLLS, B.Ed., M.A.,

CONTENTS

SIGNS USED IN DIAGRAMS

◯	player
◯̸	direction player is facing
⊕	coach
⋀	blocker
⟶	path of player
- - ⟶	path of ball
•	base

PREFACE

A wealth of books are available in many languages on the playing and teaching of a whole range of sports. These vary from the anecdotal and interesting reminiscences of leading players, to intricate stroke analyses of for example the game of golf. The number of such books which could really be classified as well-devised coaching texts is much more limited. This is particularly true in the case of *Vo'leyball* where a number of attempts have been made to contribute material designed to inform and thus improve coaching, but to date, a comprehensive text does not seem to have been produced.

In this volleyball coaching text, Keith Nicholls brings to bear considerable practical expertise and theoretical training in providing not only an analysis of the basic techniques and strategies of the game, but insight into the problems of both player and coach. In this way, the book fills a worldwide need for an authorative manual on modern *Volleyball.*

In this the first major study of the modern game to be written in the English language, the author—an international player and successful coach—makes an exhaustive study of the tactics and techniques currently in use by the worlds' best players and teams. With chapters on every aspect of the game, this book represents an A-Z of volleyball.

The aim of the author was to write a book about the modern game which was of sufficient depth to provide the background knowledge which hitherto had not been available to coaches, teachers and players in general. This was precipitated to some extent by the radical changes in technique, tactics and rule interpretations which followed on the inclusion of volleyball in the modern Olympic programme in 1964. The game of volleyball today would hardly be recognised by William Morgan the originator of the game. Nevertheless, after eight years of progressive changes, the game has now settled down sufficiently well for a comprehensive text to be written. This book documents the changes that have taken place and suggests proven ways of teaching the game. As such, it will become the standard volleyball work throughout the world for many years to come.

For the complete beginner, the first two chapters provide an outline history of the game, the equipment to be used and how a start might be made.

Chapter 4—primarily addressed to teachers and coaches—considers each technique in depth, suggests progressive steps in their teaching, points out the major faults that occur and ways in which they might be corrected. An overall method of introducing volleyball to classes of children using small game situations and the normal gymnasium equipment is dealt with in chapter 3.

Players will find the theoretical analysis of each technique extremely useful and the sections giving 'hints to players', which are based on the authors' own international experience, provide much valuable advice on achieving maximum performance.

Chapter 5 on the tactics of the game, examines all the systems for covering attacks and against the major forms of attack in use today. The advantages and disadvantages of each system are given together with methods of teaching tactical formations and of linking them together to provide an overall system for the team.

Both players and coaches will find Chapter 6 on 'training for volleyball' of particular interest. Several hundred advanced training practices are provided for each of the techniques. These practices will be most useful in training the better player. Chapter 9 reviews the latest knowledge on methods of improving human performance in volleyball. Examples of training schedules specially designed for volleyball players are given.

Chapter 7 on the role of the coach in volleyball, looks at all the duties of the coach both before and during the game. The rules governing match procedure, times-out and substitutions and their relevance to the coach are discussed. At a theoretical level, the implications of recent psychological research in human motor performance are developed in relation to the coaching of volleyball.

Further chapters deal with *officiating*—in which the major rules and game situations are discussed in the light of current rule interpretations - and with the organising of tournaments and competitions.

In addition to his experience as an international player and member of the national coaching panel, the author has considerable background knowledge in the theory of skill acquisition having completed a B.Ed. degree of the University of London and an M.A. degree of the University of Leeds. In being able to put himself into the position of the player who is having difficulty and in being able to appreciate the problems which are involved in progressing along the continuum from unskilled to skilled, he overcomes one of the major difficulties facing the experienced player who without much knowledge attempts to use his coaching ideas on his own present expertise.

Leeds April, 1972.   H.T.A. WHITING
                                                            series editor.

1 VOLLEYBALL – A WORLD GAME

From a humble beginning as a recreational activity for overweight businessmen in an American Y.M.C.A. in 1896, to the most popular Olympic sport, that is the success of volleyball.

In 1970 a survey undertaken on behalf of the International Olympic Committee into the spread of the Olympic sports throughout the world, showed that volleyball and basketball with 65 million registered players each, were more popular than athletics, swimming and football combined (Table I).

Table I

CLASSIFICATION OF OLYMPIC SPORTS

Basketball	65 million players	127	Federations
Volleyball	65 million players	110	,,
Football	25,800,000 ,,	135	,,
Shooting	25,500,000 ,,	94	,,
Athletics	19,500,000 ,,	143	,,
Swimming	10,500,000 ,,	98	,,
Skiing	8,000,000 ,,	47	,,
Judo	6,000,000 ,,	78	,,

Volleyball was invented by William J. Morgan, Physical Director of the Y.M.C.A. in Holyoke, Massachussetts in 1896. For no known reason the game was originally known as minonette.

Impressed with the increasing popularity of basketball Morgan decided that his students might have just as much fun in playing a ball over a net. For a net he used a lawn tennis net spread across an indoor court and, for a ball he used a basketball bladder since it was light and could be played on the hands without injury.

Despite a slow start the game spread through the Y.M.C.A. movement to other major Massachussets and New England cities. It was at Springfield that a Dr. T.A. Halstead, after watching the game, suggested that its name be changed to volleyball since the basic idea of play was to volley the ball back and forth over the net.

Volleyball eventually spread outdoors and became a highly popular game at summer resorts and playgrounds. In 1900, Canada became the first foreign country to adopt the game.

The Y.M.C.A. movement helped to spread the game throughout the world and it was first played in Cuba in 1905, Puerto Rico 1909, Uruguay 1912, the Philippines 1910, China 1913 and Japan 1917.

Volleyball was a very popular recreation with U.S. troops stationed abroad during the two world wars and the sight of several million servicemen playing the game during off duty periods gave added impetus to the development of the game.

Strangely enough the game did not develop as quickly on mainland Europe. Only three European countries, France, Czechoslovakia and Poland had national associations before the second world war. Although these countries had considered trying to form an international volleyball associ- ation the outbreak of war forced them to shelve the idea.

The first post-war international match in Europe took place in Paris between France and Czechoslovakia. At informal talks between represent- atives of the three countries, it was agreed that France should prepare a special foundation congress for a world association. Fourteen national associations from all corners of the world sent representatives to this meeting in Paris in April 1947. As a result the International Volleyball Federation (I.V.B.F.) was set up with its headquarters in Paris. Many other countries were quick to affiliate to this body and at the latest count there were 110 affiliated national associations.

In 1964 the game gained Olympic recognition with its inclusion in the Tokyo Games and it has continued to enjoy this status ever since. It is interesting to note that it is the only team game with competitions for men and women in the Olympic programme.

There are many international volleyball championships in addition to the Olympic Games. World Championships, European, Pan-American, Pan-Asian, Pan-African, World University championships are competed for regularly.

In many European countries, especially those in Eastern Europe, volleyball ranks high as a spectator sport. In Western Europe it is particularly popular in Belgium and Holland. The Japanese have taken to volleyball in a big way and it receives regular coverage on television. Each year the Japanese teams undertake a world tour playing the top countries as well as giving exhibition games in countries where the game is in its infancy.

With the exception of Japan the top teams in the world today are all East European. The top four countries, Russia, East Germany, Czechoslovakia, and Bulgaria have played a game of musical chairs since 1964 with continual changes in their rankings at the major championships.

The rest of the European countries are not far behind and always offer a strong challenge. In Asia, as well as Japan, both North and South Korea are outstanding in world volleyball. As is to be expected the Asian countries find that their physique is a limiting factor in international competition. The Japanese have made considerable efforts to find and develop taller and stronger players with much success.

On the otherside of the world several new powers in volleyball are emerging. Cuba, Brazil, Argentina and Uruguay are improving rapidly. Throughout the world the game is on the verge of a new phase of development. In Africa new national associations are being formed each year; in Europe the West European countries are working extremely hard to catch up their East European rivals; in Asia the Japanese are passing on the benefits of their experience in world volleyball to coaches in neighbouring countries.

Olympic Games 1972 Munich

Men		Women	
1	Japan	1	Russia
2	East Germany	2	Japan
3	Russia	3	North Korea
4	Bulgaria	4	South Korea
5	Rumania	5	Hungary
6	Czechoslovakia	6	Cuba
7	South Korea	7	Czechoslovakia
8	Brazil	8	West Germany
9	Poland		
10	Cuba		
11	West Germany		
12	Tunisia		

Volleyball although strongly promoted by the Y.M.C.A. in 1914, did not catch on in Britain until after the 2nd World War. Many of the Polish ex-servicemen who took up residence in Britain at this time continued to play volleyball through their Polish clubs in many of the major towns in England. Inter-club matches and a national Polish Club Championship helped

3

to spread the game throughout the country. In 1955 the Amateur Volleyball Association of Great Britain and Northern Ireland was formed to organise and promote the game.

A further milestone was reached when the International Volleyball Federation at their Congress in Sofia 1970 accepted the Scottish Volleyball Association's application for membership. In 1971 the English Volleyball Association was formed from the old A.V.A. A separate body—the British Volleyball Federation—is concerned with the selection and training of the British team for the Olympic Games.

Volleyball has proved to be an ideal game for schools. The recent formation of the English Schools (E.S.V.A.) and the Scottish Schools associations are evidence of the growing popularity of the game. On the continent the game is firmly established as a major school sport and the great strength of these countries at adult level stems from the good grounding their players get at school.

Schoolboys find the game very exciting and challenging. The powerful action of the smash and the daring of the recovery dives and rolls are particularly appealing to them. For girls, volleyball is a long overdue alternative to the outdoor winter games of netball and hockey. Many girls are alienated against physical activity because they dislike playing games out-doors in the winter cold. Until now there has been no alternative indoor game for girls. The increasing number of girls' schools affiliating to the Schools' Associations and taking part in the national championships confirms this view.

What is it that makes volleyball such a universally popular game?
Volleyball is a game that can be played by all ages and both sexes indoors and outdoors. It can be highly competitive requiring a high level of fitness, agility and co-ordination or, it can be a relaxing and highly enjoyable recreation.

Played competitively the game requires concentration, quick thinking and a great deal of movement. The speed of the game means that players must be thinking one moment about attack and the next about defence. They must be concentrating all the time, if they are to keep up with play. Volleyball is an all action game with none of the players acting as involuntary spectators for part of the game as in other team games such as football, hockey and netball.

As the game is played the best of three or five sets it is possible to win despite playing badly for a particular period of the game. In many sports mistakes made at the beginning of the game can have a disastrous effect on the rest of the game.

For the coach the game can be as mentally demanding as chess. Tactical formations, moves, substitutions, use of time-outs and team line-ups all have so many variations and have an effect on the quality and result of the game.

The rotation rules ensure that every player plays in every position and that

4

outstanding players in the front or back court cannot dominate the game all the time. The limitations imposed by the rules on consecutive plays of the ball mean that a player must make his shot as good as possible because he will not have a second chance to play it as in most other team games.

For the spectator the game is fast and full of contrasting action, from the power of the smash to the agile recovery shots in back court. The small playing area concentrates the action so that spectators have a clear view of the game all the time.

Although there is no time limit the most one sided of games lasts at least forty minutes. At the other end of the scale the longest international match on record took place on the 18th October 1964, during the Olympic Games, between the U.S.S.R. and Czechoslovakia lasting 3 hours and 2 minutes!

Whether you want a game that will be physically taxing or a game that will be relaxing, volleyball is that game.

How do we play volleyball?

A volleyball team consists of six players and two teams are separated by a net across a court which is 18m x 9m. The object of the game is to make the ball land in the opponents' court, force them to mishandle the ball or, return it across the net so that it lands out of court. Each team is allowed to play the ball up to three times on their side of the court before it is returned over the net. The ball may be struck by any part of the body above the waist provided that it does not come to rest. When a ball rests momentarily between the arms or hands of a player the ball is said to be carried and this is illegal. The ball must be cleanly played. If it is lifted or pushed, it is also considered to be held.

The six players on court are placed three at the front of the court and three at the back. To identify them they are numbered according to the position they are playing at the time of service. The player in the right rear position is number 1, the player immediately in front of him in front court is number 2 and the sequence follows anti-clockwise (Fig. 1). It must be noted that the number on each player's shirt serves to identify him for purposes of substitutions etc. His court number will vary with each rotation and these numbers are used mainly to make it easier when discussing line-up and tactical formations.

When the team regains the service all the players rotate one position clockwise so that each person will move around the court playing each position in turn. Once the serve has been made any player may move to any position on court and play the ball. There is one limitation on the type of shot that may be played in certain situations. The back court players, numbers one, six and five, may not play the ball across the net in the attack

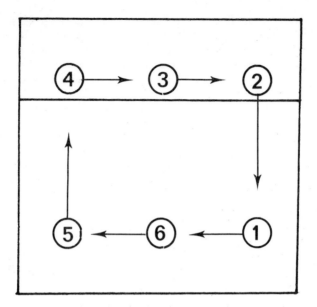

Fig. 1   Numbering and Rotation of Players

zone when the ball is above net height. This ensures that once players have rotated into the back court they cannot be used as attacking players.

The player in position *one* serves the ball across the net and into the opponents' court. If it hits the net or, lands out of court service is lost to the other side who rotate one position clockwise before serving.

After service the ball is received on the combined forearms of the player. This is the 'dig' pass. The object of this pass is to control the ball so that it rebounds high and forwards to a player in the centre front court. This player then plays the ball with both hands when it is above his head, the volley pass; high to the side of the front court. The player in this position then jumps as high as he can and 'smashes' the ball down into the other court. The opponents try to prevent the ball from passing over the net by placing a wall of hands in the path of the ball to 'block' its passage across the net. If the ball passes over the net the ball is then played with a dig pass and a counter attack is set up. The ball may be played back across the net on the first or second touch if it is tactically better to attack quickly.

At the completion of the rally, point or service is awarded. If the winners of the rally served the ball they gain a point, if they did not serve the ball they win the right to serve the next ball. Points can only be scored by the serving side. The service changes at 'side-out'.

A set is won when one side has reached a minimum of fifteen points with at least a two point lead e.g. 15:13, 16:14. Games are played the best of three or five sets.

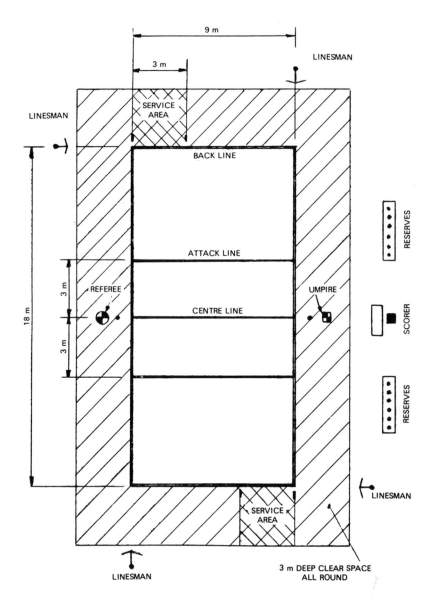

Fig. 2   The Volleyball court

CHAPTER 2

MAKING A START

The court

Volleyball is played on a court which measures 18 metres by 9 metres, the English measurements are 59 feet by 29 feet 6 inches.

The court is divided into two by a net at a height of 2m 43cm for men and 2m 24cm for women, and boys under sixteen. On the floor directly below the net is a line 9m long by 5cm wide which marks the limit of each half (Fig. 2).

Three metres from this centre line, in each half, is the attack line. A player who is playing in one of the three back court positions at the time of service may not play the ball across the net when it is above net height and he is within the area between the attack line and the net, unless he plays the ball whilst he is in the air, having taken off from behind this line.

The only other court markings are the short lines limiting the service area. This is marked in each half by two lines 15cm long and 5cm wide, drawn 20cm from the perpendicular to the end line. One line is along the continuation of the right hand side line and the other 3m to the left of the right hand side line. The server must serve in this three metres wide channel. There is no limitation on the distance the server may stand behind the base line to serve providing that he serves within this channel.

The posts

The posts should be situated one metre from the side line. This is to prevent injuries caused by players tripping over or bumping into them during the game. The posts should fit into sockets in the floor or, attach to the walls of the sports hall or gymnasium if they are one metre from the sideline. Posts with bases that rest on the floor and are supported by counterweights should *never* be purchased as they are easy to topple and players can be injured. The players in the two front court wing positions, 2 and 4, could also trip over them in the excitement of the game.

When choosing posts make sure that the following points are satisfied;

i) The posts are quick and easy to erect.

ii) The height of the net can be varied and this procedure is both quick and accurate.

iii) There is an effective means of tensioning the head and bottom lines of the net.

iv) Provision is made for tying the sides of the net to the posts so that it can be fully stretched.

The enterprising teacher or coach will find it very easy and much cheaper to make his own posts. The basic material consists of two metal tubes of diameters such that one will fit inside the other. The outer tube, about four feet long, has rings welded to it on one side so that the net can be firmly attached to it with adjustable shackles. The inner post inserted in a floor socket (which can be bought from equipment manufacturers) acts as the upright. The height of the net, which is attached to the outer tube, is varied by inserting pins into holes which are drilled through both tubes, at varying heights above the floor.

The net

The net is one metre deep and 9m 50cm long. The mesh is 10cm wide and a double thickness of canvas is stitched across the top and bottom of the net. Cables run through these canvas sheaths and attach to the posts. Wooden stretchers should be sewn into canvas sheaths at each end of the net to keep it stretched vertically. The net will project over the side lines and moveable white bands should be attached to it and positioned directly above the sidelines. These help the officials judge which balls are returned across the net from outside the court.

Playing the ball off the net is allowed in the game and is an important aspect of it. The net must be stretched horizontally by lacing the side stretchers to the posts. When the net is taut, the ball will rebound several feet and will be easy to keep in play.

It is false economy to try and save money on nets. A poor net changes the entire character of the game. The best way to store nets is to lace them to the side wall of the store room or hall. This way they do not get tangled or torn.

The ball

The ball is light, weighing 260-280gms with a circumference of 65-67cms. The ball is laceless and is made entirely of leather or is leather covered. The pressure of the ball should be 500 ± 20 gm/cm^2.

The most popular type of ball is the leather covered moulded ball which is

10

a rubber inner covered with leather strips. This combines the long life and constant shape of the all rubber ball with the feel and handling qualities of the leather ball. Balls of this type are used in all the major tournaments. Virtually indestructible and excellent to play with, these balls are the best buy for teachers, coaches and players.

At one time, the all rubber ball was very popular but in recent years the development of the leather covered ball has meant that the money saved by buying rubber balls is not sufficient to make up for their vastly inferior handling qualities. Many children find these balls painful to volley, dig or serve.

The all leather ball is very expensive and loses its shape quite quickly. For top tournament play they are excellent but for every day use they are a luxury that soon becomes a liability.

When teaching volleyball it is essential that there are at least enough balls for one between two. If the expense involved in buying sufficient proper balls is prohibitive a good substitute is the plastic ball. These balls cost very little and can be bought in various sizes and weights which is useful when introducing the game.

It is important that children are given the experience of playing with a proper ball as soon and as often as possible.

Net aerials

These are used in most levels of play to help the referee identify shots which pass across the net outside the sidelines. When the ball contacts the aerial, it has crossed the net outside the sideline.

Since the Munich Olympics, aerials are standard equipment for competitive volleyball.

Footwear

When the game is played competitively players will be jumping up and down hundreds of times each match, changing direction quickly and coming to a stop quickly. This imposes a fair amount of strain on the foot and ankle. A well cushioned and good fitting training shoe will minimise the risk of injury and is the most comfortable footwear for volleyball.

3 INTRODUCING VOLLEYBALL IN SCHOOLS

At what age can volleyball be introduced
In most countries where volleyball is a major sport it is introduced at the age of 9. A specially adapted game for younger players—Mini-volley—is widely played. The rules of this game vary slightly from country to country and efforts are being made to produce an International set of rules.

Mini-volley is played on a court approximately the size of a badminton court by four players on each side. The height of the net for each group varies from country to country. For the youngest children a net of five foot six would be suitable. It must be remembered that at this age the technique of smashing will not have been learnt and that the height that young children are able to jump is limited.

Mini-volley is played widely on the beaches in the Mediterranean countries and commercial organisations have for many years sponsored and promoted this game.

The handling rules are the same as for the full game and in essence it is really what its name implies, a miniature form of volleyball. As such it provides an excellent game for younger players—suited to their physique and ability.

The major problems encountered when introducing the game to younger players are, the size of the ball and court and the height of the net. It is difficult for the young player with smaller hands to volley the full size ball over the distances involved in a full game. A lightweight plastic ball is an excellent substitute for the proper volleyball for children between the ages of 9 and 13. Once they have developed their techniques with the lighter ball they will be able to transfer to the full-size ball quite easily.

Mixed volleyball on small size courts is an excellent game for junior and middle schools. The equipment that is normally found in these schools can be used to introduce the game. Skipping ropes can be stretched between high jump stands or canes, or tied between apparatus to make nets and small courts. At this age the main aim should be enjoyment and participation rather than the development of excellent technique. Over emphasis on the development of good technique will reduce enthusiasm for the game. The secondary school teacher will be able to harness this enthusiasm and develop techniques at the age when their physique will enable them to carry out the full movement.

What techniques do we teach first?

Unlike most other games the techniques of volleyball are each very different. There is little similarity between the techniques of the volley and dig pass, or, between the smash and block. In most other sports there are fewer basic techniques and several variations of each of these techniques.

It is important when introducing volleyball to ensure that the beginner is not faced with too many techniques at one time. The techniques should be progressively introduced as the skill of the performer increases and the character of their game changes.

The techniques of volleyball can be divided into those needed to play the game at its basic level and those which improve the quality of the game. The former consist of the volley pass, the dig pass and the service; the latter, the block and smash. The chief concern of the teacher must be the development of these three basic techniques. Once these have been learned it will be possible to progress to the other more advanced techniques. For, unless the volley and dig passes are accurate it is extremely difficult to learn to smash the ball, and until the smash is quite effective, blocking cannot be taught properly.

How can we introduce volleyball?

If the children are to learn the techniques of volleyball they need to practice them frequently. In an ordinary 6 v 6 game the number of times each child will touch the ball during the game will not be sufficient for maximum development. The level of skill in the early stages of learning volleyball is not high enough for the game to be kept going. Rallies will end quickly and the players become bored. While twelve players are on court playing and therefore practising their techniques the rest of the class are probably sitting out watching.

The best way to introduce the game of volleyball is through the use of small courts and small side games. In this way each player has maximum touches of the ball and the distances over which he must play the ball are more suited to his level of skill. When the volley pass has only to travel ten feet the beginner is able to make a fairly reasonable pass from the technical point of view. However, as soon as he gets into a full game and has to volley the ball over distances two or three times as far he tends to abandon technique in favour of brute force.

Although the use of small side games is recommended they must be used in conjunction with more formal practices and drills. Naturally the technique to be learned must be practised in realistic and competitive situations. It is at this point that small side games on small size courts are most beneficial. At some point in time the children will be wanting to play full size games and their level of skill is such that it can be played without breaking down too quickly or frequently. Specially conditioned and adapted games can be played which will serve to keep the children's interest and assist in their development.

The volleyball lesson

Each lesson should consist of the following:-
- a) Warm up games or practices
- b) Introduction to new technique or, drills for further practice and development of a technique already introduced.
- c) Practice in small game situations of the techniques and tactics introduced so far.
- d) Adapted or conditioned game

Warm-up games

i) Half-court tag;

Appoint three chasers who must try to touch with their right hand the left ankle of the other players. The players may not go outside the boundary lines of the court or pass under the net. When they are properly touched they leave the court. This is an excellent game for improving agility and getting the players used to falling, diving and rolling on the floor—an essential aspect of volleyball.

ii) Dodge ball

Still in half a court and with three chasers, players must prevent a ball hit by the chasers from hitting them on the legs below the knee. The chasers may run with the ball and must hit the ball—not throw it—with the flat of the hand. The players may stop the ball from hitting their legs by jumping out of the way or, by placing their arms in front of their legs so that the ball rebounds off. Once again a game that encourages movement, quick reactions and introduces the hand/wrist action used for the smash or overhead service.

iii) "Mine"

In groups of six, players keep the ball in the air by any legal method for as long as possible. Each time a player moves to play the ball he must shout "MINE". This helps the players get used to calling for the ball as they should do during a game. If they do not call before playing the ball, if they fail to play the ball, or if they pass the ball so that the next person has little chance of playing the ball they must leave the game and volley the ball twenty times against the wall before re-entering the game.

iv) "Keep it up"

In groups of six try to keep the ball in the air for as many consecutive touches as possible. Only legal shots may be played. This is a good game to use to introduce children to the game. Insist that they play the ball with any part of the body above the waist and that they do not play the ball on their palms when it is below head height. As they progress the methods by which they are allowed to keep the ball in the air are limited until scooping lifting and carrying movements are eliminated and only those allowed in volleyball remain. If these limitations are adopted at the outset it inhibits the children. They are more concerned with the type of movement they can make than actually keeping the ball in the air. Competitions between groups to see who can play the ball the most number of times before it hits the floor or an illegal shot is played, will encourage the children to stretch, dive or chase the ball to keep it in play.

The four games described above are examples of games that can be used to start the lesson. They are not the only ones and imaginative teachers will be able to devise other games which will suit the ability of the individual class they are teaching.

Conditioned or adapted games:

a) Quick change volleyball

Divide the class into teams of six with two teams on court and the other teams standing off court on either side of the net. A point is scored for every rally and not just when a side is serving. When one team reaches two points the other team comes off court and is replaced by the reserve team on its side of the net. The team staying on court may serve as soon as it has the ball. This means that the changeover must be quick and that the team coming on must have its court positions sorted out beforehand. To avoid injury during the changeover the team on court must always go off court via the right hand side line and the team coming on via the left side line. Holding the ball during the changeover to prevent a quick service should be penalised by loss of a point.

b) Prisoner volleyball

This is an ideal game when it is possible to have two courts playing at the same time. When a side loses a rally the player who is in position 1 is transferred to the opposing side and plays for them. The game continues until one side has "captured" all the other players. Players are won back when a rally is won. If there are no players to win back then a prisoner is taken.

c) Substitute volleyball
Six players on each side of the net and the substitutes wait on the side line opposite position 1. When a side wins service and rotates positions, the player at number 2 comes off court and the first substitute becomes the new server. When there are a lot of substitutes a second substitution can be made at position 4.

d) Timed volleyball
Teams are formed and play timed matches on a league basis. The length of the matches depends on the number of teams and courts available. To speed things up and to help get definite results in each match, score points on each rally. The side that wins the rally wins the point and the right to serve.

Choosing a drill
When a new technique is being introduced, or, one that has already been introduced is being developed, the choice of drill or practice is important. When selecting a drill or practice the teacher should ask himself the following questions;

i) What does this drill practice? Is this the technique I am trying to develop or introduce?

ii) Is it the best drill for this technique?

iii) Is it suited to the ability level of the children?

iv) Does it involve the maximum number of children?

v) Are the facilities and equipment available to make the drill possible?

vi) Does this practice use any other technique as well? Can the children perform this sufficiently well to make the drill successful?

Once a drill has been selected it must be explained and demonstrated properly to the children, for unless they understand what it is they are trying to learn and how to do the practice they will not make the progress they should.

When the drill does not appear to be successful it is pointless continuing with it. The lack of success may be due to an overestimation of the children's ability on the part of the teacher or simply that the children cannot get involved with the drill. In these cases instead of trying to make it work and wasting valuable teaching time it is advisable to modify it or to switch to another drill. The teacher must continually be evaluating each drill he uses and look for even more effective ways of teaching the techniques.

16

Movement

Movement is the basis of volleyball—movement to play the ball, movement to cover another player, movement to a new tactical position. During a game a player should never be still, his position should be changing according to each new situation created by the movement of the ball and other players. Spectators are off court not on court!

Without movement, volleyball can be a most boring game. As often as possible drills should involve movement to play the ball. In the early stages it must be emphasised to the children that they must defend a piece of territory—that the ball must not touch the ground. If the children adopt this approach the ball will never touch the ground without someone attempting to prevent it. In this way the game is lively and exciting. The static game of volleyball is a result of bad teaching.

It is important to remember that it is not sufficient just to teach the actual movements involved in the volley, dig etc. The player must be able to move into the correct court position and adopt the correct body attitude before he can make the movements involved in the technique. These preliminary movements must be learnt and drills used in teaching the techniques must involve these movements to the ball.

Teaching with small side games

The use of small side games will help the development of good techniques in volleyball while at the same time maintaining interest.

Small side courts can be made in several ways. The normal court and net can be used and divided into three courts each ten feet wide and extending to the attack line on either side. A rope can then be stretched along the length of the court dividing it in two lengthways. Other courts can be made by playing across court over this rope. Chalk lines and ribbons tied to the rope can be used to delimit the sidelines of these courts (Fig. 3).

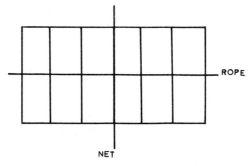

Fig. 3   Making small courts

17

An alternative method of making courts is to lower the beams to the height required (do not attach the vertical supports) and play over these. Wall bars which swing out from the wall make self contained courts needing only a rope stretched across between two sets of bars or between the bars and the wall.

One versus one games on these courts can be used to practice volleying and digging and also to teach the basis of scoring. In these situations players learn to move into position to play their shot and to identify the cues which tell them which shot to use and where they must be to play it. Serving can be made by volleying the ball or by use of the underarm serve.

In a 1 versus 1 situation all the shots are played backwards and forwards along the same line between the players. In most situations during the game the players must be able to receive a ball from one direction and play it to another. This can be practised by increasing the number of players on each side to two. Now the players can pass the ball between each other before sending it across the net. The limitation of three touches on each side need not be introduced until the players are able to control the ball sufficiently well to keep play going with only three touches.

In the early stages do not be too strict on the handling interpretations. It takes many thousands of volley passes before a fully legal technique is developed. However, carrying, holding, lifting and throwing of the ball during these games must be penalised when they are excessive.

The object in the early stages must be to determine which shot to use, where and when to make it and the carrying out of the necessary movements. This is a lot to think about and carry out and too great an emphasis on quality in the early stages will slow down development.

One of the best features of teaching through small side games on small courts is that the children quickly learn to judge the speed and force of their shots. To keep the ball in play and to score points on these small courts the children must learn to discriminate between the force needed and the flight path of the ball which will just clear the net and land in the front court and the shot which will land in the rear of the court. This fineness of touch is essential for the future development of the volley and its use in the full court game.

Once the children have developed a good level of skill in the volley and dig passes in the 1 versus 1 and 2 versus 2 games the smash, block and various tactical formations are ready to be introduced. As with the volley and dig passes the smash must be controlled if the games are to be kept going. At this stage all that is needed is for the children to be able to jump and play the ball over the net and down into their opponents' court using the correct hitting action with their wrist and palm. There is no need for an approach, the ball can be hit after jumping off the spot. In this way the children learn to control

18

their movements in the air and to control the direction and force of their smash.

As soon as they are smashing the ball it is advisable to increase the numbers to 3 versus 3. With three players, *service receive* and the idea of *setting* can be introduced. Service can be received with the dig and played forward to a setter waiting near the net. The principle of rotation can be introduced at the same time.

Following the introduction of smashing and the use of a setter, blocking by one player and some ideas on cover behind the block can be gradually introduced.

When using small side games it is advisable to change the players on each court frequently. Naturally the better players will try to play against each other and the weaker players will fall further behind because they will not be getting good service to enable them to improve their techniques. If the players move around the courts the weaker players will benefit greatly from the better passes that they will receive from the more advanced players. The better players will lose little by this process.

Volleyball is not a game that can be learnt in two weeks, or, two months. No physical education teacher would expect to teach children to play rugby, basketball or tennis in that short period of time. Volleyball is no different in this respect to those, and other sports.

A well planned volleyball syllabus in a school should extend over two years minimum and preferably three years. One of the advantages of the game is that it can be played indoors or outdoors. It is possible to allocate one term a year to volleyball by using the summer and winter terms.

The teacher who tries to take a short cut and teach the full 6 versus 6 game from the start will soon find that the techniques of the children become so bad that the game does not resemble the true Olympic game. If the small side approach is used the children will develop a strong base in the techniques as well as finding this approach enjoyable.

USES FOR GYMNASIUM EQUIPMENT

A lot of the equipment available in the normal gymnasium can be used as aids to the teaching of volleyball.

Basketball nets

These can be used for developing accuracy in volley passes and developing a good flight path for a volley pass. The aim should be to volley the ball straight into the basket without touching the ring or backboard.

Climbing Frames

Volley passing through climbing frames going up and down is an excellent practice for control.

19

Beams _____
Single or double beams can also be used for volleying or smashing practice.

Boxes and benches
These can be used to store volleyballs when not in use. Turn a box top over and it makes a useful receptacle for volleyballs. Two benches turned upside down and side by side will make a channel in which balls can be stored. Loose volleyballs can easily trip a child up and result in a broken leg or ankle.

Identification of faults
Merely providing children with a series of drills and small side games will not result in every child developing a sound volley, dig, smash etc. To carry out any shot successfully three conditions must be satisfied;
    a) The child must be in the right court position.
    b) Once he is in that position he must adopt the correct body attitude for the shot he is to attempt.
    c) He must set in motion the necessary movements at the right time and in the right order.

If it is apparent that a child is consistently unable to play a shot successfully then the teacher should look at his performance to see at which stage it is breaking down. Is he in the right position? Is he adopting the right body position?· Is his timing correct. Using this approach it is possible to find the root cause of the fault in technique. Once it has been found, corrective practices should be given.

In the sections dealing with the techniques of volleyball the most common faults and the practices which will help to correct them have been given. It is essential that faults are corrected before they become too difficult to eradicate.

The techniques of volleyball—especially the volley pass—will not be learnt quickly, they require constant practice. However, once a few children in the school have mastered them others will copy quite quickly. One of the reasons why football is relatively easy to teach is that children see so many others playing that they copy them and play out of school. Unfortunately at the present time this does not happen very often with volleyball. For many children their introduction to volleyball will be at school. Once they see others in the upper years playing they will soon copy and the teacher's job will be made somewhat easier.

Using this book
Each technique is discussed in detail and a series of practices suitable for introducing and developing them are given. In a later chapter further practices are given for training more advanced players.

20

It is not necessary or indeed advisable for the teacher to copy the introductory practices in their entirety. Different classes of children will progress at different rates and some of the suggested stages will not be needed. As the teacher becomes more experienced he may find alternative practices which suit his teaching style and children better. Above all the teacher must examine every practice and every step he uses in the search for the most efficient and effective means of teaching and developing the techniques of volleyball.

Plate 1

THE TECHNIQUES OF VOLLEYBALL

Movement on court

An essential ingredient in any volleyball game is movement. Players must constantly be moving their positions according to the changing situations. They must move to play a shot, move to cover a fellow player who is making a shot, move to a position of readiness for the next phase of the game. At every opportunity the coach or teacher should emphasise movement, should create situations in which players have to move in training sessions. Without this emphasis on movement the game is boring and the level of play will remain very low.

Volleyball is a fast game both in terms of the speed of certain shots such as the smash and serve, and fast in terms of the changing phases. One moment the player is defending, the next attacking. This means that players while waiting to receive the ball must adopt a body position that will enable them to move their whole body quickly in any direction. This position must also allow them to move their arms and hands into position for a dig or volley as quickly as possible.

The recommended position is shown in Plate 1. The feet are placed slightly more than shoulder width apart with one foot slightly in front of the other. The weight should be kept over the front foot as most of the movements will be in the forward direction.

The legs should be flexed so that movement in any direction only requires an extension of the legs. If the player is standing erect, the legs must first be flexed before movement can be made in any direction. The speed of the volleyball will not allow the extra time that this takes.

The back should be kept as straight as is comfortable. The arms are kept away from the body with the hands above the level of the knees. If the back is bent and the player leans well forward, the angle of the arms in relation to

23

his body decreases. This change would affect the quality of the dig pass as will be seen later.

Keeping the arms away from the body and above the level of knees allows a greater range of movement of the arms. If kept below the knees they could hit them when moved quickly to one side to dig the ball. If the arms are kept away from the body, it is only necessary to bring the hands together to make a dig pass, and to bend them at the elbows to bring the hands into the correct volley position.

This basic body position should be adopted at service receive, when the ball is being moved around the court, and when covering during the defensive phases. Although it will seem strange and slightly awkward at first the player will soon find that he is able to get into position for his shots much more easily and quickly and he will have more success in playing the unexpected shot.

When moving across the court to play a ball, the player should sidestep or turn to face the direction he has to travel and then use normal steps. If crossover steps are used there is always the chance that the player will get hopelessly entangled and lose his balance.

After sidestepping across court the player should ensure that his outside foot is slightly in front of his other foot. This will have the effect of angling his body inwards so that his pass will also be played into court.

Not only must the player be able to move in any direction, but he must be able to stop quickly in the correct place to play his shot. The player must learn to judge when to start to slow down, so that he can achieve a specific court position. This will only come from practice.

While the player is waiting for the ball to come to his part of the court he should not remain flat-footed. All the time he should be making very small movements on the spot, lifting his feet off the ground an inch or so each time. In this way he will be able to move more quickly to play the ball. In situations where it is necessary to get as low as possible e.g. when covering a smasher or covering close to the block, this position is achieved by spreading the feet more than shoulder width apart. Greater stability is achieved and it is easier to move from that position than one in which the legs are closer together.

Movement practices

1)   The players face the coach and move in the direction he points. The coach changes the directions quickly so that the players are learning to stop and change direction quickly.

2)   Players start on the baseline and run forward until they hear the coach shout a new direction in which to move.

3)   Starting on the baseline players run forward until one foot crosses the

24

centre line. They then return to the baseline by running backwards. This procedure is repeated to and from the attack line.

4)   The player must sidestep when he is at the net and return to the baseline by running backwards (Fig. 4).

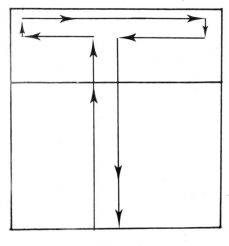

Fig. 4

In all these practices the player must keep low. Valuable time is wasted if the player stands up while running and then returns to the low position once he has stopped. Practice of movement in this way is valuable, but it must be accompanied by technique practices incorporating plenty of movement.

Techniques

A wide variety of techniques are needed to play volleyball and these can be considered under three headings.

    a) Those which use two hands above the head e.g. volley pass
    b) Those using one hand above the head e.g. tennis serve, smash
    c) Those using the hands below the head e.g. dig pass, service.

The technique used depends on the situation and the position of the player on court. The serve and smash are only used at a particular point on court and at a particular time. The volley and the dig are interchangeable in many situations. The technique used is that which will result in the greatest accuracy without contravening the handling rules.

THE VOLLEY PASS

This is the basic pass of volleyball. It is used most often because it plays the ball into the air giving the receiver time to decide where to play the ball next. The volley pass is the most accurate pass in volleyball.

The international rules which relate to the volley pass are:-

Rule 16

Article 2; The ball may be struck by any part of the body above and including the waist.

Article 3; The ball can contact any number of parts of the body down to the waist, providing that contacts are simultaneous and that the ball is not held but rebounds cleanly.

Article 4; Contact with the ball;
A player who contacts the ball or is contacted by the ball shall be considered as having played the ball.

Article 5; Held ball;
When a ball rests momentarily in the hands or arms of a player, it is considered as held. The ball must be cleanly hit. Scooping, lifting, pushing or carrying the ball shall be considered as holding.
A ball cleanly hit with both hands from below is considered as 'good'.

Article 6; Double hit;
A player contacting the ball more than once with whatever part of the body, without any other player having touched it between these contacts will be considered as having committed a 'double hit' (exception Blocking Rule 17, Article 4,b).

The volley pass can only be used when the ball being played is moving slowly and is high enough off the ground for the player to play the ball when it is above his head. This does not mean that he can only play the ball when it is above his normal standing head height. By bending his legs he is able to lower his head so that he can volley a ball as low as three feet off the ground.

A good volley is one that:-

26

a) Does not contravene the handling rules.

b) Is accurate in length and direction.

c) Has enough height to give the receiver time to get into the correct court position to play the ball.

d) "drops" onto the receiver, making it easier for him to play. It also allows him more time to look and see to where it is tactically best to play the ball.

A volley can be described as the receiving of a ball with two hands simultaneously, just above and in front of the head, and then changing its direction without it coming to rest. The rules expressly forbid the player to allow the ball to come to rest in his hands during the volley action. It is helpful if an analogy is drawn between the action of a trampolinist on the trampoline bed and the ball in the hands during the volley pass. As the trampolinist lands on the bed it gives with his weight and then sends him back into the air. At no time is he at rest during this action. In a similar way during the volley action the hands rotate backwards with the ball before volleying it forwards. The ball does not come to rest during this time. Naturally it could be argued that at some point in time the ball must be at rest, but this is only for the smallest fraction of a second.

The ball should be played slightly above the forehead and 6 - 12 inches in front of the player.

The forefingers and elbows form an angle of 90°. The player should aim to cup his hands around the ball. The thumb should be at the lower rear of the ball, the forefingers at the top rear, and the remaining fingers spread around the ball. If the fingers are correctly placed there will be a shape similar to that of the spade in playing cards, between the forefingers and the thumbs. The ball is played mainly on the thumb and the first two fingers. The other fingers help keep the ball under control. As the ball comes into the hands the wrists are cocked back and the palms turned so that they are almost facing each other. The fingers should be spread as wide as is comfortable. The ball is then played on the fingers (Fig. 5) and not the palms. As the ball touches the cupped hands the wrists are rotated forwards to volley the ball. If the angle of the arms and hands is less than 90° then the position of the thumb will be altered

27

limiting the amount of control the player has over the ball. On the other hand when the angle is greater than 90° there can be no rotation at the wrists. This makes it much more difficult to play the ball and reduces enormously the accuracy that can be achieved. Another result is that it is very difficult to play the ball upwards with this hand position. The volley tends to be very flat and almost parallel with the floor.

Fig. 5   Contact points (in black) during the volley pass

It was stressed earlier that the ball should be played above the head. If the arms are lowered so that the ball is played below head height it is nearly impossible to play the ball into the air or over a great distance without some lifting of the ball occuring. The only way to gain height or distance with this position is to lift the arms rapidly as the ball is played and this will mean that the player will very probably be penalised by the referee.

Obviously, even when the ball is played above the head in the manner recommended, it is not possible to send the ball across court using the wrist and finger action only. The volley results from a smooth extension of the whole body and finally the action of the hands and wrists. Before the ball enters the player's hands he should bend his legs slightly. The feet should be about shoulder width apart with one foot in front of the other. As the ball is played on the hands the player should extend his legs and arms to give greater control, accuracy and power to the volley. To ensure that the ball is given some forward movement as well as vertical, the player should extend mainly off his back foot so that the force of his body is applied "through" the ball and not underneath it. It must be emphasised that the whole action of the volley pass takes place with the feet on the ground. The tendency for many beginners is to spring at the ball and try to play it while their feet are off the ground. It is impossible for a beginner to play a legal pass in this way.

Footwork is essential in volleyball just as it is in most other sports. The use of the feet in the volley pass to give extra power has already been considered. This action is similar to that of the oarsman, who can row the boat reasonably well using only his arms, but he can row much better when he uses the sliding seat and is able to add the power of his feet as well. The volleyball player who trys to volley the ball using his hands and wrists only is not using his body to the maximum advantage.

There is another way in which footwork is essential in the volley pass. The player must be able to get into position to play the ball quickly so that he has as much time as possible to prepare to play the ball. This means that he must be able to predict where on court the ball can most easily be played and at what height above the ground. The player should move to the position he anticipates that he will be able to play the ball and take up the basic position for the volley pass with one foot slightly in front of the other. From this position it is easy to make minor adjustments forwards or backwards immediately prior to playing the ball. In addition to making adjustments horizontally he must also be able to make them vertically. Whatever the height of the ball the player must volley the ball at slightly above head height. He must adjust his height above the ground so that he can play the ball in this position. It follows therefore that he can volley whenever he can get under the ball to a position from which he can comfortably extend.

The selection of the right court position to play the ball is the result of experience. The beginner will often make errors in the prediction of where the ball will land and find himself too far under the ball. When this happens the volley will have a greater vertical component than a horizontal one because he is applying force directly under the ball.

The various body positions and actions in the volley pass can be summarised as follows:

Hands	Fingers spread, palms almost facing each other.
	'Spade' shape formed by forefingers and thumbs
	Wrists cocked back as ball enters the cupped hands.
	Wrists rotate forwards to play the ball.
	Hands at head height and 6-12 inches in front of the head.
Arms	Flexed so that an angle of 90° is formed between the elbows and the forefingers.
	Smooth extension of the arms as the ball is played

29

Legs   A balanced position should be established on court so that the ball is played within the base of support i.e. legs

One foot is kept slightly in front of the other.

Legs flexed before playing the ball so that it is played above head height.

There must be a smooth extension of the whole body as the volley is made.

Extend upwards and forwards off the back leg to ensure that the ball is given forward as well as upwards movement.

The volley should always be made from a balanced position. This means that the player must get into the correct position to play the shot as soon as he can. It is essential that the player is stationary as he plays the ball. If it is played while he is moving both the technique and the accuracy of the volley will be adversly affected.

Rarely does the ball come to the player from exactly the direction that he must play it. Usually he is required to change the direction of the ball. The player must turn his body to face the direction he is intending to play the ball *before* the volley is made. This is very important if maximum accuracy is to be achieved and the player is to avoid the handling faults of carrying or lifting the ball. In the case of the overhead volley the player must try to turn his body to face the exact opposite direction of his intended shot.

There are five different angles through which the player may be required to volley the ball:-

    i) return it straight back from where it came

    ii) play it straight overhead

    iii) play it at $90°$ to his court position

    iv) play it at an acute angle

    v) play it at an obtuse angle

These are illustrated in Fig. 6.

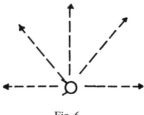

Fig. 6

To change the direction of the ball the player must first move into the court position where he expects the ball to be most easily played i.e. that point where it will be just above head height. As the ball comes to him he should turn his body so that it is facing the direction in which he wishes to volley. This means that he must be in position early enough to turn and look where he is going to play the ball and then have time to concentrate on making the minor adjustments needed to his position, to play the ball.

Fig. 7 shows the path of the player trying to play the ball at 90° to the direction it is already travelling.

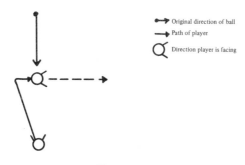

Fig. 7

N.B. Once he has found the position where the ball will be at a playable height he turns to face the direction he wishes to play it and at the same time takes a pace back. This is necessary to allow the ball to come across the front of his body. If he does not take this pace his view of the ball will be restricted, and he will have little room to make any late adjustments to his court and/or body position if necessary. In volleyball these late adjustments are often necessary as it is never possible to predict with 100% certainty where the ball will be most easily played. The skilled player will have to make less adjustment than the beginner but even he cannot allow exactly for the many factors such as spin, position of the valve on the ball, etc. which affect the flight of the ball.

It is always easier to move forward at the last moment and still play the ball with a high degree of accuracy, than it is to move backwards. The step back as soon as the player alters the direction of his body ensures that he has room to make adjustments if he needs to.

Beginners will often try to play the ball by turning their trunk only. This can still result in a good volley if the angle of change in direction is only small but it will not work for angles of 90° or more. Volleying in this way should

31

be discouraged as early as possible and the player must move the whole of his body (feet included).

There is no short cut to learning how to volley the ball through 90° or more. The only way is by hard work and constant practice.

The sideways volley
Sometimes the dig pass following a serve or smash is too close to the net. When this happens the setter cannot volley the ball in the normal way with his shoulders at right angles to the net without touching it and causing a fault. In this and other similar cases the ball can be volleyed sideways, with the shoulders parallel to the net. If the ball is to be volleyed to the right, the right hand must be dropped slightly so that the left hand exerts more pressure on the ball and therefore directs the ball to the right. The arms will play a far greater part in this volley than normal as the rotation of the wrists is very restricted. In the case under discussion the right upper arm should be almost parallel with the shoulders and the left arm will come across and above the head. The ball is then volleyed when it is over the right shoulder. Once again good footwork is essential if the player is to place his body correctly to allow the ball to be volleyed in this position.

It must be emphasised that this type of volley should only be used in the circumstances described or in similar situations where there is not time or room to turn to face the direction the ball is to be played before the volley is made.

The rolling volley
As the volley is the most accurate pass in volleyball it should be used as much as possible. However, there are many situations when the techniques already described will not result in a legal, or, accurate volley.

Some of these situations are:-
a) when the ball has a flat, low trajectory
b) when the ball is dropping low and to the side of the player
c) when the ball is dropping close behind the blockers.

Earlier it was suggested that a low ball could be volleyed by lowering the body so that the ball is still played above head height. This is very easy when the ball is dropping. When the ball is not dropping but moving horizontally—after a bad dig for example—and this method is used, the angle of the volley will be very low unless the player extends his arms strongly, but this will result in an illegal volley. In this instance the player should try to roll backwards so that his hands will be below the ball on contact. When the force is applied from this position the force is under the ball and will give the height needed.

As the ball comes towards the player he should lower his body position so that his head is at ball height (the back should be kept as straight as possible and not bent forward). His arms and hands should be raised ready to play the ball. The feet are placed about shoulder width apart with one foot slightly in front of the other. If, for example, the right foot is forward it must be flat on the ground. The player is on the toes of his left foot which is placed about nine inches behind the right. When the ball is almost in his hands the player falls back, rocking on to the heel of his left foot and then his back. The hands and arms, which have been kept high, play the ball in the normal way but as the legs cannot be used, must be extended slightly faster than in the normal volley.

The timing of the volley is crucial if the ball is to be played before the player has rolled too far back. The angle of the volley pass depends on the relative positions of the head and ball. The lower the head in relation to the ball, the higher the ball angle and vice-versa.

Once the player has played the ball he must get to his feet ready to take further part in the game. This can easily be achieved by placing the heel of the right leg as close to the seat as possible as soon as it has left the

ground in the roll back. After the ball has been played and the player has rolled onto his back, he should use the momentum gained to rock forwards over his right heel to a standing position. Some coaches feel that this style puts too much strain on the knee and have adopted a different technique. When the player is on his back his feet are spread about two feet to two feet six apart with his left foot firmly placed on the ground and the knee pointing to the right at an angle of approximately 70°. The right leg is also bent, almost on the ground and pointing in the same direction. Immediately after the ball has been played the right arm should be pulled back so that the hand can be placed on the ground as the player rolls forwards. With the aid of this hand the player comes to his feet, pushes hard with his right foot and turns his trunk to the left so that he is standing again.

The low ball to the side

To play this ball and the ball dropping close behind the block, the same basic rolling action is used. If the ball is to the right, the right foot should be stretched out far enough for the ball to be played in front of the head after the player has moved his weight across on to this foot. From this position the player rolls back as already described and volleys the ball.

If however, the direction the ball is to be volleyed is different to the direction from which it has come, then the player must pivot on one foot so that he faces the right direction before he plays the ball. Naturally, if the ball is to his right he can only pivot further to his right and volley to his left and vice-versa.

The overhead volley pass

There are many times during a game when for tactical reasons, or because of the position of the ball, it is necessary to pass the ball overhead.

This pass can only be made when the ball can be played at normal head height. Unless the player can get his body directly under the ball and use his legs as a source of power this shot is impossible without contravening the rules.

The hands should be held directly over the head with the arms flexed, elbows to the front. It is not possible to use the normal wrist rotation to play the ball, so most of the power for the volley must come from the arms and legs. The arms are smoothly extended over the head as the ball is played.

This is a difficult shot to play and should only be used in a game after it has been well practised in training. To help improve awareness of where the ball will go the player should try, before playing the ball, to face an object immediately opposite the point he is trying to reach. As the ball can only be played along the line of the body this will help him see where he will send the ball. In the front court it helps if the player uses the line of the net as a guide to his position.   .

Consistent accurate volleying can only come from practice. The player must be prepared to move quickly into position for each shot. Laziness in getting into the right position results in inaccurate volleys.

A good volley is essential if the game being played is to be of good quality.

Stages in the introduction to the volley pass.

V1 Hand position on the ball

Each player has a ball, throws it into the air and catches it just in front of the forehead. The ball must be caught and held in front of the forehead. Develop this practice to include throwing the ball up and the player turning through 180 or 360 degrees before catching the ball. This will help the player get used to preparing his hand position while moving and in the shortest possible time.

Another useful practice is to put the ball on the ground in front of the player and get him to crouch down and place his hands firmly on and around the ball. The teacher then checks to see that the thumbs and forefingers are in the correct position. Once this position has been achieved the player lifts the ball up to his forehead. He will then be able to see and feel the correct position of the ball in relation to the body and the arms and hands in relation to the ball. This can be developed so that one player rolls the ball to his partner who must stop it and bring it up to the forehead, using the hand grip that he has just learnt.

At this stage it is useful to point out to players that although the ball may not be caught and held in the hands during the volley, it is essential that it fully enters the hands so that the fingers will be able to get a good grip on the ball during the volley action. The hand position they have been learning enables them to achieve this grip.

V2 Moving to the ball

In order to play a volley pass during the game the player must be able to select the best spot on court to play the dropping ball. This ability must be learnt and the following practices will help to develop this ability.

The player throws the ball into the air so that it will land about ten feet away from him. Instead of letting the ball touch the floor he must move forward and catch it in the volley position. Alternatives to throwing the ball are strongly bouncing it on the floor in front of the player and catching the rebound on the way down, or throwing the ball high on to the wall and again catching the rebound.

These practices and, indeed the volley pass, can be made easier for the players if they put their hands up close to their forehead in the volley position, and look forward through the spade shape made by the hands at the ball, as they move into position. By looking through the gap between the hands it is very easy to get into the correct court and body position to play the ball. In most situations involving catching the ball the performer will put his hands in the waiting position in good time and not wait until the ball is almost on him before making a movement of the hands. The same principle applies in volleyball. Once the hands are up in position the player can then concentrate on the timing of the shot, where he is to play it, etc.

V3 Partnerwork

In pairs fifteen feet apart throw the ball to and fro making sure that each time the ball is to be caught the player moves so that he is able to catch the ball in the correct position. To make it easier the ball should be thrown up into the air so that it 'drops' in front of the player.

Once the players are finding it reasonably easy to catch the ball in the correct position, vary the length of the throw so that they have to move greater distances backwards and forwards and have to make quick decisions concerning which direction and how far in that direction they have to move.

A further progression is to vary the height of the pass so that the player must learn to adjust his body position in the vertical direction as well as in the horizontal. The height is varied by throwing the ball the normal height but at a steeper angle so that the player has to move further forward to play the ball and therefore it will have dropped nearer the ground when he gets there.

Do not be in too much of a hurry to move on from this practice. Further progress in the volley pass depends largely on the ablility to predict the court position in which to play the ball, the height it will be off the ground when the player gets there and how long before the ball reaches this position. The players must learn to watch the flight of the ball in the early stages and try to predict these factors from the speed and angle of release of the ball.

V4 Catch and return

Instead of the player catching the ball he should return it with a two-handed throwing action once the ball is firmly in his hands. As the ball is thrown the fingers are squeezed from the forefinger to the little finger. This will lead to a slight rotation of the wrists similar to that needed for the volley pass. Gradually the amount of time the ball is held in the hands is cut down until the ball is played with a volley action.

It is important that even at this early stage the legs are brought into the volley action. Once the player has found the correct court position to play the ball he should be waiting in a flexed position, one leg in front of the other. Just before playing the ball he should smoothly and slowly extend off the back foot to bring the *whole body* up to meet the ball. There should be no seperate movement of the arms or hands towards the ball. The extension of the body continues as the ball is played by the hands.

Only one of the pair should be practising the volley at a time. At first the volley that is made will be of poor quality and very inaccurate. If this volley is used as the feed for the next player's attempt then it will give him little chance of making a good shot. If one person volleys and the other catches the return, progress will be much faster.

The players will now have a basic idea of what the volley pass is and will be able to play the ball in a way which resembles the movement they are trying to learn. What they must be given next is plenty of practice in a small game situation. Put the net or rope at a height of ten feet. This will ensure that they keep their passes to each other high. This will give both of them more time to play the ball. Time is very important for the beginner. The small

36

courts will mean that they will not have to volley over a great distance. They can therefore concentrate on developing technique and a good flight path for their pass instead of on increasing the length of their pass. Once they have a reasonably good volley they will be able to work on increasing the length of their pass without ruining their technique.

The teacher will have to spend some more time on improving the various aspects which make up the volley pass, e.g. the hand action, use of the feet, etc. The following practices will be useful in this respect.

Drills for improving and developing the volley pass

Practices for improving the hand action

1) Two players sit opposite each other and volley the ball. By putting them in this situation they can use only their arms and hands when volleying. They do not have to think about using their legs and moving into position to play the ball. This enables players to focus their attention on their hand action.

2) In the same position but players use only their forefingers to volley the ball. This immediately prevents them from holding the ball and gets them used to the forward rotation of the fingers in the volley pass. It is helpful if they point their forefingers at their eyes just before playing the ball and rotate them forwards as the ball is played so that they finish up pointing at their partner's eyes. Gradually the rest of the fingers and the thumb are added until the full volley action is achieved. Insist that the flight path of the volley is such that the ball drops on the partner. If the path is flat players will have little time or chance to play the ball.

3) In the early stages, beginners have a tendency to keep their fingers stiff when volleying the ball. If this is so, get them to bounce the volleyball on the floor just as they would a basketball. Show them the difference between the control they have over the ball with relaxed fingers compared to stiff fingers. This applies just as well to the volley pass. Get the players to squeeze the ball with their fingers as they bounce it. If they try and use this squeezing action as they volley the ball, they will not play it with stiff fingers.

Practices for getting the hands into position quickly

1) Three players sit on the floor in a line 6 feet apart. The middle player must always face the person playing the ball. The two outside players volley the ball to and fro, over the head of the middle player. Every now and then the ball is played to the middle player. The centre player will have to keep turning to face the person playing the ball and in turning will lower his hands to the ground to help him turn. This means that he has to raise them very quickly to the volley position if he is to make a good volley when the ball comes to him.

37

2) In pairs playing the ball across the net each player standing three feet from the net. After volleying the ball across the net each player must touch both hands on his knees. This cuts down the time the player has to play the ball. It also means that he must raise the arms quickly to the volley position each time.

Positioning the ball in relation to the body
The best practice for this is heading the ball between two players. If the ball is to be kept in the air then both players will have to move their feet so that they position their head well under the ball. The same kind of footwork and almost the same positioning is needed in volleyball.

Practices for improving the extension of the legs
Players stand in the centre circle on a basketball court and try to throw the ball into the basketball ring. The ball must be held with two hands in front of the forehead at the start. The only way the players can do this with any degree of success is if they extend the whole body off the back foot as the ball is thrown. The same action is needed in the volley pass.

Practices for control of the ball
1) Each player has a ball and must volley the ball above his head while he lowers himself until he is lying on the floor. From this position he must stand up while still volleying the ball. The ball should be kept close to the head all the time.
2) At the beginning of a lesson or training session when players have their tracksuits on, start them volleying the ball to each other ten foot apart. They must then take their tracksuits off and put them off court while keeping the ball going between them. At the end of a lesson get the children to do this by taking off their vests, undoing their plimsoles and taking their socks off. This is a most hilarious spectacle!
3) This is a drill that the coach or teacher should get someone else to demonstrate. The reason for this advice will be obvious once the teacher has seen someone else demonstrate it. Two players 15 feet apart volley the ball to each other. Immediately after they have volleyed the ball they should make some action e.g. clap their hands, turn round etc. Their partner must reproduce the same movement before he plays the ball.

Some common faults in the volley pass, their cause and correction

1. Fault; Volleying at chest height

Reason	*Correction*
a) Player does not get his hands up into the 90° position before he plays the ball, instead he waits until the ball has dropped to his chest.	1) Practice volleying across the net while standing only two feet away. If the arms are dropped it is impossible to get the ball over the net.
b) His court position is several feet to the rear of the correct place to play the ball.	2) Throw the ball to the player at varying heights and lengths getting him to catch and hold it in the volley position.

2. Fault; "Poking" at the ball

Reason	*Correction*
a) The hands have not been cupped ready to receive the ball. Instead the fingers point towards the ball and "poke" at it.	1) Stand the player four feet from a wall. Starting from the 90° position throw the ball at the wall using rotation of wrists, so that it hits a point several feet higher. The return is caught in the volley position and then thrown back again by rotating the wrists.
b) The fingers and wrists are not relaxed.	2) Get the players to volley an overweight ball e.g. basketball or netball. The extra weight will mean that they have to relax their fingers and wrists or they will find it painful!
	3) Get two players to play the ball quickly to each other using a basketball chest pass. The ball must not be caught but sent back to the other player immediately. This can only be done if the fingers and wrists are relaxed so that the ball can enter them and be brought under control.

3.   Fault; "Lifting" The ball

Reason   *Correction*

Instead of playing the ball when it is in front of the forehead, the hands are dropped a few inches when the ball is in them. The arms and hands are then lifted back up as the ball is played.

1) Stand the player at the end of a gymnastic box with his elbows resting on the top and his hands/arms forming the 90° position. Volley the ball to him from about three feet away. He will be unable to drop his hands as he volleys the ball back.
2) Hang a ball from a beam. The player must then volley it. He will not be able to drop his arms as he volleys the ball without losing contact with the ball.

4.   Fault; Turning the ball with the hands.

Reason   *Correction*

This is the result of not turning to face the direction it is intended to send the ball before it is played.

1) Walk the player through the movements emphasizing the changing feet positions.
2) Stand the player three feet away from the wall. The coach throws a ball over the player's head. The player must turn and trap the ball with his hands against the wall. If he can get used to tracking the ball and turning in this situation he should have not further difficulty in the game situation.

5. Fault; "Flapping" at the ball

Reason	*Correction*
The player has the wrong hand position. His hands are flat and facing the ball with the result that it is impossible to cup the hands. The wrists are flexed forwards as the ball is played.	Take the player back to the first stages and show him the correct hand position. Use the practice as in Fault 2 (1)

6. Fault; Ball goes straight up in the air and not forwards

Reason	*Correction*
The player is too far under the ball, so that his hands play the ball when it is directly above his head.	Throw the player balls of varying height, length and position and get him to head them back. If he is to head them back then the ball must be on his forehead which is almost the correct position. Next get him to catch the ball in the correct volley position.

7. Hitting the ball

Reason	*Correction*
The arms are brought up to the volley position much too late. As a result it becomes one continuous movement of the arms up to the head and to the ball. There is no control of the volley and often a slapping sound is heard.	1) Throw a number of balls to the player in quick succession so that he does not have time to lower his arms each time. 2) Volley in pairs close to the net keeping the ball as low as possible. To keep the ball going the hands will have to be kept up.

8. The pass has a flat trajectory

Reason	*Correction*
a) There is no use of the legs. b) The body position is too high so	1) For the legs: stand on the centre line of a basketball court and

that the force is applied from directly behind the ball.

c) The ball is played too far in front of the body so that once again the force is applied from behind the ball.

throw the ball into the basket using a full extension of the body.

2) For body position; Use the practices already described in Fault (1) 2, Fault (6).

9. Fault; Taking the ball in an unbalanced position

Reason

This usually happens when the player has to move across the court to play the ball. In doing so he uses a cross step instead of a sidestep so that if he is late in reaching his position one of his feet is still in the air, or they are too close together. As a result he is unable to use any leg movement in the volley.

Correction

The player must use a sidestep and not a cross step. He should also aim to get the leg on the side he is moving to, well past the ball. This will give him a stable and balanced position.

10. Fault; Leaning backwards as the ball is played

Reason

The player does not use his legs to give more power to the volley. Instead he leans back before playing the ball so that a forward movement of the back will give the ball the desired extra power. This movement however often leads to a flat pass.

Correction

1) Sit the player with his back to the wall and throw balls to him to volley back. This will get him used to volleying the ball without the back movement.

2) Use one of the practices described earlier for encouraging use of the legs.

11. Fault; Volleying the ball while off the ground

Reason

This happens because the player is too far forward and instead of moving his feet to bring him into the correct position, he jumps and tries to play the ball in the air.

Correction

The best correction for this is pure practice of the heading and catching drills followed by plenty of work which makes the player move back and forwards to volley.

This is not an exhaustive list of faults or corrective practices by any means. It is given in the hope that it will discourage the coach from merely telling a player to 'move your feet' or 'use your legs' and encourage him to be more constructive in his coaching. Only when a coach is looking for the reason for a fault in technique and devising suitable corrective practices is he giving the players the maximum help.

Drills for the volley pass
A large number of drills and practices for the volley pass are given in this chapter. The volley must be practised continually if it is to become really accurate and effective. The coach or teacher must have a large number of drills in his repertoire so that the sessions are interesting and do not become repetitive. There are several types of volley pass and many different angles through which the player must volley. The player must practice all these thoroughly so that during a game he is able to play the ball in each situation accurately and efficiently.

Practices for the volley pass

1)   Volleying the ball into the basketball net. Vary the position each time.
2)   Volley once above the head about three feet high, and then volley the ball to partner.
3)   Volley once above head as partner moves to a new position. The second volley must be played accurately to him.
4)   One player receives a series of volley passes from a line of players facing him. He must return each ball to the player who sent it to him.
5)   Player (1) volleys to (2) who returns the ball to him. As (1) volleys the ball across to (3), player no (2) turns to face (3). Fig. 8

Fig. 8

6)   (1) volleys to (3). Player (3) volleys to (2) who then volleys out to (4). (Fig. 9)

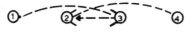

Fig. 9

7)   (1) volleys to (2) and receives the return volley. The ball is then volleyed
across to (4). (Fig. 10)

Fig. 10

8)   The coach feeds a line of players with volley passes. After volleying
the ball back to him the player goes to the back of the line.

9)"   Two lines of players opposite each other. After volleying the ball to the
front player in the opposite line, the player then moves to join the end of the
opposite line. (Fig. 11)

Fig. 11

10)   Player moves to Position A, opposite the coach to receive and return a
volley pass. (Fig. 12)

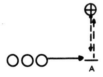

Fig. 12

11)   The player has to run back to Position A to receive the ball from the
coach. (Fig. 13)

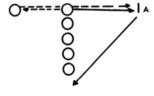

Fig. 13

44

12)   The player moves diagonally forward to Position A to play the ball. (Fig. 14)

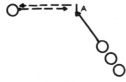

Fig. 14

13)   Similar situation to (12) but the player moves diagonally backwards to play the ball.

14)   The player stands fifteen feet away from the coach with his back to him. When the coach volleys the ball he tells the player to turn. The player must then turn and run forwards five feet to play the ball.

15)   Pass and follow using three players. Two players start in one place and the other is ten feet away facing them.

16)   Alternate short and long passes making one player move each time.

17)   Coach makes one player work by varying the height as well as the length of the pass.

Changing the direction of the ball; acute angles

18)   Volleying the ball around a triangle.

19)   Four players in a square. The ball zig zags between them. (Fig. 15)

Fig. 15

20)   Eight players standing in two rows opposite each other. Each player is ten feet from his opposite number and six feet from the next player in his line. The ball zig zags between the players. (Fig. 16)

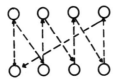

Fig. 16

21)   Six players form a circle and a seventh stays in the middle. The ball is played in to the centre player and around the circle in a series of triangles. (Fig. 17)

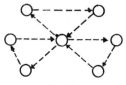

Fig. 17

22)   Pass and follow drill in a triangle using four players. (Fig. 18)

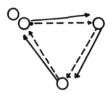

Fig. 18

23)   Seven players in a circle. Each player volleys the ball to the third player to his right. (Fig. 19)

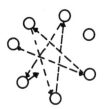

Fig. 19

24)   Four players stand in a ten foot square. Two other players stand in the centre. Two balls are used. The balls are passed around the players in a series of triangles. (Fig. 20)

46

Fig. 20

25)   Seven players in a circle. Two balls are used. Players volley to the second player to their right. (Fig. 21)

Fig. 21

26)   Similar drill to (19) but with eight players who pass and then follow. (Fig. 22)

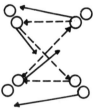

Fig. 22

27),   Same number of players, starting positions and volley passes as (26). However instead of moving to the spot where the volley has been played, the player moves one place to his right.

28)   Pass and follow in a triangle using nine players. (Fig. 23)

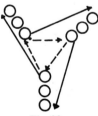

Fig. 23

29) Five pointed star shape formation with an extra player at one point. The ball is passed to the second player on the right. The player follows his pass. (Fig. 24)

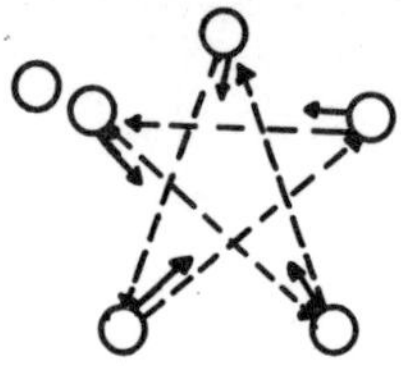

Fig. 24

30) Three players are used with one player standing at point A with his back to the other two. As player (1) plays the ball he shouts. The receiver, player (3), must turn, move forwards five feet and play the ball to no (2). After each volley he returns to point A. (Fig. 25)

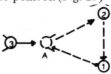

Fig. 25

31) Eight players are used to form a fifteen foot square with two players at each corner. The ball is played around a ten foot square. Each player must move five feet forward to play the ball. The ball zig zags between the players. After playing the ball the player moves one place to his right. (Fig. 26)

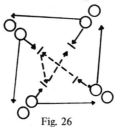

Fig. 26

32) Two players stand opposite each other ten foot apart. They both play two corners of a square. Player (1) must move to and from point A each time. (Fig. 27)

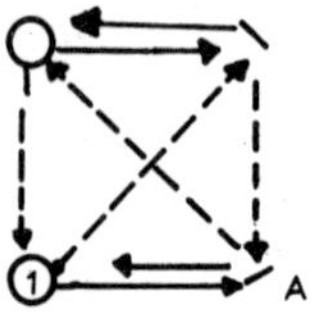

Fig. 27

Volleying the ball through 90°

33) Four players volley a ball around a square.

34) Pass and follow version of (33) using eight players. (Fig. 28)

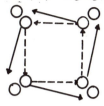

Fig. 28

35) Using eight players a pass and follow drill around a square with a different line up. (Fig. 29)

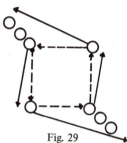

Fig. 29

36) Eight players stand so that they form two squares side by side. The ball is passed around the players at 90° each time. (Fig. 30)

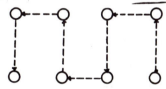

Fig. 30

37) As (36) but using one extra player so that it becomes a pass and follow drill. (Fig. 31)

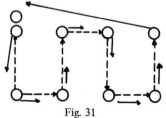

Fig. 31

38)   Three players form corners of a square. Player (1) must also play position 3 by running to and from the positions. (Fig. 32)

Fig. 32

39)   Similar to (38) but with only two players. Player (1) also acts as player (3) and (4) as 2. (Fig. 33)

Fig. 33

40)   One player stands in a corner and plays the ball alternately to the wall on his right and then the one in front of him.

41)   As (40) but using three players. After playing the ball the first player moves to the end of the line.

42)   As (36) except that the player must move forward five feet to play the ball.

43)   Three feeders are used. The player runs zig zag between positions 1, 2 and 4 to play the ball. (Fig. 34)

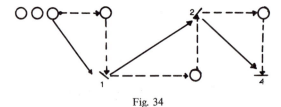

Fig. 34

44)   Two players are used and the ball is volleyed around a triangle. Player A must play position 1 and 2. This drill combines practice for one player in playing the ball through $90°$ with practice for the other player in volleying the ball through an acute angle. (Fig. 35)

50

A poorly formed block give the Czechoslovakian player No. 7 a chance to score

The Volley Pass. The 90° position of the forearms and hands. (see page 27)

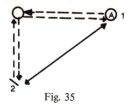

Fig. 35

45) Two lines of players stand ten feet from each other and ten feet from the wall. The first player must volley the ball against the wall and then return to the end of his line. The next player volleys the rebound through 90° to the front player of the other team.

46) Four players volley a ball around a square. Each player moves forward ten feet to play the ball.(Fig. 36)

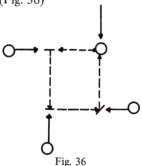

Fig. 36

Volleying the ball through an obtuse angle
47) Players form a triangle so that they volley the ball through obtuse angles to each other. (Fig. 37)

Fig. 37

48) As (47) but as a pass and follow drill.(Fig. 38)

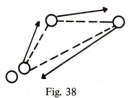

Fig. 38

51

49) Four players form a diamond shape and volley the ball around the diamond. (Fig. 39)

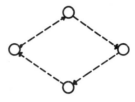

Fig. 39

50) As (49) but pass and follow.
51) Six players in a circle passing the ball around the circle.
52) As (51) but with an extra player to make it a pass and follow drill. (Fig. 40)

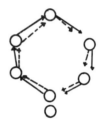

Fig. 40

Overhead volley
53) Player (1) volleys the ball to (2) who volleys overhead to (3) and then turns to face the return pass from (3). (Fig. 41)

Fig. 41

54) Four players in a line. The coach volleys a ball to the first player who volleys overhead to (2) and so on. As soon as (2) is playing the ball another ball should be sent to the first player. (Fig. 42)

Fig. 42

55)   Six players form a triangle. The three players in the middle of each side of the triangle must play an overhead pass. (Fig. 43)

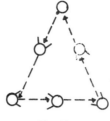

Fig. 43

56)   Player (1) receives a volley pass and plays it overhead to the second player in his line. Player (2) then volleys the ball to the front player of the next line. He then volleys the return pass overhead. (Fig 44)

Fig. 44

57)   Two players are used. After receiving the ball and playing it above his head the player turns 180° and volleys the ball back overhead.

58)   Players (1) and (2) stand in a line twenty foot apart. The other players stand to the side between the two players. Player (1) volleys the ball half the distance between him and (2). The first player in the other line must move across and play the ball overhead to (2). The next player must play the ball overhead to (1). (Fig. 45)

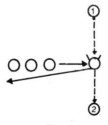

Fig. 45

53

59)   Four players in a square volleying the ball overhead around the square.
(Fig. 46)

Fig. 46

60)   Six players volley the ball overhead around a circle. (Fig. 47)

Fig. 47

61)   Three players in a triangle. Player (3) volleys the ball in front of player
(1) so that he can volley it overhead to (2).(Fig. 48)

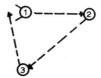

Fig. 48

62)   The players remain in a triangle but the positions are changed so that
the person playing the overhead shot has the ball coming to him from an
acute angle.(Fig. 49)

Fig. 49

54

63)   Player (1) must run forward to Position A to receive a pass from (2).
He plays the ball overhead to (3) who volleys it back to (4). After playing the
ball the players go to the end of the other line.(Fig. 50)

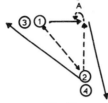

Fig. 50

The volley pass; hints for players
Always be expecting the ball to be played to you either voluntarily or as a
result of a bad shot from another player. Turn to face whoever is playing the
ball on your side and adjust your court and body position so that you are
ready to volley the ball if necessary.

Once you have decided that the ball is going to come to you, watch the ball
in the early stages of its flight. As you become more experienced you will be
able to estimate quite accurately from the angle of release and the speed of
the ball at this time how long the ball will be in flight, how far it will travel
horizontally and where on court will be the best place for you to play the
ball. The earlier you can make these predictions the more time you will have
to prepare for your pass.

When the ball has to be played below normal head height lower yourself as
you move into position instead of waiting until you get to the spot. In this
way you will be ready and waiting for the ball as it comes down. Small
corrections in the height of your position can easily be made to bring you
into the exact position.

Always raise your arms to the 90° position as early as possible. Look through
the gap between the hands at the ball and move until the ball is filling that
gap. In this way you will be able to pick the right spot every time. As you
become a better player you will find that making this movement early means
that your attention can then be focussed on other aspects, such as where to
play the ball to etc.

Having decided where the ball is going to drop and having put your hands
up ready to play the ball, you must start deciding where you are going to play
the ball to. This is governed to some extent by the position on court where
you have to play the ball, its height above the ground, the team line up you
are using etc. Very often your team mates will be shouting to say where to
play the ball so you should be listening for them. If the ball is in a difficult

55

playing position don't try the impossible, play the safe and straightforward shot. It is always better to keep the ball in play than to try a difficult pass from an even more difficult position.

Whenever possible use the volley pass instead of the dig pass. The volley is more accurate and easier for the next person to play than a dig pass. In training practice volleying from different heights and positions so that you will be able to use this pass more in the game.

Lastly—and perhaps most important—remember that you will not learn to volley unless you practice and practice and practice. The volley is fundamental to the game and it is impossible to spend too much time on it.

THE DIG PASS

When the ball to be played is too low, too fast, or, too far to the side to volley, the dig pass is used.

The dig pass involves receiving the ball on the outstretched forearms. By extending the legs as the ball contacts the forearms it is possible to control the speed, length, height and direction of the rebound.

After a hard serve or smash, the ball travels too fast for the player to allow the ball to just rebound off his arms. The player must control the ball by absorbing some of the power on the fleshy inside of the forearms. It is important to remember that in the majority of cases the dig must take the speed out of the ball and the action of the dig itself should not increase the speed of the ball. If the arms swing into the ball then the speed of the arm movement will be added to the existing speed of the ball, and one of the objects of the dig pass, to reduce the speed of the ball, is destroyed.

It is important that a quick and easy method of gripping the hands is chosen so that the forearms are brought together to form a rigid, broad platform for the ball. In the early days of volleyball the fingers were interlocked, but this has proved to be too slow and complicated for the modern game of volleyball.

The recommended hand grip can be achieved by placing the fingers of one hand on top of and at right angles to the fingers of the other hand. The hands are then closed by bringing the thumbs together, so that their outside edges touch from the tips to the heel of the hand.

The elbows as a general rule should be locked so that the arms are kept straight. This prevents the ball from rebounding back onto the player's arm or head. When the ball is extremely low or some distance in front of the player, he may find it necessary to bend slightly at the elbows so that he can get his arms between the ball and the floor. For all other shots he should keep the elbows locked.

The angle of the arms in relation to the body at the time the ball is played determines the flight angle of the pass. The closer the player is to the net when he plays the ball the higher his arms should be and vice-versa. A low arm angle results in a longer pass, a high angle gives more vertical than horizontal travel to the pass (see Figs. 51 & 52).

During the game the player should ensure that his arms are kept away from his body and clear of the legs. This will make it easier and quicker to prepare for the dig.

Fig. 51   Low arm angle in the dig pass   Fig. 52.   High arm angle in the dig pass

Arm movement should be cut to a minimum so that the speed is taken out of the ball. When the ball is travelling very fast, a slight give with the arms on contact may be necessary. The arms should *not* be swung upwards as the ball is played.

As in the volley pass the use of the legs is important. Firstly, the player should move to the spot where the ball must be played from. At this point his body position should be low, legs spaced forwards and backwards, back as straight as is possible and comfortable, arms extended ready to play the ball. If the ball is played in mid or back court, then the player must 'guide' the ball to the setter by extending his back foot upwards and forwards as he plays the ball. The player should always try to position himself so that he plays the ball in the midline of his body. If it is played to either side of this line the ball is liable to fly off the arms in a different direction to that intended. This is because the body is not stable and the speed of the ball could knock the arms out of the way.

When the ball is played at the side of the court it must be 'guided' back into the centre. This is easier if the player positions himself so that his front foot is also his outside foot. When the other foot is forwards the player will have to 'pull' the ball across his body with his arms. To play a ball that is well to the side of the player back into the centre, the inside shoulder should be dropped slightly so that the arms are inclined inwards and present a larger playing surface to the ball. The outside leg should smoothly extend upwards and inwards on contact and the ball will than be guided inwards.

Sometimes the ball is coming so fast to the side of the player that he does not have time to move all his body across and behind the ball. In these circumstances it is tempting to just swing the arms out to the side and into the path of the ball. On many occasions this will be successful but if the player also moves the leg on that side across as well, so that the ball is played within his base of support, i.e. his legs, he will be more successful.

Often when the ball is travelling very fast and low the player will find that he will make a better dig pass by rolling onto his back as he plays the ball. This enables him to get his arms well under the ball and play it high into the air. This technique is shown below.

The dig pass should be high enough to give the setter time to get into position to play his set. As with the volley pass the player should try to make the ball 'drop' on the receiver's head.

Whenever possible the player should try to turn to face the direction he intends to play the ball, before he plays it. In doing so he must take care to see that he doesn't turn too far with the result that he is unable to present a strong platform to the ball.

Common faults in the dig pass and their cause

Fault	Reason
1) Ball flies straight up in the air	a) Player is swinging his arms as he plays the ball so that it follows the direction of his arm movement—upwards b) Angle of his arms in relation to his body is too high.
2) Dig pass is too low	a) Arm angle in relation to his body is too low. Possibly because he is bending his back too far forward. b) No extension of the legs as the ball is played.
3) Dig pass consistently too short.	a) No use of the legs. b) Arm angle too high so that the ball has too much vertical travel. c) Forearms absorbing too much of the ball's speed.
4) Ball hitting the top of the arms above the elbow.	a) Player is too far forward as he plays the ball. He must move back so that he plays the ball further in front of his body.
5) Ball flies off the arms to either side.	a) Ball is played on the hands instead of on the forearms. b) Ball is played to the side of the body without the player bringing the leg on that side of the body, across to produce a more stable position. c) No leg movement so the ball is not 'guided' in the right direction. d) An uneven platform is made by the forearms so that the ball only contacts one of them. e) Player has turned too far in the direction he intends playing the

Fault	*Reason*

ball and is unable to present a
broad and strong platform to the
ball.

6) Ball is played backwards instead of forwards.	a) Arms are bent instead of locked at the elbows. b) Player is leaning backwards as the shot is played because he has positioned himself too close to the ball.
7) Player plays the ball with bent arms instead of straight ones.	Fault obvious—try throwing him a high dropping pass to be returned with a low dig pass.

A summary of the body positions and movements during the dig pass

The hands;	Kept apart during the game and brought together as early as possible for the dig. Hands linked as described.
The arms;	Locked at the elbows. Well clear of the body and kept above the waist during the game. Forearms pulled well together to make a flat platform for the ball. No arm movement at the shoulders when playing the ball. The ball is played an arm's length away from the body. If the ball is very fast the speed is taken out of it by a very slight backward movement of the arms on contact. The ball is played on the fleshy part of the forearm between the wrist and elbow.
The back;	The back is kept as straight as is comfortable. The player should always try to get under the ball by lowering the body and moving the feet. This removes the temptation to lean forward to play the ball. If the player leans forward the angle of his arms drops and the pass will be low.
The legs;	One in front of the other. Bend them before playing

60

the ball. As the ball is played the back foot extends smoothly upwards and forwards to give more control to the pass. When playing a ball passing to the side the foot on that side should be moved past the arms to make a firmer base when playing the ball. The outside foot should be the forward foot when playing at the side of the court.

Teaching the dig pass

An important point to remember when teaching the dig pass is that part of the technique is the forming of the platform for each pass. Very often teachers allow children to keep their hands clasped together throughout the entire practice for the dig. It is essential that beginners practice making the platform as often as possible.

Whenever possible the players make their partners move to play the ball. The person who feeds the ball should move to a new position and provide a target.

In the game situation most digs are made towards the net. In practice it is wisest to make all digs towards the net so that players learn to judge how far they are from the net each time, and to give the ball the right amount of force to reach the setter at the net.

Stage 1 Forming the platform

Show the hand position and the formation of the forearm platform. Practice forming the platform quickly by bringing the arms together. Ensure that the elbows are locked and the shoulders pushed forward to bring the forearms closer together.

Each player throws a ball into the air, forms the platform with the arms parallel to the floor and lets the ball bounce on the platform. Emphasise how far the ball will bounce on its own. Demonstrate what happens if the arms are swung into the ball.

Players then throw the ball so that it will land about five feet away from them. They must then move into position, form the platform and let the thrown ball rebound off the forearms.

Stage 2 Introducing the leg action

1) Two players stand opposite each other and hold each other's hands. Both players then make the dig platform as best they can in this position. A ball is placed on the forearms of one player. It must then be transferred from one platform to the other. The player with the ball extends his legs and the other flexes them so that the ball rolls onto his arms. The see-saw action of the players gives them the feel of the movement of the legs in the dig pass.

2) Each player throws a ball into the air, allows it to bounce once and then digs it when it is on the way down again.

3) Continuous digging. Each player throws the ball into the air and then using the dig pass plays it against the wall. He will then find that he will have to move into position and use his legs if he is to keep the ball rebounding against the wall. If he swings his arms, control of the ball will soon be lost.

Stage 3 Movement to play the ball

1) In pairs, one player feeding the ball each time and the other digging. The digger must start on a line which is five feet behind the place where he will have to dig the ball. He must adopt the basic stance while waiting on the line. When the ball is thrown he must move forward into position to dig the ball. After each dig he must return to the line.

2) In pairs, one player always volleying the ball and the other digging. The player volleying the ball varies the height and direction of his pass so that the player digging the ball must be constantly moving to play the ball. Each dig pass must go back to the player volleying the ball.

Stage 4 Changing the direction of the ball

1) In pairs, one player volleys the ball to his partner who is standing about ten feet from him. After volleying the ball he moves ten feet to his left. The second player must dig the ball to his partner in the new position. After playing the ball he also moves ten feet to the side so that he is back opposite his partner. The ball is then played in the opposite direction.

2) In threes, with two players standing fifteen feet apart, two feet from the net. Opposite one of these players, 15 feet away, is the third player. This player must dig the volley pass sent to him by the player opposite him. The dig pass should go across to the third player. The ball is then volleyed back to the original player so that it follows a triangular path.

In the small game situations that the teacher uses, the ball will not be hit very hard and the practices given so far will bring the dig pass up to the standard needed. Further practices are given in Chapter 6. These practices should be used to develop the dig pass to the standard required for the full 6 versus 6 game.

Hints for players;

The dig pass is perhaps the easiest technique to grasp in volleyball and therefore the one least practised. This is unwise because the dig pass is used at the most crucial part of the game-service receive. If the team cannot play a good dig pass to the setter, the whole attack of that team will be weakened. The first pass, as the dig pass on service receive is called, is crucial in volleyball. It follows therefore that every player should work on his dig technique until he can play a good dig from every kind of service and in every court position with the maximum reliability.

While waiting for service or to receive a smash put the arms straight out in front, locked at the elbows. All that is needed to make the platform is to put your arms together. This takes but a fraction of a second. If your arms are down by your side you will first have to bring them up to this starting position and this takes more time than you have to spare. Remember that on most occasions when you are going to use the dig pass, the ball is moving very fast. This means that you have very little time to move your arms into position.

Always put your outside foot forwards when you are at the side of the court. This means that you are facing inwards, the direction your dig pass must go.

If you have to move to a different position to play the ball move there with your arms extended. You will then find little difficulty in positioning yourself so that you are playing the ball the correct distance from your body.

When you are waiting for the serve to cross the net try to predict as early as possible where the ball is going. Will it cross the net on your side of the court? How fast is it going? How high is it? From these questions you will soon be able to decide whether the ball is likely to come to you or not. In the former case you should start to line yourself up with the ball so that it is coming for your chest. This will put the ball in the correct position in relation to you for the dig pass. If it is coming to you, start to lower your body as you move to the best place to play the ball. Don't wait to do this until you get into position as you may not have enough time left.

Once you are ready and waiting for the ball, try to turn your body as much as possible—without risking a bad shot—towards the player you intend should receive the pass.

Just before the ball contacts your arms, smoothly extend you body off the back foot. Try to stay with the ball as long as possible. In this way you will resist the temptation to swing your arms at the ball.

The success of a dig pass depends as much on your footwork as the positioning of the arms. Always keep light on your feet so that you can move quickly to play the ball.

DIVES AND ROLLS
Not every ball that has to be played during a game is high enough, or close enough, to use the volley or dig passes. In these circumstances the player must use another technique of preventing the ball from touching the floor.

There are two main techniques used for extreme recoveries; the forward dive and the rolling dig. It must be emphasised that these are only used when it is impossible to play the ball with either of the other passes.

The forward dive

When the ball is travelling low to the side or front, or is dropping steeply to the floor some distance away, the player must dive and play the ball on the back of his hand before landing. In this way the ball will be kept in play and played high enough into the air for another player to volley. The full length dive is one of the most exciting sights in volleyball. Although spectacular the dive is not very difficult to learn, and contrary to what the spectator would imagine does not hurt the player.

Technique of the forward dive

The player dives upwards and forwards, reaching forwards with his arms. The ball is played on the back of the hand, the fingers of which are kept stiff, by forcefully flicking it upwards. The hand should be well under the ball so that it will be played upwards. The arm should not make a large movement because at the time of contact the player is only a short distance off the ground and the arms are needed to help soften the landing. The head should be kept back so that the face does not touch the ground. As his hands make contact with the ground the player should try to extend his arms. This action enables him to lower his chest slowly down to the ground until it makes contact with the floor. His back is arched with his knees bent, heels above the seat. This bow shape helps the player to land on his chest and to prevent his knees from crashing to the ground. With this technique the landing is controlled and soft.

As soon as he has landed, the player must get to his feet quickly so that he can take part in the game again. The easiest way for him to do this is to push strongly with his arms so that his chest comes off the ground. At the same time the knees are brought forwards so that the feet come between the hands. The player can then stand up. If this action is done as soon as the chest touches the ground there will be no chance of banging the knees on the ground.

Teaching the forward dive

Naturally it is not wise just to throw the players a ball

and tell them to dive. As soon as players hurt themselves they will be put off the dive. If the method suggested is followed it will be possible to get most people doing the dive in ten minutes. Children find it particularly easy because they have the supple backs that are needed for this activity.

Stage 1
In pairs, one player does a handstand and the other catches both feet at the ankles. The player is then lowered slowly down to the floor with the head back so that the chest touches the floor first. This can only be done if the player relaxes his back.

Stage 2
From the press-up position, players kick their heels up and forwards over their seats. The head should be held back so that the face does not contact the ground. The back should be relaxed so that the chest can touch the ground first. If the back is not relaxed the whole body will land on the floor at the same time, which needless to say is none too comfortable.

Stage 3
From the crouch position the player must turn through 180 degrees. After turning, the player goes straight through the press-up position to the bow shape on the floor. This action should be completed as quickly as possible.

Stage 4
From the crouch position with one foot slightly in front of the other, the player dives up and forwards to land in the bow position. It is essential that the player dives up rather than at the floor. If he dives up he will have time to get his hands and then chest down to the floor before the rest of his body.

Naturally this is the most difficult stage. If the players attempt this stage before they have mastered the bow position fully they will land very heavily.

As the confidence of the player increases get him to take a step forward before he dives, then two steps and so on.

The hand action
The ball is hit on the back of the hand. The fingers should be kept stiff so that the hand makes a strong striking surface. On contact with the ball the hand is quickly flicked upwards. The movement must be made as short as possible. Remember that the player has to play the ball when he is only a matter of inches off the ground. If the movement is large he will not have time to get his hand down to assist his landing.

Practices

1) In the press-up position the player must play a ball thrown two feet in front of him. The ball must be hit at least six feet in the air.

2) As soon as the ball has been played the player kicks his legs up and forwards to land in the bow position.

3) The player is now ready to try the full movement. The ball must be thrown so that it drops for at least four feet. If the ball is thrown higher the player will have problems with his timing. If it is thrown lower he will overstretch trying to play it and forget his technique.

Some teachers and coaches teach this activity on mats to start with but this makes the activity unreal. The whole point of the activity is to learn how to land without getting hurt. As soon as the mats are introduced it is suggesting to the learner that there is a possibility of hurting himself. Another point is that once having taught the activity on the mat it is still necessary to overcome the fear of attempting it without a mat.

Once a player has learnt it he will soon tell the others that it is painless and they will copy him. If the players are not taught this technique their game will be the worse for it. The whole idea of volleyball is to prevent the ball from touching the floor and this technique enables players to play balls in difficult positions without injuring themselves.

The same technique can be used to play balls landing to the side. All that is required is for the player to pivot so that he can play the ball in front of himself. If it is a few paces away then he can run forward and dive in the normal fashion.

The one handed rolling dig to the side

This is the technique used by most ladies teams in preference to the dive, for obvious reasons. The ball is played on the underneath by sweeping the arm forwards and upwards. When played to the side it involves stretching the body as far as possible towards the ball. When used for a ball that is in front of the player it involves running to the side of the ball.

Technique of the one handed rolling dig to the side

When playing a ball to the right the player should stretch the right leg as far to that side as possible. This has the effect of lowering the player so that the ball can be played close to the floor and on the underside of the ball. It also means that the player has less distance to fall to the floor after contact with the ball thus minimising the discomfort!

The action of playing the ball involves sweeping the outstretched right arm forwards and upwards to contact the ball with the wrist or closed fist. After playing the ball the player falls onto her side. To regain her feet she can continue rolling over her shoulder, or stop her sideways movement and roll back to her original position. Many coaches feel that it is unwise to roll over the shoulder as this could bring the player into the path of another player.

When teaching the roll, start by getting the players to stretch as far as they can to the side without losing their balance, swing the arm back a short way, then forwards and upwards. They will then fall onto their side in exactly the same way as in the real situation. They should experiment with ways of regaining their feet until the whole movement flows smoothly. The secret of the technique is to stretch the leg as far as possible.

Playing the ball dropping forwards of the player
In this situation the player must very quickly run forward in a low position. at an angle which will bring her to the side of the ball. Once she has done this the ball is played with the normal sweeping action.

Very often the forward ball that the player must go for is at the side of the court. This means that the player must put herself in a position so that her body is parallel to the side line and she is facing into court. This will enable her to play the ball to her fellow players and not straight back across the net.

The serve
The Rules governing serving are;

RULE 13

Article 1; Service is the act of putting the ball into play. This is done by the right hand back-line player, who hits the ball with his hand (open or closed), or any part of the arm, in order to send the ball over the net into the opponents' court.

The server stands in the service area and hits the ball. At this moment of contact the service is completed.

The ball is struck after having been thrown in the air or released from the hand. The server is not allowed to strike the ball resting on his other hand.

After striking the ball, the player may land on the line or inside the court, so long as at the moment of impact he was behind the back line and within the service area.

If, after having been thrown or released from the hand, the ball falls to the ground without being hit or contacted the service is re-taken. However, the referee will not allow the game to be delayed in this manner.

The service is considered good if the ball passes over the net without touching it, and between the vertical net bands. The service must be made immediately after the referee has whistled. If the service is made before the whistle, it must be taken again.

Article 2; Duration of service;
A player continues to serve until his team commits a fault.

Article 3; Serving faults;
The referee will blow his whistle and signal 'change of service' when one of the following serving faults occur.

(a) The ball touches the net.

(b) The ball passes under the net.

(c) The ball touches one of the aerials (supposed to be extended indefinitely) or crosses the net outside of them.

(d) The ball touches a player of the serving team or any object before entering the opponents' court.

(e) The ball lands outside the limits of the opponents' court.

Article 4; Serving out of order;
If the service is made by the wrong player, the referee shall whistle 'change of service' and that side shall lose all the points scored whilst the wrong player was serving. The players of the team that was at fault shall revert to the correct positions.

See also Articles 5 - 7; Rule 14, Articles 1 & 2 and Rule 15, Article 1.

Extracts from the Official (I.V.B.F.) Commentary on Rule 13.
If the server throws the ball in the air but doesn't hit it and if it touches some part of his body as it falls, this counts as a fault and the ball is given to the other team.

Service cannot be made with two hands (e.g. with a dig).

At the moment he hits the ball, the server may not touch or step on the back line of the court. However, he may jump or move forward. As soon as the ball has been hit, the server may land on the end line or inside court, as he completes the serving action.

The service must be made as soon as the referee blows his whistle. The referee will allow a delay of about five seconds after blowing his whistle.

The server may make a second and last attempt at service for which he is allowed an additional five seconds.

A team can only score points when it is serving. For this reason it is essential that the service is legal so that the team is in a position to take advantage of their opportunity to score. It is pointless for players to try and score an ace with their service and hit into the net or out of court. When a player makes a bad serve he loses two possible points for his team. The point

68

his team could have scored if he had got the ball in play and the point the opponents may score from their service.

Every player must be able to serve consistently and with a reasonable amount of accuracy. There are several different types of serve and the one used should be the one which enables the player to get this consistency and accuracy.

Types of service
    (1) Underarm
    (2) Tennis
    (3) Hook or Windmill
    (4) Floating

Underarm Service
This the most simple and reliable service. It is the type recommended for beginners and girls.

Technique for the underarm service
The ball is held on the outstretched left hand at waist height about two feet in front of the right shoulder. The left foot should be kept about two feet in front of the right with the weight on the back foot.

The right arm is swung down from well behind the body, almost brushing the thigh, towards the ball. Just before the ball is contacted the ball is flipped a few inches into the air by the left hand.

As the hitting arm swings through, the weight should be transferred from the back foot to the front foot. This weight transference plays a great part in adding power to the service. Smaller players and girls will find great difficulty in getting the ball over the net without the aid of this transference.

The ball can be contacted with the heel of the hand, the wrist, or the inside of the clenched fist. Players should experiment to see which striking surface gives them the best results.

Teaching the underarm service
This is a very simple action for the player to learn. The main problems for the teacher or coach are to see that the arm is swung straight down and through like a pendulum, and that the weight is transferred in time with the arm swing.

Practices
(1)   Players hold the ball in the serving hand and stand with their legs spaced correctly and the weight on their back foot. The arm is swung through to bowl the ball so that it passes over the net. Make sure that the weight is transferred to the front foot as the arm swings through.

(2)   Standing 15 feet from the wall, the ball is held in front of the hitting shoulder. The player swings the arm through to hit the ball *out of the hand* at the wall. At this stage the player needs to concentrate fully on the arm swing and contacting the ball. This is made easier if he does not have to think about timing the arm swing with the flip up of the ball.

(3)   This is a practice to improve the timing of the weight transference with the arm swing. The player must serve the ball at the wall to hit it above a line ten foot high. The ball must bounce off the wall and travel as far across the gym as possible. The aim should be to try and hit the opposite wall. If the timing is right and sufficient force is used, the players will be able to get the ball most of the way across the average size gym. Without good use of weight transference the ball will travel only a short distance.

The players must now be given plenty of opportunity to serve in the real situation. They will not find it difficult to adjust to flipping the ball up before hitting it, if they have not already done so.

Common faults in the underarm service

Fault	*Reason*
1) Ball hits the roof	a) Player is hitting the underneath of the ball. This could be because the ball is held too high, or too close to the body.
	b) Player is swinging his arm upwards and not forwards through the ball.
	c) Ball is thrown too high and out of timing with the arm swing.
2) Ball consistently fails to gain enough height to pass over the net.	a) Ball is hit from directly behind instead of from slightly underneath.
	b) Arm is not being swung through correctly. Possibly being brought around the side.
	c) The ball is flipped up too early for the arm swing so that on contact it is too low.
	d) Ball is thrown too far in front of the body so that it is only just contacted by the player.
	e) Player is not making use of weight transference so that the ball has too little power.

The only way to correct these faults is to take the player back to the early practices and watch each serve closely. Check the various positions of the ball and body each time. Practice is essential if a player is to develop a good serve.

The tennis service

The tennis serve is a more difficult serve to make and receive. As its name suggests it is hit from above the head. It is a serve that requires a reasonable amount of arm strength to perform successfully. In addition the server must be able to time accurately the movement of the striking arm with the dropping ball.

Technique of the tennis service for a right-handed player

The player stands facing the net with his left foot approximately 18 inches in front of the right. The ball is held by the left hand just above head height, 18-24 inches in front of the right shoulder.

To hit the ball the player uses the palm of the hand. The fingers are kept together and pulled back so that the palm is as rigid as possible. With the elbow pointing to the front, the right hand is placed on the rear of the ball. The ball is tossed about two feet in the air as the right hand is withdrawn to the ear. At the same time as the hand is moving down to the ear the back is arched. Both the back and the arm are then extended to contact the ball sharply as it drops down. When the player becomes more experienced he can use a greater amount of back and arm movement in order to increase the speed of the serve.

Teaching the tennis service

(1) Players stand 10 feet from the wall with the ball and hands in the starting position for the tennis serve. The hitting hand is pulled back to the ear and then extended to hit the ball off the other hand.

Gradually increase the distance from the wall. A line drawn along the wall ten foot off the ground makes a good point for the server to aim at. The ball must

achieve this height within twenty feet, if it is to pass over the net.

(2)   In the same starting position as for (1). The players toss the ball six inches into the air and withdraw the right hand the same distance, before making the striking action. Gradually increase the height of the toss up and the distance the hand is withdrawn.

Timing the arm movement with the dropping ball is quite difficult and most bad serves are a result of an error in timing. If the player is introduced to the tennis serve in the way described he will learn the timing quite quickly.

Hook service

This is the big serve, the power serve of volleyball. At one time it was the most popular type of serve, but as the technique of the dig pass developed its potency became reduced. It is still very difficult to receive and can be used to good effect in a game by players who have mastered the technique.

Technique of the hook service for a right-handed player

The player stands sideways to the baseline with the feet astride. The ball is thrown above and in front of the head with the left hand.

As the ball is thrown up, the weight of the player is on his flexed back foot and the right arm is outstretched just above and outside the right knee.

The arm swings up along the plane of the body to hit the ball with the palm of the hand slightly behind the head. To give extra power to the serve the rear leg is extended and the weight transferred to the front foot in time with the arm swing. This body shift also helps to bring the head slightly forward of the dropping ball, enabling the player to contact the ball in the best position. If the ball is hit directly above the head, it will be hit too late and will not gain enough height to pass over the net.

The wrist should be kept loose and the hand allowed to cup as it contacts the ball. This will help to curve the flight path of the serve and keep it in court. The arm should also be slightly bent at the elbow. If it is rigid then the ball will gain too much height and will not be too difficult to receive.

There can be no doubt that this is a difficult serve to master and to be able to play with the consistency that the modern game demands. With the fast arm swing there is no room for error in the throwing up of the ball, or the timing of the swing with the dropping ball.

Teaching the hook service

(1)   In pairs with one partner standing on a bench, arm outstretched to the 'side, holding a ball in the palm of his hand. The other player stands at right

72

angles to his partners arm, with the ball positioned above and very slightly in front of his head. From this position he will be able to practice the arm swing without worrying about throwing the ball up or timing the swing with the ball.

(2)   An alternative to the partner holding the ball is to suspend a ball from a beam at the required height.

(3)   Once the player has got the feel of the arm swing and body movements he must try to coordinate these with the throw up of the ball. Start by restricting the length of the arm swing and the height of the throw up. Gradually increase both until the full serve is reached.

This service requires constant practice and should only be used in matches once the player has mastered it in training.

Floating service

In the past ten years the Japanese have developed the technique of serving the ball so that its flight pattern is very unpredictable for the receiver. During the latter part of its flight a ball served with this technique will suddenly change direction in either the vertical or horizontal plane.

This change can be most disconcerting for the receiver. He will be just about to play the ball when it runs out of steam and drops suddenly, or swerves to one side. It is possible for an expert server to hit the ball so that after crossing the net it passes outside the sideline, the receiver does not attempt to play it thinking that it will land out of court, but at the last moment it swerves back into court.

The serve gets its name from the way in which the ball appears to float through the air, often wavering from side to side in the middle part of its flight.

These flight characteristics are achieved by hitting the ball so that it does not spin and so that it achieves a velocity of 19 m.p.h. (30 km/h). To prevent spin the ball must be hit through its centre of gravity. At the required velocity the flow of air around the ball causes the ball to waver as the drag forces reach a critical point. As the ball slows down it will fall away towards its heaviest point, the valve. If the valve is positioned on the right at the time it is hit then the ball will fall away to the right. By placing it at the bottom the ball will dip very suddenly and by placing it at the front it is possible to make the path of the ball flatten out during the last few feet. This creates the impression that the ball has suddenly picked up speed again. When used effectively the ball will often hit the receiver's upper arms because he has misjudged the landing place.

To obtain maximum effect the ball should be the minimum weight allowed by the rules and the surface as smooth as possible. A rough surface alters the flow of air around the ball and helps to create spin. For these reasons it is more difficult to make the all leather sewn ball float than the leather covered moulded ball.

The technique of the floating service
It must be pointed out that there are many different styles used to hit the ball so that it will float. It does not really matter what style the player adopts as long as he achieves the following:-

a) The ball is hit so that it does not spin.

b) The ball achieves the speed necessary for the ball to float.

Style 1
This style is based on the tennis smash technique. The hand is kept stiff and in line with the forearm. The wrist stays rigid throughout the whole movement. The ball is hit from above net height if the player is tall enough, or as high as the player can reach without spoiling his technique. The ball must be hit sharply and squarely with the palm of the hand.

Style 2
Using a technique very similar to that of the hook service, the player also tries to contact the ball sharply and squarely, with the minimum of follow through. Again the arm and wrist must be kept rigid. There are two stages in the movement of the hitting arm. The first brings it up to within a couple of feet of the ball and the second accelerates it from this position to strike the ball. This ensures that the ball is hit from directly behind and not underneath. The ball can be struck with the palm of the rigid hand or on the fingers of the clenched fist.

Style 3
This style makes it easier for the player to ensure that the ball does not gain any rotation as a result of the throw up. It also enables him to position the valve on contact more accurately. It does, however, require good coordination of the arm movement.

The player stands sideways on to the baseline leaning over his back foot. The ball is held in the left hand. The right arm is kept straight and just below the ball. The two arms move upwards and forwards in unison. When the ball is about two feet from the hitting position the arm holding the ball accelerates and releases the ball in the path of the right hand. The right arm then comes through to hit the ball sharply and squarely.

To gain the speed necessary for the ball to float the

player will have to stand quite a way behind the baseline. It is not uncommon to see top players standing as much as 20 feet behind the line.

It is possible to vary the point on the opponents' court where the ball is going to fall away by increasing or reducing the distance the server stands behind the line. If the player wants the ball to land nearer the net he should start further back and vice versa.

Which serve?

For beginners there is no doubt that they must be taught the underarm service. They should use this service until they are reasonably experienced. Once the player is able to smash the ball and play a reasonable level of volleyball it will not be too difficult for him to learn the tennis serve. The timing needed for the tennis serve is not unlike that used in the smash. The hand action is also very similar.

Each serve has its advantages and disadvantages. The underarm serve is the easiest to use and the most reliable. Once the player has mastered it he will rarely fail to get the ball into play. It is also the easiest to receive because the curve of the flight path means that the ball must travel upwards to cross the net. This makes it a very slow and simple serve to dig. It is almost impossible to vary the pace of this serve.

The tennis serve is hit at net height, or just below, which means that it drops much steeper and faster then the underarm serve. It is possible to vary the speed of the tennis serve and to add spin to the ball. The area of court that it is possible to serve into with this serve is less than the underarm serve. The trajectory of the serve makes it very difficult, if not impossible, to serve into areas of the court close to the net. If enough height is given to the underarm serve it can be played to almost any part of the court.

The hook service has a tendency to dip very suddenly. This combined with its speed causes many problems for the poor 'digger'. However the length of the hook serve is very consistent, and the amount of court it can be served into is less than with the other two serves. Most players who have developed this serve have a particular rhythm, which means that the ball nearly always travels the same distance. The server has less control over where the ball is hit with this serve. It is a very difficult serve to master with sufficient consistency to warrant its use in a match, but when a player has mastered it, it can often be used to good effect. However, the number of points scored with this serve must be balanced against the number of times it is unsuccessful.

The floating serves are the most difficult to receive. Not every player is able to develop his technique sufficiently well to be able to make the ball float. Once a player has achieved this he has a powerful weapon. Even the world's best players find trouble digging a good floating service. The characteristic sudden drop of the floated serve means that most areas of the court are vulnerable. To use this serve there must be a large area behind the base line so that the player can hit the ball with the correct amount of speed and still get it into court. One of the main weaknesses of this type of service is that players often hit the ball too hard and it goes out of court.

Whichever serve the player decides to use he must practice it thoroughly. It is no use trying every service in a match just to find one that works. The most important thing that a serve must do is get the ball in play. If the player can do this and at the same time make it more difficult for the opponent to receive the ball, then he is giving his team a bonus. It is pointless to go all out for the ace serve each time, score twice and make five foul serves.

Serving like all other techniques of the game must be practised. The practices should be related to targets so the player is not just mechanically hitting the ball over the net but trying to control his movements accurately.

The smash or spike

The smash or spike as it is sometimes called, is the attacking weapon in volleyball. It entails a player jumping as high as possible into the air near the net and hitting the ball strongly down into his opponents'

court. It is said that the ball just after impact is travelling at 100 m.p.h. Japanese scientists have shown that it takes 0.33 secs for a ball smashed by a good player to travel to the base line of the opposite court, which means that the average speed is 57 m.p.h. It is obvious from these figures that the smash is more than a player jumping up and belting the ball with his hand. It is a very complex technique that requires athleticism, good timing, quick thinking and plenty of practice.

The smash is the finishing touch to the team's play. It is the shot designed to win the rally for the team. As a result the smasher has the spotlight during a game and every player wants to be a specialist smasher. Unfortunately, the physical requirements for a top level smasher are more limiting than for any other role in volleyball. The player must be tall (over six feet is usual), and have a good vertical jump. Smaller players with exceptionally good jumps are often able to make the grade as well. It is important to remember that the ball must be hit at a minimum height of eight feet to clear the net and in a match it needs to be even higher in order to pass the blockers. Perhaps the best smasher ever is the almost legendary Boegajenkov of Russia whose vertical jump has been measured at 42 inches!

The smash can be divided into four stages;
  a) The approach to the net
  b) The take-off
  c) The movements of the body in the air prior to hitting the ball
  d) The hitting action

a) The approach to the net

The smasher does not stand by the net for the smash. He starts his smashing action from the attack line, ten feet from the net. This approach gives the player time to move into the correct position to play the ball. In addition it helps him to gain the maximum vertical jump for the smash. Obviously, the higher he is able to jump the greater is his smashing potential.

When the player is smashing in either of the wing positions he should start his approach from the junction of the sideline and the attack line. If he starts from further in court he will find difficulty in getting into a good position to smash a set near the edge of the court.

During the approach to the net, the smasher's shoulders should be facing towards the net and not the setter. If his shoulders are towards the setter he will find it more difficult to smash. Firstly, he will be hitting the ball from a position in which he cannot see the block or court clearly. Secondly, it will restrict his movements and reduce the effectiveness of his smash.

The steps that the player takes towards the ball must bring him to a position where the ball is dropping about eighteen inches in front of his hitting shoulder. He must also achieve a position from which he can get a good take-off. Some players take two steps, and others three, towards the ball, depending on the distance they have to cover and individual preference (Fig. 53). The approach steps bring the player into a position with both feet close together and the legs flexed (Fig. 54).

The first step brings the player in towards the net. The final step brings him towards the dropping ball. When the player begins his approach he has a *general* idea of the court position where he will hit the ball. During the approach he gets more information from the set pass and is able to select the *particular* court position. Any necessary adjustments to the line of

77

his approach are made by pivoting on the foot during the last step.

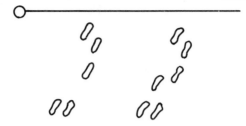

Fig. 53   Two step approach to the net (left) and a three step approach (right)

The approach to the net must be smooth so that the player is able to make the best use of the forward movement he has gained during the take-off phase.

During the last step the trailing foot must be brought forward quickly to join the other one for the take-off. The take-off is from both feet. If the smasher is right-handed the front of his right foot should finish about six inches behind the front of the left foot. This allows the player to get a better attitude in the air and increases the strength of the shot.

The last step, when both feet are off the ground at the same time, must be kept low over the ground. The feet should just skim the surface of the floor. By keeping low the player makes the movement much smoother.

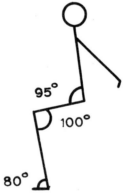

Fig. 54   Recommended position and joint angles prior to take off in the smash

The smasher should land with his legs flexed and arms well behind the shoulders. From this position he is able to get a vigorous take-off. During the approach the player should lower his body position and swing the arms well

78

back. If the player waits until he has landed before carrying out these actions, he will waste all the forward momentum he has gained.

The approach to the net does not necessarily have to be straight. The player may curve his approach so that he is able to hit the ball in a different direction to that he was originally following. Most smashes are hit in the direction of the approach. As will be seen later this helps to make the smash as strong as possible. By altering the starting point, the angle of the approach to the net and the path of the approach, the player is able to change the direction of his shot before he hits the ball. These changes in direction can be gradual or they can be relatively sudden—occurring in the last step. Sometimes the player turns in the air just after take-off. This turn is made possible by a change in the foot positions at the end of the approach.

It must be remembered that the smashing action starts with the approach to the ball. The approach should not be thought of solely as an aid to gaining a higher jump.

b) The take-off

The take-off begins as soon as both heels touch the ground after the approach. The player must rock over the heels and onto the toes in a continuous movement. In this way he is able to convert a certain amount of his horizontal momentum into vertical momentum.

As the heels rock over, the arms swing forwards and upwards as strongly as possible. The hip, knee and ankle joints are vigourously extended. In this way the maximum impulse is generated at take-off. The approach and take-off should be as fast as possible. The quicker it is, the less time the blockers have to prepare the block.

The take-off must be two footed. In this way the player gains maximum height with maximum control. Prior to taking off, the player is moving towards the net. He may not touch the net or cross the centre line during the smashing action. This means that he must check all forward movement with the take-off action. By landing with both feet flexed and close together after the approach, the player is able to check this movement.

c) The movements of the body in the air prior to hitting the ball

During take-off the arms are swung forwards and upwards. This action continues as the player leaves the ground. The right arm flexes at the elbow. The hand comes back past the ear with the elbow pointing forwards.

The left arm reaches up towards the ball. This action drops the hitting shoulder in relation to the left shoulder. The position of the player's trunk and arms are now similar to those of a tennis player just after the ball has been thrown up. The actions of the smasher and tennis player up to contact of the ball are almost identical.

79

The back is arched so that it can be used to add extra power to the smash. If the arms are forcefully extended during the take-off the back will arch naturally.

As the ball drops closer towards the hitting shoulders the left arm is brought down, thus raising the right shoulder and arm. This action is essential if the player is to hit the top of the ball. Without this action the player will probably hit the ball from directly behind. When the ball is hit from this direction it travels forward a long way before landing—possibly out of court. The action of dropping the left arm also brings the right shoulder and arm forward towards the dropping ball.

d) The hitting action

The player is now in a position to start the hitting action. The trunk moves forwards towards the ball. The hand which has been kept by the ear now comes upwards and forwards. The fingers are kept together and the wrist loose. The ball is hit with the open hand and not the clenched fist. In this way maximum control over the direction and trajectory of the smash is obtained.

As the hand nears the ball the wrist is extended. In this way the ball is hit downwards and forwards across the net. The contact with the ball must be sharp so that the ball is not dragged or pushed.

After the ball has been hit the hand must be brought down without touching the net. If the elbow is rotated outwards so that it is parallel with the shoulders the hand will be brought in close to the body, thus avoiding the net.

The smash is a powerful action which requires good timing of the body movements. It is a fast action and once started cannot be stopped. For this reason it is essential that the player has positioned himself correctly before he starts the hitting action.

To obtain a powerful smash the player must use the combined forces derived from the extension of the back, shoulder, elbow and wrist. This is achieved by hitting the ball when it is in line with his right shoulder. If the ball is hit outside this line the smash will be weaker. This is because the player is only using the forces derived from an extension of the elbow and wrist.

Most smashes are hit along the line of the hitting shoulder. The smasher can alter the direction of his smash by angling his wrist just prior to its extension. In this way he can hit the ball from one side and this will send the ball away from the line of his shoulder. It is essential that players learn to vary the line of their smash so that they can hit the ball past a block.

The hook or windmill smash

As its name suggests, this type of smash involves a circular movement of the

80

arm. At the time the ball is played the smasher is sideways to the net. The ball is hit with an action similar to that of the hook service, when the ball is above and just behind the head.

This type of smash is mainly used when the ball is set several feet back from the net. In these circumstances the ball is hit from as high as possible so that it passes over the top of the blockers. When a smasher finds that he has gone too close to the net for the set he may alter his actions so that he can play the ball with a hook smash, instead of a tennis smash.

The right arm of the player starts from a position in which it is across his chest. It then swings back and up in a wide arc. The ball is hit with the open hand. Top spin can be added to the ball by bringing the hand up and over the ball during contact.

The weakness of the hook smash is that the player has little control over its direction or length. It is not a smash that should be attempted by inexperienced players.

Tactical Ball

There are many occasions when it is not practical or wise to smash the ball hard across the net. The block may be well formed, the set badly placed for a smash, the smasher slightly off balance, or there may be a particular weakness in the opponents' defensive line up. In these instances players should use a tactical ball. There are two types of tactical ball:-

a) The dump
b) The soft smash

a) The dump

The dump is a ball placed just over, or to the side of the block. The actions of the player for the dump are the same as the smash until the last phase, the hitting action. Instead of hitting the ball by bringing the arm and hand through strongly, the player stops the action just before he contacts the ball. At this point his arm will be almost straight. The ball contacts the end joint of the fingers and is played by slightly extending the wrist. The amount of movement allowed by referees varies greatly from country to country. Just as with the volley the dump is very subjective. In some countries the ball seems to stay on the fingers a long time, while in others only the slightest touch is allowed. The player must disguise this movement as much as possible so that although he has decided to dump the ball, he must make his actions as close to those of the smash as possible until the last moment.

With practice the dump becomes a very potent shot. An expert in the technique can place the ball accurately just over the net or to the side. The ball then drops into a space and the defenders have very little time to move forward and play the ball before it touches the floor. However, if it is not well disguised, or is used too frequently teams will easily play the first touch and the attacking shot has been wasted.

b) The soft smash

This is exactly what its name suggests. The smashing action is slowed down so that the ball can be played more accurately into a space or to a particular player in the opposing court. The dump can be read by experienced back court players because at a certain point, just before the ball is played, the arm straightens. With this shot they are unable to get any clues apart from the speed at which the smashing action is carried out.

Using this method the ball can be placed accurately in gaps which are not in the immediate area of the block. When a defender is too far forward a soft smash can be placed behind him near the baseline. Another situation in which it can be used is to place the ball in the centre of the back court. The back court players will be expecting a fast, hard smash. The ball dropping in front of them will catch them by surprise.

Teaching smashing

The smash is the most popular technique in volleyball. Every child sees himself as a smasher extraordinaire and cannot wait to have a go! This poses problems for the teacher. He must see that this urge is satisfied to a certain extent to maintain interest, and yet he must ensure that the beginners get a good grounding in technique. As soon as the child gets the opportunity to smash, his prime object is to hit the ball as hard as he can, regardless of technique. Many children will find the smashing action requires more physical ability than they possess. This does not mean that the teacher should forget about these children. If he organises any game, whether it be a small-side or full-side game, it will break down if the child cannot smash the ball across the net.

The method of introducing the smash proposed will help to solve these three problems. The child has the opportunity to hit the ball, the teacher can give the child a good basic technique and all children will be able to smash the ball sufficiently well to keep the ball in play.

The aim is to get every child capable of jumping off the ground using a two-foot take-off and hitting the ball in a controlled manner while in the air. In the early stages of teaching volleyball the players will be playing on small courts. This means that they must learn to control the amount of force they use to hit the ball so that it stays in court. The smasher who likes to use brute force will soon find that he is hitting the ball out of court so often that he gets fed up and starts to soften the smash.

Stage 1:

1) In pairs standing ten feet apart. One player acts as the feeder each time.

82

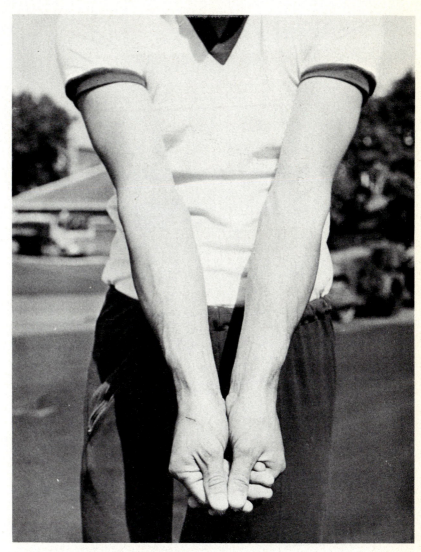

The Dig Pass - The recommended hand grip (see page 56)

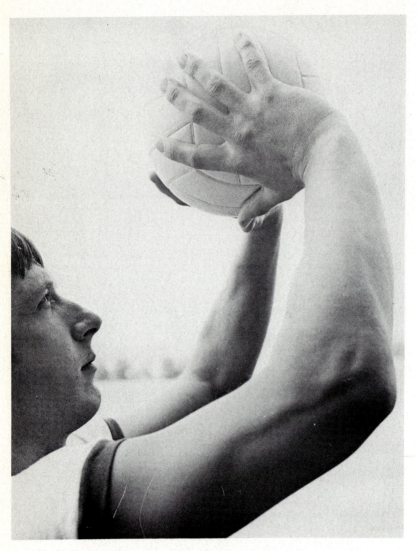

The Volley Pass. The position of the fingers around the ball (see page 27)

He throws the ball into the air so that it drops in front of his partner. The partner must jump up and play the ball on the finger tips of one hand, back to his partner. Emphasise the swinging of both arms back behind the body before take-off and upwards on take-off. The ball should be played from as high as possible. Demonstrate how the height of the jump is affected if the player does not crouch before take-off.

2)   The same as (1) except that after throwing the ball up the feeder must crouch down. The smasher must then play the ball down to him. Vary the distance between the two players. Vary the position of the feeder after throwing the ball up so that the smasher gets used to controlling the ball.

Stage 2:

1)   The same situation as in the previous stage. The players must now hit the ball with the palm of the hand. It must be hit from as high as possible. Do not allow the ball to be hit with a bent arm. If the ball is hit with a bent arm, the speed of the ball will be too great for the feeder to catch.

2)   Players stand fifteen feet apart with one player holding the ball in his left hand above his head. He must hit the ball with the palm of his hand so that it bounces to his partner. The ball must be hit *above* head height. If it is hit from a lower position it is an entirely different technique to that which the players must learn for the smash.

Stage 3:

1)   Players stand in front of a net or rope with a ball. They stand four feet from the net and throw the ball fifteen feet into the air. Then, using the technique already practised, they jump up and hit the ball across the net, from as high as possible, using the palm of the hand. The emphasis should be on control.

2)   In pairs standing at the net. One player stands sideways by the net and throws the ball up into the air so that it lands about two feet in front of him. The other player stands about six feet from the net. He must then take one pace in towards the ball and jump up to play it in the normal way. The take-off must be from two feet. This practice serves as an introduction to learning the approach and also to timing the take-off with the dropping ball.

Stage 4:

1)   This is a practice for introducing the approach. Draw two 4 foot circles in line with each other between the net and the attack line. The players start on the attack line, place their preferred foot in the first circle and move off that foot to land with both feet in the second circle.

On landing in the second circle they should have legs flexed and arms well behind the body so that they can get a good jump. After jumping up they should land inside the second circle. If they do, it will show them that they managed to check all forward movement during the take-off.

2) Now go back to Stage 3 (2) with the player making a full approach.

Stage 5:
1) Gradually throw the ball farther away from the setter each time. This means that the smasher must not only judge how long the ball will take to come down to a height at which he can hit it, but also where he can hit it. His approach must bring him to this spot at the right moment.

Players should not attempt this stage until they have mastered the complete movement of the smash as in Stage 3 (2). If they try to smash a ball set in this way before they have learnt how to combine the approach, take-off and hitting action into one smooth and controlled movement they will ruin their existing technique.

2) The setter now throws the ball above his head and then volleys the ball for the smasher to hit. This will soon show the players how accurate their volley is. It also means that the smashers will have to hit balls which are inconsistent in height and length. This will be useful practice for picking the correct approach and timing.

In schools, teachers will find that they only need go as far as Stage 3 in the first instance. This will teach the children enough to be able to use the smash in small-side games. As proficiency improves then the extra stages can be taught. By the end of stage 3 all players should be capable of jumping up and hitting the ball in a controlled manner back across the net. This will greatly increase the enjoyment they find in small-side games.

Common faults in smashing
The majority of smashing faults arise from an incorrect approach to the ball. Incorrect positioning in relation to the ball greatly reduces the effectiveness of the hitting action.

Approach faults
1) After his approach the player is in a position where the ball is dropping inside the hitting shoulder.

To play the ball he will have to reach across his body, or drop his left shoulder to bring the right shoulder across behind the ball.

2) The player's approach has brought him to a position where the ball will have to be played outside his hitting shoulder. This makes the shot very weak.

3) The approach has brought the player too far behind the ball. He can only just play the ball and it will probably be hit from so low that it goes into the net or block.

84

4) The player misjudges where the ball will drop and has to alter the angle of his approach at the last moment.

In each of these cases there is no simple corrective practice that will cure the fault in a short time. The faults stem from wrong predictions about where the ball will land. The player should be given a large number of sets which are consistent in length. The teacher or coach should watch each smash closely and tell the player how close to, or far away he is from the correct point. The only way to cure approach faults is for the player to have guided practice.

Take-off faults

1) *One footed take-off.* This may be caused by a late approach of the player, who then jumps forward off one foot to try and contact the ball before it is too late. Continually taking off on one foot is a bad fault because it leads to a poor position in the air and the likelihood of net faults.

2) *The player travels into the net during or after the smash.* This means that the player has not been able to check the forward movement he has gained from the approach. Make sure that he is landing in a flexed position, heels first at the end of the approach. In this way his forward momentum can be checked during the take-off.

3) *The take-off is very slow.* The player is obviously not obtaining the height or speed of which he is capable. there may be several reasons for the slow take-off. The player may not be linking the take-off to the approach. Instead of commencing the take-off as soon as the heels land, the player waits until he has landed fully. The arms must be swung upwards and forwards vigorously from behind the body during the take-off. The player may have a tendency to jump into the starting position for the take-off. This will mean that his legs have to flex a lot to enable him to regain his balance before take-off.

A method of practising the approach and take-off with some method of judging performance, is to approach and try to smash the basketball ring or back-board.

4) *Taking off too early.* This is because the player is starting his approach as soon as the ball leaves the setter's hands. His approach should begin as the ball is nearing the highest point of its path.

Faults with the hitting action

1) *The ball travels a long way before landing.* This is because the ball is hit from behind instead of on top. Check the movement of the non-hitting arm to see if it is helping the player to bring the right shoulder up as high as possible before the ball is hit.

2) *Player follows through after the smash to contact the net with his hands.* The elbow should be rotated outwards so that it is parallel with the

shoulder. This will bring the hand down in front of the chest away from the net.

A summary of the body position and movements during the smashing action.

The legs: A 2 or 3 step approach is used. During the approach the shoulders should be towards the net. The player lands in a flexed position on both feet at the end of the approach. A two footed take-off is used. As the heels land after the approach the player should rock over onto the toes to get a fast and smooth take-off. The take-off must be as fast as possible. The hip, knee and ankle joints should be vigorously extended.

The arms: The arms should be swung well behind the body during the approach. As the take-off commences the arms should be swung forwards and upwards as fast as possible. This aids take-off, helps arch the back and gets the arms ready for the smash. The left arm reaches for the ball. The right hand comes back to the ear, elbow pointing to the front. The left arm is pulled down to raise the right arm. The ball is hit sharply with the open hand. The force for the smash is derived from extension of the back, shoulder, elbow and wrist. This is most effective when the ball is hit in front of the shoulder. After the ball has been hit the elbow is rotated outwards so that the hand comes down close to the chest.

Hints for players.
The best piece of advice anyone can give about the smash is to THINK BEFORE YOU HIT. It is no use possessing the world's hardest smash if you can't beat a block or get it into court. Remember that while you are trying to get that ball over the net and down into your opponent's court, two or three of their players are trying to stop you. If you just blast away then you are helping them. A good smasher is one who thinks about each shot and makes sure that he makes best use of each set. The player who blasts a super smash past a block and then hits the next few into the block or out of court is not a good smasher. The French call this type of player a 'smasher bestial' for obvious reasons!

To smash you must get yourself a good approach. After blocking or defending in back court, get yourself in a position near the attack line for an approach. Your smash will be all the better for it.

Watch the set as it leaves the setter's hands. Look at the angle of release, estimate the speed of the ball. You will need this information to enable you to predict where you can hit the ball from. You must be thinking about the position right from the first moment the set comes towards you, otherwise you will not have time to think about other aspects of the smash.

Start your approach for the smash as the ball nears its highest point. As you become more experienced you will find that the timing will become automatic.

The angle of approach to the ball will greatly determine the direction of the smash. Position yourself so that you have as much court as possible to hit into. If your approach is too acute you will find that you will have to hit the ball across your chest to get it into court. The angle of the approach is partly determined by the position where the ball will drop. If it is well to the side of the court then the best angle of approach will be straight. To hit the diagonal shot from this position you would need to start from well outside the court which in this instance is impractical.

As you are taking off, start to look for your opposing blockers. Are they beginning to form up? Will they get there in time? To be able to think about these things, the movements you are making must be well learned, this will come from practice. You must also be confident that you have picked the right spot for the smash and that you have timed your approach well because you must take your eyes off the ball at this stage.

Look to see if there are any obvious gaps in your opponents' defence. You should already know what defensive system they are using and be looking at the weak points of that system for a target.

When you are playing in position 4 your best shot is the diagonal shot. This is because the ball is coming straight to your shoulder from the setter. The block will also be easier to pass on the inside. If the block lines up exactly with your hitting shoulder when the ball is set a couple of feet in from the sideline, it will be so far across to the centre of the court that it will leave a huge gap down the side line. Usually the blockers line up a bit wider for a smash from 4. It is only a matter of a foot or so, but every little helps.

Use your wrist to turn the ball past the block, or if there is a gap, through the middle of the block. As you are about to hit the ball you should be looking for a gap in the block. If the outside blocker does not get his hands angled into court then smash the ball off his hands so that it rebounds out of court. To do this you must try and pivot towards him just before you play the shot. This will enable you to hit the shot accurately and forcefully.

Vary your smashes so that the block does not find it easy to line up in your path. If you hit 90% of your shots on the diagonal then the blockers will soon realise this and set the block to cut out all diagonal shots.

If a block is beating you consistently, don't just carry on blasting the ball hoping to get through. Try hitting the ball from higher up. Although this will make it a slower smash, it will stand a good chance of going over the block. Try a few dumps over or round the block. The object must be to become unpredictable. When you are smashing you have the advantage that you know where you are going to smash the ball. Keep that advantage by hitting each ball according to its position and the circumstances at the time and not to a fixed predetermined pattern.

If you get a bad set don't glower at the setter or make comments to him. You must hit whatever is set to you and made as good a shot as you can. Not every bad set is the fault of the setter. The pass to the setter very often leaves a lot to be desired. Even so every setter can have an off day or put one or two bad sets up during a game. If you think you have a right to criticize the setter if he gives you a bad set, remember he has the same right when you make a bad smash from a good set. If the setter gives you a good set, thank him, he will be pleased to know that you recognise the part he played. It is said that behind every successful man there is a strong woman. The same can be said about a smasher. Without a good setter who knows just where to put the ball for a particular smasher, that smasher will not be so successful.

Every ball that is above net height should be played with an attacking shot. Some smashers will only hit those sets that are perfect. The rest they volley or lob over. This is not good enough. Try to hit over every ball that you can with the smashing action. This does not mean that you must hit every ball the same way. If the set is difficult then hit the ball over using a wrist action and not the full shoulder, arm and wrist movement. In this way the ball will be passing over the net and down into the opponents' court. This is a more difficult ball for them to play than a volley.

You must practise the smashing action until the action becomes almost second nature to you. In this way you will be able to concentrate more on what you are going to do with the ball. I want to finish with the same advice given at the start of this section. THINK BEFORE YOU SMASH.

Blocking

The main attacking weapon in volleyball is the smash or spike; an opponent hits the ball from above the net, across and downwards into the other half of the court. Blocking is the counter to the smash.

To form a block, front line players of the defending team jump vertically opposite the smasher and place a wall of hands in the path of the ball, hoping to deflect the ball into his court.

The rules governing blocking

Rules 17 and 19 govern blocking.

Rule 17

Article 4a) The blocking action is made near the net and consists of attempting to stop the ball coming from the opposite side with any part of the player's body above the waist.

The block can be performed by any or all of the front-line players. Any player is considered as having the intention to block if he places one or both hands above the level of the top of the net, whilst in a position close to the net.

A block is a blocking action in which the ball is contacted by one or more of the players concerned.

Article 4b) Any player taking part in a blocking action in the course of which the ball is contacted, shall have the right to make a second play at the ball. Such a second shot, however, shall count as the second of the three hits allowed to the team.

Article 4c) If the ball touches one or more players in the block, it will be counted as only one hit for the team, even if these contacts are not made simultaneously by the players in the block.

Article 4d) The three back-line players may not block at the net, but may play the ball in any other position near or away from the block.

Article 4e) The hands of the blockers may reach over the net. However, the blockers shall not contact the ball over the opponents' court until after the completion of the opponents' attack.

Article 5 When the ball, after having touched the top of the net as well as the opponents' block, returns to the attacker's side, the players of this team have the right to three hits.

Rule 19

Article 1 Touching the ball with the hands over the net in the opponents' court, before opponents' attack is completed, shall constitute a fault.

The block is most commonly thought of as the main defensive weapon in volleyball. This is a correct, but also an incomplete definition. In the modern game the block is an important attacking weapon. A good team usually gains about four points per set from its blocking. It is true to say that the team that gains control at the net wins the game. If the block is strong the opponents' attack is unsettled.

The smash will win service and the block, points. For unless the opponents' attack can be prevented from crossing the net, or its effectiveness be reduced so that a successful counter attack can be set up, points will not be scored. This is something that tends to be overlooked by team coaches and by players. Much time is spent practising the smash and little, if any, on blocking. An equal amount of time should be spent on both in training.

How many blockers?
The number of blockers depends on the position of the attack i.e. wings or centre and the build-up of the attack.

Two-man block
In the wing positions a two-man block should be used whenever possible. When the attacking team uses feint attacks or builds up attacks quickly, the centre blocker may not have enough time to move across and complete the block. He must make the attempt each time; this will give his team confidence, keep the pressure on the smashers and sometimes he will just get a touch to the ball which may help his team in the back court. (Fig. 55)

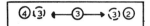

Fig. 55   Two man block

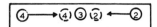

Fig. 56   Three man block

Three-man block
A three-man block is used when an attack is made through the middle section of the court. The two wing players, (nos. 2 and 4), move in towards the centre blocker (no. 3) and place their hands next to his in the air. (Fig. 56)

One-man block
At certain times during a game (e.g. when a ball has been volleyed or dug too close to the net so that an opponent can smash it back; during a rally when a team has not been able to reform properly along the front line, or, when feint attacks are used), a one-man block has to be used. It must be stressed that wherever possible two-man blocks should be used at the wings and three-man blocks in the centre.

Block leaders
When two or three players form a block it is essential that a block leader is chosen. It is the responsibility of the block leader to see that the block is in the right position. Without a block leader, front line players will all try to set

the block, with the result that a great deal of bumping occurs along the net, which could cause net faults, and the block itself will be unco-ordinated.

Some teams use the wing players, (nos. 2 and 4) to lead the block for a wing attack and no. 3 when a centre attack is made; other teams use no. 3 to lead the block in all positions. The latter system is the most difficult to play and demands a great deal from the player in this position. If the centre blocker is late moving across to the wings when he is the block leader the block will not be set. At all levels of play the wing system is the most widely used. Even in this system the centre blocker is required to move very quickly to complete the block against a wing attack. Most smashers when confronted with a block will try to turn the ball inside the block along the diagonal. The middle player (no. 3) must close up to the block leader to cut out these shots. For this reason many teams switch their best blocker into the middle.

To be effective a block must be in the right place at the right time. This means that there are two aspects to consider, *positioning* and *timing*.

Positioning

Many players can be seen hopefully blocking opposite the ball. Hopefully, because in this position they are lucky if they contact the ball. It is easiest for the spiker to hit the ball along the line of his body. A good spiker will also be able to angle his shot by using his wrist, but the amount he can do this is limited and a well set block should be able to cut out these shots. It follows, therefore, that if the blockers block immediately opposite the ball, they will only contact the ball if the attacker approaches the net at right angles, or turns the ball into the block. (Fig. 57)

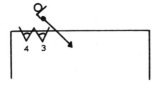

Fig. 57

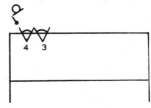

Fig. 58

The block can be thought of as similar to the parry in boxing; just as the boxer places his palm in the path of his opponent's fist, so the blockleader must place his outside hand in the path of the smasher's hitting hand (Fig. 58). This means that providing the block times its take-off correctly, it has a very good chance of blocking the shot. Most smashers will attempt to turn the shot inside the outside blocker and the centre blocker must close up tight to block this shot.

91

The block leader should concentrate on watching the smasher and not the ball. The smasher must hit the ball, so he will be adjusting his body position and timing in relation to the ball. Watch him and he will show you where the ball is and therefore where to position the block.

When the block is set correctly the amount of court the smasher is able to hit into is reduced to a small amount down the line, and a larger area inside the block. (Fig. 59)

The area down the line is very small, difficult to hit into and easily covered by one player. To hit into the other side of the court the player will have to hit across several hands in the block.

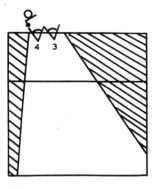

Fig. 59

Timing

The smasher can hit the ball at any point between the highest point he can reach and the top of the net. The point at which he hits it, is determined by his own preference and the timing of the block.

If the block is late the smasher will hit the ball from as high as possible before the block comes up. If the block is early, from as low as possible, as the block goes down. Timing is crucial in the blocking action.

The block should take off just after the smasher. If the blocker is to stand a chance of blocking the smash he must get his forearms at least across the net. To do this he must be a minimum height off the ground. This height is determined by his own height and the distance he must jump before he can put his arms across the net without touching it. It follows, therefore, that when he is below this height on the way up, he is not able to block at his most effective. The same holds for his descent. If he takes off the same time as the smasher he will only be able to block well during the time he is above this minimum height. The smasher however is able to hit the ball throughout the whole time his hitting hand is above the net. The blocker must try to be

92

in a good blocking position at the time the ball is struck. This is best achieved if the block takes off just after the smasher.

It is often useful for the block leader to set the timing of the take-off in all three positions. More experienced players will develop their own timing pattern according to their jumping ability and speed of take-off.

In positions 2 and 4 the blockers should stand about six feet in from the side lines. This shortens the distance they have to move to form a centre block. It also means that they are inside the position where they are likely to block. As they get the smashers line of approach they will be facing him and therefore more likely to position themselves in the exact spot for the block.

The wing players should watch closely the player opposite them so that they are not caught unprepared by a parallel, short, or overhead set. The middle blocker must also be watching the setter's hand and body to see where the set is going.

All blockers should sidestep along the net when moving to a new position. In top level play the centre blocker often finds it difficult to get across to close the block using the normal sidestep approach. Many top players use a normal running approach, take off using a full arm swing, and turn their trunk in mid-air so that their hands are correctly placed. This is a very difficult technique but one that experienced players may find suits them. Beginners and players of average ability should not attempt it as they will find less success using it.

The take-off should be always from two feet. When a one-foot take-off is used the blocker will not be able to control his flight or landing, and a net or line fault will probably result. If the blocker is late in reaching the block he should close the gap between the blockers by tilting his arms to one side and not by jumping off one foot at an angle.

To obtain maximum height above the net the blocker must bend his knees before take-off. The Japanese players execute a full knees-bend before the take-off. The recommended angles of the various limbs are shown in Fig. 60.

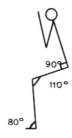

Fig. 60   Recommended joint angles for the take-off position in blocking

The arms must not be swung forwards and upwards, this action is too slow and also causes many net faults. Instead the arms should be extended vertically from the ready position i.e. with the arms bent and the hands in front of the chest at shoulder height. The hands should meet, with the fingers spread, when the arms are fully extended. The outside hand of the wing blockers should be angled inwards to deflect line shots back into court. Care must be taken to ensure that there is no gap between the blockers or between each blocker's hands.

The rules allow the hands to be passed across the net provided that the net is not touched. When the ball is set close to the net the blocker's hands should reach across the net to "cap" the ball just after it has been hit (Fig. 61). On contact with the ball the hands should be flexed strongly downwards. If the set is far away from the net the blocker's arms should be kept higher and not reach as far across the net as they do when the set is near (Fig. 62). A smash from a ball set back from the net will pass higher across the net than a smash from a close set.

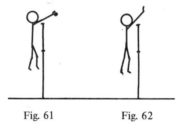

Fig. 61   Fig. 62

Once the blockers are in the air they must watch the spiker's arm and wrist to try and predict the angle of the shot. If the shot is going to be made round the block they must move their arms sideways into the path of the ball. Blockers should not assume that once they are in the air their work is finished.

After the blocking action over the net has been completed, the blockers must bring their arms back to their own side without touching the net. The arms should be lifted quickly and brought back to the side of the head. As the arms bend, the elbows should move backwards so that the hands come down in front of the body without contacting the net. On landing the legs should be bent to absorb any movement, thereby preventing the blocker from touching the net or crossing the centre line. When the blockers touch the ball but fail to block it into their opponents' court, they must shout "touch", so that the rest of their team know that they have only two touches left to play.

If the ball is not blocked out completely the blockers must turn immediately on landing to look for the ball—they may be able, or required to play the ball again. When the ball passes into back court the blockers

94

should quickly move out to the attack line ready to smash. In doing this, care must be taken not to obstruct a penetrating setter, or to lose sight of the ball in case they have to play it.

During the game the blockers cannot afford to wait until the set has been made before they start to form up as this will probably lead to a badly positioned and formed block. The blockers must be constantly assessing the game and trying to anticipate where their opponents' attack will take place.

If the blockers are to anticipate the type and position of the attack they should understand the factors that determine the attack produced by a side. There are many factors determining the attack but the most important of these are the following:-

a) The serve

Servers and blockers should work together as the server can almost force the attack to be made into the strongest blocking position of the serving side. During the service receive, the setter always turns to face the side of the court that the ball is served to, which means that his easiest set is forwards to the smasher on that side of the court. If the setter has to move forwards quickly to play the ball it is exceptionally difficult for him to play an overhead shot. When the setter is making an overhead set his hands must be directly above his head and this should be a clear indication to the blockers of the direction of the set.

The server should serve to give his blockers the best possible help. The strongest blocking position against a right-handed smasher is the left of the front court i.e. positions 4 and 3. In this position the smasher will find it more difficult to hit a diagonal shot. To make this shot he must hit the ball across his body and the face of the block. To exploit this advantage, serves should be made along this side of the court (i.e. into positions 2 and 1) and blockers switched along the front line to provide the strongest blocking combination.

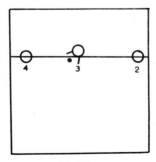

Fig. 63

95

b) The first ball

The first ball is the pass the setter receives from service, or after an attack has been received in back court. If this pass is too short, only reaching the attack line, too close to the net, or too low, the variety of sets that the setter can give is reduced.

When the setter moves towards the attack line to receive the ball (Fig. 63) he has only two real choices; he can set the ball overhead to position 2, in which case he will try to get under the ball to play it, or he can turn before he plays the ball and set to position 4 which can easily be seen by the blockers. Blockers should assess each situation to see what choices are open to the setter, watch the setter for movements which will indicate where he is sending the ball, and then move early into position.

When the first ball pushes the setter far out to the side of the court, it is very difficult for him to play a set across the full width of the court and blockers should expect a set in the middle of the court, or close to the setter.

Short sets can only be given when the first ball is of good height and length and straight to the setter. A ball to the setter which is more than three feet from the net is difficult to set and blockers should not expect a short set to be given. However, it must be remembered that the standard of setters varies considerably and what one is able to do another cannot. The blockers must decide what set is likely to be given according to the ability of the setter. Each setter has obvious preferences for a particular type of set and also weaknesses in certain sets. Similarly they prefer to set to particular spikers along the front line. Blockers should watch closely for this in the opening set so that they can adjust their blocking tactics accordingly.

Obviously, numerous examples can be given but only through experience will blockers be able to recognise all of them during the game. What the blockers must do, is to be alive to all the possibilities open to the setter with each ball and then to watch the setter's body and hand positions closely to see what set he has chosen to make. The work of the blockers starts as soon as the serve is hit and *not* when the set is played to the smasher.

c) Setter's body position

When the setter is in position to receive the ball, the body and hand positions he adopts can tell the blocker much about the set that will be played. Different types of set need different hand positions in relation to the body. (Figs. 64, 65, 66).

Similarly when the setter takes a low ball, with or without a backward roll, it is very difficult and often impossible for him to send the ball anywhere but forwards and this eliminates the short set, high set close to the setter and the overhead set.

Fig. 64   **Overhead set.**
Hands are directly above
the head and there is a
noticeable backward movement
of hands and body

Fig. 65   **Normal set.**
Hands above and in front
of the head

Fig. 66   **Short set.**
Hands are kept high
almost above the head.

There are exceptional setters who are able to put practically any set up from any position. It will soon be clear to the blockers that such a setter is playing and they must then watch very closely for any signs or particular movements that will help identify the set quickly.

d) Spikers
The position of spikers along the front line will often determine where the setter puts the ball. Setters will try to use their most effective spikers as much as possible. If there is a left-hander on the front line the setter will try to use him to best advantage, or if one particular spiker has been consistently beating his block on that line up he is likely to be used. Blockers should assess the capabilities and strengths of each spiker and switch the strongest blockers to cover the dangerous spiker.

When the setter is playing one of the wing positions it is not very often that he will spike, so the best blockers should switch to cover the other positions.

Most spikers have obvious preferences for certain shots and the setters will try to give the correct sets for these players so blockers should be especially prepared for these shots.

When blocking a left-handed spiker from position 4 the block should position itself further to the side of the court than for a right-hander so that the line shot which is the easiest shot for this player is well covered. Similarly, when the left-hander is in position 2 the block should set itself nearer the centre to cut out the shot inside the block.

e) Blockers
Just as the blockers will try to switch their most effective combinations against the best spikers the setter will try to direct the attack through the weakest block. Where there is a small blocker the block is particularly weak, so the server must place his serve so that the attack does not come through this blocking point. The blockers should try to switch their smallest blocker

opposite their opponents' setter if he is setting from the side, or switch him to position 2 where he is likely to be most effective.

Successful blocking is the result of good technique, experience and a sound understanding of the factors affecting the build up of an attack. It is not enough for a blocker to be tall or to have a high vertical jump. He must be capable of reading his opponents' game and adjusting his movements and body and hand positions accordingly. Good blocking is the secret of the success of most of the world's top teams.

Major faults and their correction

Fault	*Reason/Correction*
1) Touching the net on take-off	a) Too close to the net before take-off.
	b) Arms swinging instead of extending vertically.
2) Touching the net.	a) Arms pushed across the net before enough height has been reached.
	b) Failure to raise arms after blocking.
	c) Excessive use of the arms during the "capping" action.
3) Touching net on landing	a) Player unbalanced on take-off and thus cannot control descent and landing.
	b) Forgetting to bring hands well back before turning to see where ball has gone.
4) Crossing centre line on take-off.	a) Too close to net prior to blocking.
	b) Player could be standing too far back while waiting to block so that when he moves in to block he oversteps.
	c) Crossing the legs when moving into position.
5) Ball passes over top of block consistently.	a) Blockers reaching over the net instead of for height when the ball

	is set back from the net.
	b) Blockers taking off too late. Should take off just before spiker.
	c) Blockers too small.
6) Ball rebounds out of court.	a) Outside man's hands are not turned inwards.
	b) Hands not forced down on contact.
7) Ball drops between blockers and net.	a) Hands not reaching over net.
8) Ball passes inside the block.	a) Block leader picking line too far to the side.
	b) Centre blocker putting his hands flat instead of turning his inside hand slightly towards the spiker.
9) Ball passes between hands of both blockers.	a) Blocker too late to get fully into position with other blocker.
	b) Blockers not moving their arms to join up both pairs of hands.
10) Ball passes through arms of player.	a) Player is blocking too high when ball is set close to net.
	b) Elbows are too wide, player must keep arms straight and force elbows in.
11) Ball touches top of block and rebounds into blockers' court.	a) Blockers took off slightly too late.
	b) Blockers pushing their arms and hands down too early.

Practice and experience will eradicate the majority of these faults.

Teaching blocking

The block when performed during a game is a highly complex skill. The blocker has to move into position at the net, find the correct place to take-off, jump, adjust his arm and hand position in the air, block the ball, land, look for the ball and move out ready for the attack. Obviously it is impossible to teach a beginner the complete skill immediately. The teacher or coach must break the skill down into progressive phases that can easily be taught and learnt.

The phases are:-

a) Take-off, arm and hand action.
b) Moving along the net and taking off without committing net faults.
c) Setting the block in the wing positions.
d) Moving into position for a two-man block and carrying out the complete blocking action.
e) Three-man blocking.
f) Block and then picking up balls that fall in the vicinity of the block.
g) Block and then move back for the attack.
h) Moving from covering the smash to the block.

It is important that the blockers being taught or coached understand the theory of blocking and can see its relationship with other phases of the game. Even though blocking is introduced in stages, the learners must understand that they are only learning a part of blocking and that as each new stage is introduced it is related to work they have already covered.

The game of volleyball has many phases and these must be fused together to form a smooth pattern of play if a team is to be successful. This fusion will not suddenly occur, it is the result of constant practice and an awareness of the part each phase plays in the total game. Blocking follows a smash and is itself followed by an attack therefore training for blocking must regularly involve these changeovers.

In training sessions blocking practice can be combined with smashing practice. Smashing should rarely take place without a block.

In the schools situation the teacher who is using the small game approach is only concerned with a one-man block. When a player has learnt the technique of blocking on his own, it is not too difficult for him to go on to multiple blocks later. The teacher's objective should be to get every child in class able to jump up, reach over the net and block a ball without touching the net. This is all that is needed in the small-side games and is quite enough for the young player to be thinking of at one time.

Phase A; Take-off, arm and hand action
1)   Stand the players opposite each other at the net. They then jump up and touch each other's hands above the net. After a few attempts point out that a two footed take-off should be used. Demonstrate the starting position for the hands and the action of the arms.
2)   Have a small competition to see who can do the most blocks without

100

touching the net. Practice continuous blocking i.e. taking off again immediately on landing.

3) Place box tops, benches or chairs on one side of the net, two feet from the centre line. One partner stands on the box top holding a ball just above the net on his side. His partner must jump up, reach over the net and place his hands on the ball without touching the net.

Emphasise that the fingers are spread and relaxed. The hands must be placed firmly on the ball. Players should try to force the ball down out of their partner's hands.

4) This time the players jump up, reach over the net and bring the ball back to their own side of the net.

5) Take the benches etc. away. The ball is now thrown up close to the net. The blocker must reach over the net and block the ball as it comes down.

Phase B; Moving along the net

1) In pairs opposite the net blocking each other's hands. After blocking, take one pace to the right and block again. Insist on a two footed take-off.

2) This time take two steps to the right block, one step to the left block and so on.

3) Same situation as Phase A (3). Blocker blocks the ball after taking one pace from the right or left.

4) Same situation as Phase A (3). Blockers take one pace and then reach over and bring the ball back to their side of the net.

Phase C; Setting a wing block

1) One player holds the ball in his outstretched hand in front of his right shoulder. Starting from the attack line he walks to the net. The blocker must move along the net until his outside hand is in line with the ball. Vary the angle and speed of approach to put the blocker under pressure. When using the court for this purpose assume that all pairs to the right of a line down the centre of the court are blocking in the right wing position and all those to the left in the left wing position. This means that all the smashers on the left side of the court will angle the approach to the right and vice versa.

2) Instead of walking in, the player now runs in, jumps up and places the ball above the net. The ball should again be in line with his shoulder. The blocker will now have to line up the block and make the blocking action.

3) In threes with two players on one side of the net. These two act as setter and smasher. The setter throws the ball straight up into the air. The smasher who is standing by him jumps up and hits the ball softly across the net. This means that the blocker must not only position himself correctly but learn to time his take-off. Gradually increase the length of the approach of the smasher. Also vary the distance the ball is hit from the setter.

This is as far as the teacher needs to go in the class situation. In the small-game situation the player will not have a great deal of distance to cover to block and the attack will be quite straightforward. What the children need is plenty of blocking practice on their own in these situations before they attempt two or three man blocking. Further drills and practices for blocking and how to coach players in the other phases of blocking mentioned earlier are dealt with in chapter 6.

Hints for players
When you are blocking it is important to remember that the rest of the team is lining up around you. If the block is badly positioned the back court players do not have any effective means of setting the back court defence. For this reason all players must attempt to block in every position and all players be capable of setting a block.

Even if you cannot get right across to block it is worth making the attempt to get as close as possible. If you make no attempt, the smasher will only have one man to beat and this is not too difficult for him. If you are moving across and making some effort at blocking, the smasher must take you into consideration. He will be less confident in his smash than if you did not bother to come across. The same applies when you are smaller than average and can only block a foot or so above the net. By being in the block you put more pressure on the smasher.

The block may score points for the team not only by preventing the ball passing over the net, but also by forcing the player to hit out of court. If there is a strong block the smasher will try to hit round it or over it. When the block is really well set it leaves only a very small amount of court open to the smasher. Many times he will be inaccurate and the block has in fact scored a point for the side.

If you block a player out several times in succession, be prepared for the tactical ball just over or to the side of the block. Watch the smasher's arm, as it must straighten to play these shots from as high as possible. You should be able to stop a lot of these from going past you.

When your side is serving, get up to the net so that you are ready and waiting for the smash. If you are standing on the attack line talking to other players you will be cutting down the time you have to prepare for the block. As soon as you are at the net identify the three front court players and the setter. With some advanced line-ups it is not so easy to identify the front court players. Remember who is in which position, this will be useful for spotting fake attacks.

Many teams use fake attacks to try and deceive the block. The Japanese mens team is well known for its ability to confuse some of the world's best blockers. Several players will approach the net at once from different angles calling for the ball. The blockers have to decide quickly which one is going to hit the ball.

The first thing to look at is the timing of the approach and take-off of the smasher. If he is to hit the ball his approach must be timed very well with the set pass. If he is acting as a fake smasher his timing will be slightly out. Some smashers who know they are not going to hit the ball only make a half-hearted approach run. This will help you to decide quite early not to block him. The position of the setter on court and in relation to the ball will give you some clues as to the destination of the set pass. The angle of the pass immediately after leaving the setter will give some clues as to the distance it is likely to travel from the setter. If it is very steep then it is likely to be short set, or a high set quite close to the setter.

Once you are certain that you will not be required in the block go to your defensive position as quickly as you can. If you have completed the blocking action and have not prevented the ball from passing over the net, look for the ball as you come down to land. Never start wondering how the smasher managed to get the ball past your superbly set block as you come down! Your full attention must be on the ball and its present whereabouts.

If you are a blocker, you are both an attacker and the first line of defence for your team. To be as effective as possible you must be lively and thinking all the time. The good blocker in a match has blocked many hundreds of times in training. His technique has become automatic and he is able to concentrate on what his opponents are doing and what he must do to counter them. Use every opportunity in your training sessions to get some practice in blocking.

SETTING

The volley pass that is placed high above and close to the net for a front line player to smash across the net, is called the set pass. A team's attacking strength is dependent on its ability to place these set passes accurately. Consequently, most teams make certain players into specialist setters. Their prime job when in the front court is to make these set passes for the other two front court players to smash. As teams become capable of more advanced play, one of the back three players "penetrates" into the front court and sets the ball. This means that a team can then smash through all three attack points in the front court i.e. positions 4, 3, & 2. This aspect will be dealt with more fully in Chapter 5.

The setters must develop their volley technique so that they are consistently able to volley the ball accurately to the smasher. In addition to having a good volley technique the setter must be quick and agile. The ball that comes to him to set is known as the first pass. The first pass may be low or high, travelling fast or slow, to his side or behind him. In all these situations his team mates will be expecting him to put up a good accurate set for the smasher. He must be able to move quickly into the best position to play the ball no matter what its height or speed.

The setter dictates the pattern of a team's play. He must decide where he can best set each ball that comes to him. When the first pass to him is of good length and height he must decide which attacking position to use according to the tactical situation at that time. It is this factor which discriminates between the good setter and the outstanding setter. Many of the setters in international volleyball have equal physical and technical ability. What sorts them out is their ability to decide where it is tactically best to set the ball at any particular time. It is generally acknowledged at the present time that the world's best setter is Nekoda of Japan. There may be other setters in the world with as good a technique as him, but none can compare in terms of his ability to choose which set to use, and where to put it. When the complexity of the Japanese style of volleyball is seen and the short amount of time the setter has to decide which player to set to is realised, his performance seems quite incredible.

Types of set

There are several types of set. The sets differ in terms of their length or speed. Types:

    a) High set to the wings or centre.
    b) Overhead set.
    c) Parallel or shoot set.
    d) Short set.

a) High set

This set is the most used in volleyball. It is usually played to the wing position. As a team becomes more advanced tactically the ball will also be set from one of the wing positions into the centre.

The height of the pass will vary slightly according to each individual smasher, but generally it should reach a height of 15 feet. This will give the smasher time to make his approach and take-off after the ball has left the setter's hands. This will enable him to position himself more accurately. The set should have a flight path which makes the ball drop towards the smasher. When viewed from the side the path of the set looks similar to that of a wave.

If the ball does not drop in this way it is more difficult for the smasher to hit. He will have to intersect the ball as it goes across court. This means that his timing and positioning must be perfect. If the ball drops he will find it easier to locate the smashing position. In addition he can divert his attention to considering where he is going to hit the ball once he has selected his line of approach. He can do this because he knows that the ball is dropping almost straight in front of him.

104

It is important that setters develop a certain consistency of length and height. The smasher will then be able to get a general timing and positioning for that setter. If one set is outside the sideline and the next ten feet in, the smasher will not be able to develop a rhythm and his smashing will inevitably be below his potential.

The set pass should preferably land in the outside four feet of the court if it is being set to the wings. The distance from the net should be between 18 and 36 inches depending on the smasher and the strength of the block.

When the ball is set to drop in the outside four feet of the court the smasher then has the shortest distance to travel to the ball. He will be waiting out at the sideline to start his approach. When the ball is set further in than four feet his approach to the ball will be acute and this will cut down the amount of court that he has to hit into (Fig. 67). It will also mean that the centre blocker does not have so far to come across to block. The block will therefore be stronger with a consequent effect on the smash. By setting near the outside of the court the setter gives the smasher more court to hit into and the chance of hitting the ball between the two blockers.

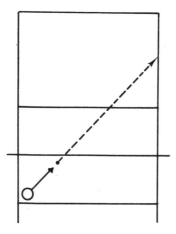

Fig. 67   Unless he hits the ball across his body (probably directly into the block), the player has only the court to the right of the dotted line to hit into, because the set is too far in court

If the ball is set closer to the net than 18 inches, the block will be able to reach well across the net and reduce the chances of the ball passing to the side of them and still landing in court (Fig. 68).

105

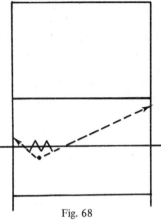

Fig. 68

When the ball is set further back from the net than this, it makes it more difficult for the player to smash the ball over the net and blockers, into play (Fig. 69). If the ball does go over the blockers, then it is bound to land in the rear half of the court, which makes it more predictable for the defence.

Fig. 69   When the ball is set well back from the net it must be hit from higher to ensure that it passes over the block and into court. This means that the ball will most often fall in the rear of the court

b) The overhead set:

The setter must be able to set the ball to any part of the front court. This means that he must be able to set to the area behind him as well as in front of him. If he only sets the ball forward, the attack of his team becomes much more predictable and therefore easier to block.

The obvious difficulty with the overhead set is that the setter cannot see the smasher behind him. He must gauge the distance the set must travel by estimating how far he is from the sideline in front of him. He will then have an idea of the distance between himself and the opposite sideline. The smasher should be standing on the sideline waiting for the smash, so this distance now becomes the distance the set must travel to reach the smasher. The ability to estimate these distances accurately and to relate them to the amount of force needed to play the ball is essential to the setter.

The technique of the overhead set is the same as that for the overhead volley. When making this set the player must position himself so that the ball is not in front of his head but above his head. In this way he will be able to volley the ball without any fear of contravening the handling rules.

The overhead set will naturally follow the line of the setter's shoulders. It is essential that he positions himself, prior to playing the ball, so that his shoulders are in line with the place where the smasher should hit the ball. This means that he must line himself up with a point in front of him which is in line with the smashing position.

The overhead set is a difficult set to play but it has many advantages for the team. Firstly, it means that all areas of the court are available as attack points. Secondly, the setter can play the ball to his best smasher even though he is facing the opposite direction. Thirdly, it has a surprise value which means that the block will not always be formed completely, thus enabling the smasher to have an easier shot.

c) The short set:

This set is played close to the setter and can be in front of him or behind him. The ball travels a maximum distance of three feet into the air. It is a highly effective shot when timed correctly. The smasher should make an approach close to the setter, then take off and hit the set as it comes up to him. It is important that the smasher does not wait for the set to be made before taking off.

When performed correctly it appears as though the smasher is hitting the ball out of the setter's hand. This form of attack can be devastating when used so quickly that the blockers do not have time to move to take off. The masters of this form of attack are the Japanese. Vivid memories of an international match played against the Japanese in London, in 1969 are recalled. Playing in the front row as a blocker in position 3, I turned to watch our serve travel across the net. I had hardly tracked the ball to their side of the court before they had smashed it back to our side. The first pass to Nekoda, the setter, was very fast and low. While he was preparing to set the ball, Minami, the captain, approached the net took off and smashed the short set a fraction after it left Nekoda's hands! I drew some consolation from the fact that they were able to do the same thing with almost equal success against the best teams in the world in the World Cup the previous week.

The short set does however require a very good first pass to the setter. The setter must decide very quickly if the ball is close enough to the net and travelling at a suitable height for him to place it accurately above the net for the smasher.

The short set rarely travels more than an arm's length away from the setter and its trajectory is very steep, almost vertical. This means that the setter

107

must play the ball almost directly above his head. He should try to position himself so that his head, the ball and the point where the smasher's hand is waiting for the ball are in a straight line. The pass must go straight to his hand for maximum effectiveness. It can be seen that for this reason the smasher must time his approach accurately. If the smasher is late, then the setter can make slight allowances by setting the ball slower so that the smasher hits the ball as he rises, or he can let the ball drop a little lower before he sets it.

With the overhead short set the setter has little opportunity for controlling the timing. He must aim to pass the ball three feet high and about two feet behind him. This should then place the ball in the path of the smasher.

The short set when used in conjuction with other types of sets greatly increases the variety of a team's attack, and therefore makes it more difficult to block against. The short set does require an understanding between setters and smashers. Each smasher will hit the ball at a different height above the net and angle to the setter. The setter must learn to adjust the speed and angle of his pass to suit the individual smasher. Some smashers like the ball an arm's length away from the setter because they feel it gives them more room to move and therefore increases the range of their shots. Others disagree and like it as close to the setter as possible to make it a much faster movement. The important thing for the setter is to practice often with the smashers and to experiment to see which is the best position and angle for each smasher.

c) The parallel or shoot set.
This is a fast low set across to the wing or centre player. The smasher must time his approach so that he is in the air as the ball comes across to him. This means that he will begin his approach before the setter has played the ball. The ball is hit about two feet above net height. Its exact height will vary according to the jumping ability of each smasher. It is a difficult set to smash, because the player must intersect the ball as it passes across the court.

When timed correctly it gives the blockers very little time to form up. Usually one blocker will be able to get up in time but the middle blocker is very often too late.

Rule changes affecting the block in the early 60's greatly increased the potential effectiveness of the block. In recent years the pattern of attack has changed to try and counteract the increased strength of the block. The high passes to the side and centre of the court give the block time to get into position. The introduction of the short and parallel sets has meant that the block no longer has as much time. However, what is gained on the swings is lost on the roundabouts. These sets require a higher standard of setters and smashers, perfect timing and understanding between the two players.

When making a parallel set the setter should watch the approach of the smasher as well as the ball. The setter must predict at which point the smasher wishes to hit the ball above the net. He must then give the ball enough force and speed to reach the player at this point at the right time. It is extremely difficult to set the ball in this way and only good club setters and smashers should attempt this shot.

Sometimes the ball is set about six feet away from the setter so that it is a cross between a short set and a parallel set. This is often very effective when hit from the centre of the court.

Jump Sets

Further variety to the sets and therefore the attack pattern of a team is obtained by using jump sets. Sometimes the setter has to jump as high as he can and play the ball while he is in the air, because the first pass is too high. He must make sure that he gets his hands up into the volley position as early as he can. If he brings them up and volleys the ball in one movement he will be volleying from a poor position and will have little control over the set.

On other occasions it is very effective if the setter fakes as though he is going to smash the first pass and then jump sets the ball instead. When a jump set is used in conjuction with a short set and smash movement it greatly increases the speed of that movement. Instead of waiting for the ball to drop low enough for the setter to play while on the ground, the setter and smasher can play the ball a second or so earlier. This second can often make all the difference to the success of the attack.

Needless to say the setter must be very experienced to be able to use jump sets to their maximum advantage. The smashers must also be able to alter their normal timing so that they can get into position for the smash at the right time.

The position of the setter.

The team's potential for attack depends on the quality of its setter. The setter must be able to deceive the blockers. If the blockers know well in advance where the set is going to go, then they will have more chance of blocking out the attack. The setter must adopt a body position which will enable him to pass the ball forwards or backwards very quickly. If he is to pass the ball forwards then the ball must be in front of him. If he is to pass the ball overhead then it must be above his head at the time he plays it. The blockers know this and will watch the body position of the setter to see where the set will go.

The setter must therefore adopt a body position prior to playing the ball that will enable him to play the ball in any direction with the minimum of adjustments. The recommended position is shown in Fig. 70. It can be seen from this that the trunk is leaning backwards slightly. This position means that the setter can play the ball in any direction without giving the blockers a great deal of warning. To volley the ball overhead the setter must let the ball come a little closer to him before he plays it. To play the ball in a forward direction then is just as easy. This position will allow the setter to play the ball quickly to any direction and does not give the blockers a great deal of help. It does require that the setter gets into position as early as possible. Speed of movement is one of the essential requirements of a setter.

Fig. 70

Hints to players

If you are a setter, or are intending to specialize in setting, you must be prepared to train hard and often. Your volley pass must become very well controlled and accurate. You must be able to play the ball to any part of the front court, from varying positions on court and various angles. This will only come from long and repeated practice.

Not only must you practice your handling technique you must improve your fitness. In a good level of volleyball the setter travels a greater distance and plays the ball more often than any other player on court. Fatigue must not be allowed to impair the quality of your pass. You must work on your speed of movement about court. Very often you will have to move across court to play the ball and then move back again for the next phase of the game. If you are slow in either direction then your standard of play will be less than it ought to be.

It is essential for the setter to dominate the front court. When the first pass comes into the attack zone it is your ball nearly every time. When the first pass is a bad one confusion is likely to occur if the setter does not call for the ball, yet still moves after it. Another player will probably decide to play it because he has not heard the setter call for the ball. Very often the result is that the two players collide as they both try to play the ball at the same time. This problem can be avoided if the setter makes a habit of calling for the ball every time it is travelling into the front court to a different position to either his intended or present position.

There is another time when the setter must call to the other players. This is during service receive. With some line-ups and formations the setter is not always in the centre of the court. It is helpful to the rest of the team if the

110

setter announces just before the whistle is blown for service, "Setter at 4", or wherever he is. If you give your team this help it will result in the first pass being played in your direction. It is amazing how much players need this reminder. The smashers may be still thinking about the smash they hit out of court. The serve comes to them and they cannot see the setter or remember where he is supposed to be. The reminder that you give your team just before the serve is hit will usually bring the other players back to the present.

If you are a penetrating setter or have executed a switch with another front court player, then the place the first pass must travel to is a different place to the one it went to last time. It is helpful if you shout out the position you want the ball as early as possible. Although you may feel a bit self conscious calling for the ball all the time, it is essential if the team is to achieve its full playing potential.

When you go to a gymnasium or hall to play a game take a good look around the hall so that you can identify various points which will help you orientate yourself during the game. Look above the net to see if there is a rafter or girder which will help you to know how far from the net you are. It is amazing how easy it is to 'lose yourself' in the early parts of a game in a new hall.

It is important for you to know the strengths and weaknesses of your smashers. You should also know how high or fast they prefer the set. You must assess the strength of each blocking combination on the other side of the court. Look, to see if one of the blockers is particularly small or unable to jump very high. All this and much more information is necessary for you to decide where to place the set. Naturally, you will find on many occasions that the first pass you are given dictates the direction you must play the set pass. On other occasions the first pass will enable you to choose the direction the pass will go and the type of pass you give.

When you have a good pass, you must decide on the basis of current form, the strengths and weaknesses of your attackers and your opponents' blockers, the current state of the game, your form and your coach's instruction, where you play the ball. What is certain is that wherever you play the ball you will disappoint at least one smasher. Smashers are a greedy lot always wanting the set to come to them and very often complaining about the quality of the pass when they get it. The best advice to give a setter is to ignore them. You must decide where the ball goes as you are the one that must play it. Whatever you do, do not set the ball to them just because they complain they have not had a set for a long while. Very often during a game it is not possible for you to set to a particular smasher for a long while due to the nature of the first pass you are receiving. If a particular smasher is getting past his block every time then it is logical to use that particular attacking point as long as the smasher

111

maintains his supremacy. The setter is the most maligned player on court, yet the most essential. Always turn to face the direction of your pass before you play the ball (except of course in the case of an overhead set). If you do not, you run the risk of a bad set or illegal volley. Whenever possible use the net as a guide to the direction your pass will go. Remember your pass must be between 18-36 inches away from the net when it reaches the smasher. If you judge the distance you are from the net and the angle your shoulders are to the net before you play the ball, you will be able to predict where your pass will go. This will enable you to make minor adjustments to your position before you play the ball.

When you are waiting to receive service, it is as well to let the smasher you hope to send the ball to know that he will receive the pass, and the type of pass. This does depend on the first pass to you being good enough. If it is not very good then play the best set for the ball you receive. Do not automatically send the ball to the smasher you warned. You must make the best of every first pass even if it means changing your original plans.

Players will often call for a short or parallel set, and in the case of the former make an approach towards you. This does not mean that you must give the ball to them. You should look upon this call as an indication that they are prepared for the set if you can give it to them or if you think that they are in the best position for an attack.

Once you have set the ball do not stand back and look at it thinking what a good set it was. You must move into a position to cover the smasher in case the ball is blocked back into your court.

As a setter you must expect your work to go relatively unnoticed. Most people watch the smasher and he is the one who receives the praise and adulation. You will have to be content with knowing that it was your good set which enabled him to have a good chance of a successful smash. As a setter you must be prepared to work very hard on your technique for many years before you become really proficient. Setting is without doubt the most difficult role in volleyball. To be successful you will have to make hundreds of thousands of sets and play in innumerable matches before you will have the experience to cope with the pressure of top level play using multiple fake attacks.

5 THE TACTICS OF VOLLEYBALL

Team line-ups

In common with other games volleyball has tactical formations to cover all the phases of the game. However, before the coach can utilise these formations, he must place six players on court in a rotational order. The order in which he places them and the starting point of each player will have a great bearing on the pattern of play adopted and the potential of the team. Remember that once the players have been placed on court and the game started the rotational order cannot be changed until the end of the set.

When deciding where to position the players the coach should decide first how many setters he intends to use.

The six setter system

With teams just starting to play (especially school teams), the usual system is to make every player the setter when he is in position no. 3. This system uses no specialist setters.

Advantages

1) Requires no switching of players to bring the setter into a particular position.
2) It is very simple because every player knows that he will be the setter when he is in position 3, and that at all times the player in that position is the setter.

Disadvantages

1) It often means that the person with the worst volley pass is setting.
2) The best smasher may also be setting while the best setter is smashing. This greatly reduces the attacking potential of the side.

113

3)   With the setter in position 3 there is little variety of attack. The attack will come through the wing positions only.

The three setter system
With this system the team is divided into three specialist setters and three specialist smashers. Very often this system is referred to as the "system of pairs". Each setter is paired with a specialist smasher (Fig. 71).

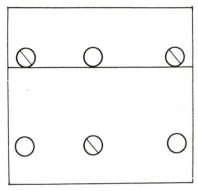

Fig. 71   Distribution of setters and smasher in the 'system of pairs'
N.B. The crossed circles indicate smashers, the plain circles setters

Advantages
1)   When a team uses this system they always have at least one setter in the front line.
2)   A team is able to take advantage of the specific abilities of players.
3)   It is a relatively simple system to introduce and use.

Disadvantages
1)   At one stage during the game the team will have two setters and only one smasher in the front row.
2)   It requires three specialist setters. It is often difficult to find three setters or even three players who wish to become setters.

The two setter system
This is the most widely used system. There are four smashers and two setters. The setters are diagonally opposed in the line up so that there is always one of them in the front row.

Advantages
1)   The attacking potential of the side is increased by having four smashers.

he Japanese smasher No. 2 directs the
ash through the hole in the block

A fast wave attack leaves the smasher with
only one blocker to beat

pical fast attack by Japan leaves the
in disarray

The tactical ball should be played from as
high as possible so that it will clear the
block

An excellent block by No. 3 gives Japan's No. 8 little chance of a successful smash

Although the dive looks spectacular it easy to learn and safe to use

The ball is hit from as high as possible with the open hand

Players may reach across the net to blo

2)   There will always be two smashers and one setter in the front line.
3)   This system can easily be fitted into advanced tactical situations and formations utilising switching or penetrating setters.

Having decided on the number of setters he is going to use, the coach must now fit the smashers into the other positions. He must avoid putting the two best smashers in positions which will mean that they are both in the front line together. This will mean that the two weaker smashers will be in the same line. The coach must try to balance his line up so that weaknesses like the one described above are avoided.

Normally coaches place the two best smashers so that they are diagonally opposed. This means that there will always be a strong smasher in the front line. Of course this is not possible when the pairs system is used. With this system there will be two good smashers together in the same line at one point in the rotation.

The coach must take into account individual differences in ability of smashers and setters. If one setter is better than the other how is he to be placed in relation to the smashers? Some coaches would argue that it is best to put the weaker smasher with the best setter and vice versa. In this way the best smasher will be able to make more of the weak set, and the weaker smasher will have more chance of succeeding because he has a good set. On the other hand some coaches say that this dilutes the teams' strength. They prefer to have a strong combination of setter and smasher and rely on them to win enough rallies and points to keep them in the front row for the majority of the game, and to carry the weaker combination. There is no clearcut answer to this dilemma. The coach must make up his own mind according to the strengths of his players and the strengths of his opponents. If the opponents have a particularly strong combination which will win quite a few rallies for them it is often wise for the coach to put out a strong combination so that his team does not get demoralised by the success of the other team.

Some smashers and setters form a combination which is very successful, because each player understands the other's game. This understanding can often make players play better when they are teamed together than when they are apart.

If there are two left-handed smashers then they must be placed diagonally opposite each other in the team. If they are both on the same front line then the coach is not using them to their full potential. A left-handed smasher is more difficult to block against in position 2. In the same way, for the reason already discussed in the section on blocking, the right-handed smasher is harder to block in position 4 and easier in position 2. The coach should try to have a right-handed and left-handed smasher in the front row.

Having placed all six players in rotational order, the coach must now

115

decide who starts in which position on court. The starting positions will be determined by the strength of the opponents front line, which team has service and the strength of the various members of the team.

Obviously it is best to start with the best smasher in position 4. He will be able to play in all three front court positions and help the team off to a good start. If he is right-handed, he will start the game smashing from the strongest attacking point.

Many coaches place their best smashers so that they will be in the front row at the same time as their opponents' best smasher. In this way each smasher balances the other and often they take the responsibility for blocking each other.

Some players will find that they are able to consistently smash past particular blockers or, block out consistently the opposing smasher. In these instances, and many others, the coach should take into account his opponents line up when planning his own.

Switching

Once the ball has been served, players may change their positions on court. It is often advantageous if players in the front row change places so that the setter is playing in the position best suited to the particular style of play. This movement of players is known as switching.

Smashers are sometimes switched so that they play in the court position best suited to their ability or the current tactical situation.

In the back court, players are switched so that they also play in their best positions. This is a particularly noticeable feature of the Japanese team's play. In some systems the setter is switched to the right of the back court to make it easier to penetrate during a rally. Very mobile and athletic players are switched to the wings to pick up the balls dropped just over and to the side of the block.

A good coach will ensure that he capitalises on each players strengths by switching him into the best position as often as possible.

Penetration

Penetration involves bringing the back line setter into the front court to take over the setting from the front line setter. Penetration can be used during service receive and/or a rally. There are several advantages in using penetration. The main advantage is that it enables a team to use all three front court players as smashers. This increases the attacking potential and allows a team a greater variety in attack. The opponents must now be ready to block in three positions instead of only two. Penetration will be dealt with in greater detail later in the chapter.

Compared with many other games a volleyball court is small for the

116

number of people on it. For this reason many people new to the game assume that it is very easy to stop the ball from touching the floor. However, the speed of the game and the smashed or served ball is such that a player must position himself in the place where the ball is likely to go, before it has been hit. In this way he will only have to make small movements to play the ball. Each player will have an area of court to defend and will know his responsibilities. Volleyball is a real team game. Unlike other sports, one good individual will not win a volleyball game for a team. He must be supported by solid team play in all phases of the game.

The coach must select tactical formations for his team to use at the following times.

1)   Service receive
2)   When his smasher is hitting the ball
3)   When the opponents are smashing the ball

Service Receive

W + 1 system

This is the simplest service receive formation. There are several ways in which it is modified depending on the number of setters used by a team.

The basic form is shown in Fig. 72. It can be seen that the five receiving players form a W shape and the remaining player, the setter, is at the net waiting to receive the first pass.

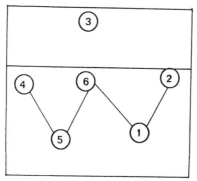

Fig. 72a   The W + 1 service receive pattern

The two wing players should stand about an arm's length away from the sideline. This will mean that any ball that passes more than an arms length to the side of them is passing out of court. The outside foot should be the forward foot so that the body is inclined into court and the dig pass will be more accurate.

The two back players must position themselves mid-way between the wing player nearest them and the centre player. It is essential that they are able to see the server.

The forward centre player is in line with the two wing players. This player is the player who normally plays in position 6. The player in position 3 is waiting at the net to set the ball.

The depth of the service receive formation will vary with the individual server. If the server is hitting the ball deep, then the service receive players move nearer the base line and vice-versa. In general the service receive line-up covers the middle third of the court. Depending on the server the distribution of the receiving players can be changed width or length ways.

The service receive line up should be curved slightly. This means that the players on the right of the formation are slightly further forward in court than those on the left. This serves several purposes. It brings the receivers round to face the server and the direction from which the ball will come. They will then play the ball with their bodies behind it. In this way the ball is less likely to fly off the arms out of court. A ball that is served to this side of the court has travelled a greater distance than a ball served to a point as far forward on the other side of the court. This means that it is likely to drop further forward in court than if it had travelled the same distance in a straight line.

When looking at diagrams of any tactical formation in this book it is most important that the reader does not assume that the position of each player on court must be exactly the same as it is in the diagram. Every situation during a game is different and the line-up must be adjusted accordingly. The positions shown are the basic recommended positions, adjustments to which are made to suit each particular situation.

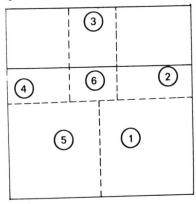

Fig. 72b   Division of court area in the W + 1 service receive pattern

It is important that players realise that when they adopt these positions at service receive, or for that matter any formation, they are defending an area of court and not a particular position. From the position where he is standing the player should be able to move easily to cover his area of court.

The division of responsibility for each player in the W + 1 service receive formation is shown in Fig. 72b. The three front court players in the lineup, nos. 4, 6, 2, cover the court in front of them and up to a pace behind them. The two back court players 5, and 1, must divide the rest of the court between themselves. The setter no. 3, must watch the serve as it comes over the net. If it is going to fall in the front court, near him and the net, he must accept responsibility for playing it. If he decides to play it he must call for the ball to let his fellow players know.

Calling.

It is imperative that players shout "MINE" if they are going to play the ball. This shout will warn other players and avoid the situation where two players both go for the ball or, both leave the ball. Nothing is more demoralising for a team than to see two players both watch the ball land between them. There is no such call as "YOURS" in volleyball. If the player is not going to play the ball he should say nothing. If nobody else calls and the ball is within playing distance he must call and play the ball himself. Once a player has called for the ball he must make every attempt to play it.

Advantages of W + 1 system with centre setter

1) It is a very simple formation for players to learn and play. The W formation gives them something tangible to look for to see if they are in the right position.
2) There is the minimum of movement of players away from the positions they will adopt for most of the game. When used with the No. 6, 2 - 1 - 3 defensive system there is practically no extra movement of players.
3) All the players can see the server and the court is well divided amongst the players.

Disadvantages

1) There are only two attack points, 4 and 2, open to the setter.
2) To play this line up all the time involves using the six setter system which is the least efficient of all the setter systems.

Overlapping

There is one important rule that limits the positioning of players at the time of service receive. That Rule is Rule 5 Article 3:-

Position of player:

At the time the ball is served;

Players of both teams must be within their courts in two lines of three players, taking positions as follows: The three players at the net are front-line players, occupying from right to left, positions 2, 3, and 4, while the three players in the back are back line players, occupying from right to left, positions 1, 6 and 5. The positions of the players on the court must conform to the rotational order recorded on the scoresheet; namely:

In the front line, 3 must be between 2 and 4, and in front of 6.

In the back line 6 must be between 1 and 5, and behind 3.

Consequently, 2 must be in front of 1, and 4 must be in front of 5.

Official I.V.B.F. Commentary on Rule 5.

At the time the ball is served (i.e. the moment the ball is hit by the server) the back line players must be at least a little behind their corresponding front line players. It is a fault if a back line player is the same distance from the net as his corresponding front line player. The position of players is judged according to the positions of their feet.

It is at the moment the server hits the ball that the player must be in the correct position. Any positional fault must be signalled by the umpire or the referee, as soon as the ball has been hit.

If one of the teams makes a positional fault and the service is also incorrect, it is the positional fault which is counted.

When the service is incorrect (touches the net or goes out of court) and the receiving team is out of position, it is the fault of the receiving team that is counted.

Although at first glance this may appear to be a very difficult rule to grasp

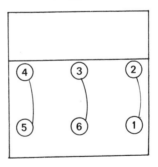

Fig. 73   Overlapping pairs–vertical direction

120

it is really quite simple. Think of it in terms of paired players. Each player is paired with the one in front or behind him (Fig. 73). The two players may be anywhere on court providing the front court player has some part of his foot in front of the front part of his partner's foot. The players are also paired with the players on either side of them. They must always keep part of a foot to the side of their partner's feet (Fig. 74).

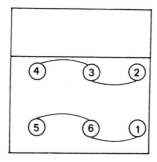

Fig. 74   Overlapping pairs horizontal direction

Some examples of illegal line ups are shown in Figs. 75 & 76. The effect of this rule is to limit to a certain extent the distribution of the players during the initial part of each rally.

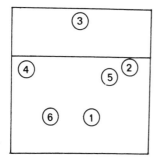

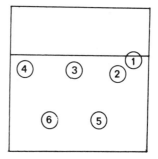

Fig. 75   An illegal service receive line-up   Fig. 76   An illegal service receive line-up

In the other service receive line-ups that are covered in this chapter the overlapping rule must be strictly observed. In each of these line-ups there is a distinct possibility of overlapping. The players must be well aware of this possibility and take great care when positioning themselves.

121

Modified W + 1 service receive formation

Type 1–Setter at the wing

When a team is using the pairs setting system, or the two setter system, there will be times when the setter is not at position 3. This means that the system described previously, the W + 1 system, must be modified either to bring the setter into the centre or to leave him at the side.

When the setter is in position 4 he can stand at the net and set from this position. The centre player, no. 3, comes back to the attack line in the centre to act as a receiver (Fig. 77 & 78). When the player in position 2 is a left handed smasher this is an effective lineup because the ball is most likely to be set across to position 2. A left-handed smasher is in a stronger smashing position at position 2 than a right-handed smasher. If however, the player at position 2 is a right-handed player, this is not such an effective line up. In this case it is best if the team operates a lateral switch between players 4 and 3 as soon as the ball is served.

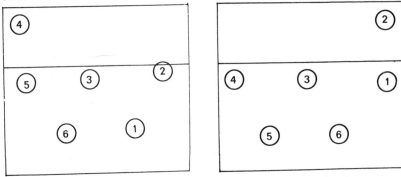

Figs. 77 & 78   W + 1 receive formation with the setter at the wing

When the setter is in position 2 and the player in position 4 is right-handed this is a strong service receive formation. Already the reader will be able to see how essential it is to understand the strengths and weaknesses of each system under different conditions. Later on in the chapter he will see how it is possible and indeed necessary to vary the service receive system according to the position of certain key players on court.

Type 2–Using a lateral switch

When the setter is in position 4, and the smashers on the front line are right handed it is best that the setter and the smasher in the centre change places as soon as the ball is served, i.e. switch. Their court positions before the ball is served are shown in Figs. 79a & 79b.

122

It is important to notice that the overlapping rule is not contravened in this instance. Player 4 is to the left of player 3 and both are in front of their respective back court players.

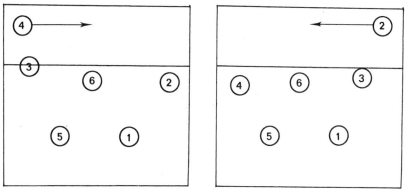

Figs. 79a & 79b W + 1 service receive formation with lateral switch

As soon as the ball is served, player 4 runs into the centre of the court to take up the position normally held by player 3 in the basic W + 1 system. The same system can be employed on the other side of the court when the setter is in position 2. By switching in this way the attacking potential of the front line is increased.

It is helpful for players to remember the following two points which will help them get into the correct position.

i) If they are a setter they will always set at the net so they stand at the net in all three positions.

ii) If they are a smasher they will always start their approach from the attack line at the wings.

Advantages of modified W + 1 wing setter

1)   It involves little movement of players and therefore less possibility of error or confusion during receive of service.

2)   When setting from position 2 the setter is playing the ball towards the strongest attacking point for a right-handed smasher.

3)   When setting from position 4 the setter is playing the ball towards the strongest attacking point for a left-handed smasher.

4)   It enables a team to use the pairs or two setter system.

5)   When the setter is at the side the variety of attack is increased. He can set high passes to the wing or centre positions, parallel sets to the wing or centre, and short sets in the centre. He can also smash the first pass if it is good enough. By eliminating the overhead pass he is increasing the potential

123

accuracy of his setting. The centre player is in a strong position to make an attack and force the opponents to be prepared to block in the centre.

Disadvantages
1) When the setter is in position 4 and the smasher in position 2 is right-handed he is setting to a potentially weak smashing position.
2) When the setter is in position 2 and the smasher in position 4 is left-handed he is setting to a potentially weak smashing position.

The advantages of the modified W + 1 lateral switch
1) Avoids the weakness of Type 1 when the setter is at 4 and the player in 2 is right-handed. The setter can now set to position 4.
2) Avoids the weakness of Type 1 when the setter is at 2 and the player in 4 is left-handed. The setter can now set to position 2.
3) There is the minimum of movement involved in the switch and therefore less chance of errors being made during receipt of service.
4) Allows a team to play the pairs or two setter systems.

Disadvantages
1) Limits the variety of attack to a forward or overhead set.

The coach must be flexible when he uses these systems. If the setter is in position 4 and the player in position 2 although right-handed is the best smasher in the team it is often wise to let the setter stay where he is, rather than switch him into the centre. If he goes into the centre he will be forced to give an overhead set to the player, or the same set that he would have given him if he had not switched. The other smasher, now in position 4, may not be such a good smasher as player 2. Even though the smasher in 4 is hitting from the best smashing position he may not be as effective as player 2 smashing from the weaker position. The coach must adapt the systems to suit his players and not the other way round.

Penetrating setters during service receive.
The service receive formations that have been covered so far all result in only two smashers being used. This means that the opposing blockers and defence need only concentrate on two attack points instead of three.

By bringing the back line setter through to the front court as the ball is served a team is able to use all three front court players as attackers. The variety of attack is therefore increased, with increased problems for the opponents.

There are two different line-ups that can be used to enable penetration to take place. One line-up involves receiving service on five players and the other on four.

Receiving on five players

The team should line up as in Fig. 80 when a setter is to penetrate from position 1. The setter must make sure that one of the feet of player 2 is in front of his forward foot, so that he is not overlapping.

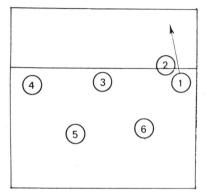

Fig. 80   Penetration from position 1 (one) at service receive

The three smashers are all waiting in the vicinity of the attack line. Player number 2 must cover for the penetrating setter. Any ball served at the penetrating setter is the responsibility of player 2. Players 5 and 6 must cover the back court between them.

As soon as the ball has been hit the penetrating setter should move into the front court. Some coaches advocate sending the setter round the outside of player 2. In this way it is argued he does not obstruct the view of player 2 as he comes into the front court towards the first pass.

Other coaches send their setter forward between players 2 and 3. This is a much quicker route than outside player 2. However, it does mean that he is obscuring the view of these two players as he moves forward. He may also find that he has to move backwards, towards the outside of the court, to play a first pass that is too long. The player coming round the side would not have this problem as he would be coming forward to the ball.

The penetrating setter must move to a position in front court which will enable him to set to all three smashers. Ideally, he wants to achieve a position with two players in front of him and one behind him. He must also aim for the same spot each time so that the receivers know where to dig the ball to. The recommended position is between players 2 and 3.

When penetrating from position 6 the line up takes a W shape (Fig. 81) with player 6 standing close behind player 3. There is one great disadvantage when penetrating in this way from position 6. The penetration takes place in the centre of the court, which is the easiest place to serve to. A well placed

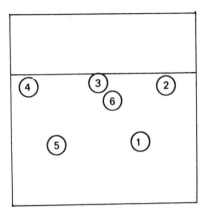

Fig. 81   Penetration from position 6 at service receive

serve could cause some confusion between players 3, 6 and 1 as to who plays a ball coming to that area. An alternative line-up is given later in this chapter.

Many teams do not bother to penetrate from position 5. Teams that use penetration usually have two setters. When one setter is at position 5, the other is at position 2, the best setting position. The primary object of any service receive line-up is to play the service in such a way that a successful attack will follow. When the front line setter is in position 4, or position 3, the attacking potential is considerably less than when penetration is used. If penetration is to take place from position 5 the attack potential must be greater than that obtained by leaving the setter in position 2 at the net. The penetrating setter would go to a position as shown in Fig. 82. This would mean that the smashers in front of him would be 3 and 2. Setting to them from this position would be no different from the situation where the setter is in position 4. As we saw this is not so effective when the smasher in position 2 is right handed.

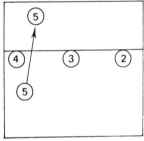

Fig. 82   Penetration from position 5. The path of the setter and the final position he would take up in the front court are shown

126

Most coaches use penetration from positions 1 and 6 only. If they penetrate from 5 they will, as we have seen, have a weaker attack unless the player at 2 is a left-handed smasher.

Receiving service on four players

In the same way that switching players are vulnerable to accurately placed serves, penetrating setters and the players in front of them are a target for servers. Penetration from position 6 is particularly vulnerable to an accurate serve. For this reason many coaches move the penetrating setter and his forward partner nearer the net out of the way.

Once these two players have been moved forward the rest of the players form an arc (Fig. 83). As soon as the ball is served the setter moves forward into his setting position and the smasher moves back to the attack line ready for an approach. As the smasher moves back he must ensure that he does not get in the way or vision of the receivers. Once the smasher is experienced he should be able to make this movement quite easily and effectively.

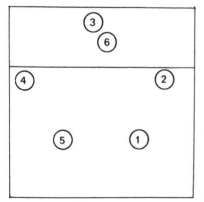

Fig. 83   Penetration from position 6, receiving on four players only

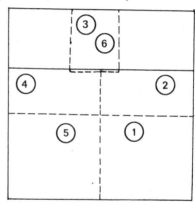

Fig. 84   Division of court areas when penetrating from position 6 and receiving on four players

The four players who receive the ball must all cover more court. The division of responsibilities in this system is shown in Fig. 84. To make this work the receivers must all be good diggers and able to move quickly to play the ball. It is essential that they call for the ball so that they do not find themselves taking the ball when it is not theirs to play. If the ball is served just over the net the centre smasher—3—must be prepared to dig the ball as he moves out to the attack line.

In addition to making it easier for the receivers to see and play the ball, receiving on four players has another advantage. The centre player, because

127

he is unlikely to play the ball, is now able to concentrate on making a short smash or fake attack through the middle. The opponents must be constantly expecting an attack through the centre. If the centre player has to receive the service he has very little time to make an approach for the short smash after he has played the first pass.

For the same reason there are two other occasions when teams use four players only to receive service. These are penetration from position 1 and when the setter is at position 2.

The line-up for penetration at 1 and receive on 4 is shown in Fig. 85. The four receivers form an arc to receive the ball. When the setter is at 2 it is possible to receive on four players by putting player 3 at the net and forming the usual arc (Fig. 86).

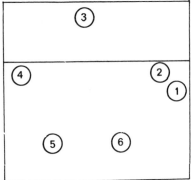
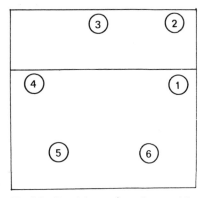

Fig. 85   Receiving on four players and penetrating from position 1

Fig. 86   Receiving on four players with the setter in the wing position

Advantages of penetration on service receive.
1) It increases the attacking points open to a team from two to three.
2) It enables a team to use the strongest attacking point—4—without having to switch front court players.
3) If a team has a good setter and he is in the back row, he is made use of. This is especially beneficial when the front line setter is not of the same calibre.

Disadvantages of penetration
1) It needs a great deal of ability if players are to make it work. All the team must be able to dig the ball very accurately. If the setter has to chase the first pass he will have little chance of making penetration more effective than the alternative simpler systems. The receivers must be able to move quickly to play the ball. They will be covering more of the court than normal, especially if they are receiving on only four players.

128

2) The setter must be very fit and of a high standard. It is much more difficult to take the ball after running forwards into the front row. He must be able to set all the different types of set and to decide which set to use very quickly.

3) The penetrating setter is an obvious target for the server. Unless players are quick to take the responsibility for the ball the setter will not be able to get into the front row. When the setter has to dig the ball he should play it across the court for the front line setter to take.

4) There is always the danger that the setter will not return to the back row after setting the ball. He may then be tempted to smash or block the ball.

Choosing a service receiver system

It is most important that the coach looks at the various service receive systems in the light of his teams' ability. The system he chooses must be related to the ability of his team. He should not pick a system because it is fashionable. His players may not have the ability to play that kind of system

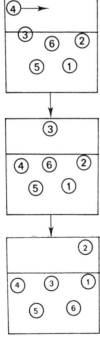

Fig. 87 Combining the W + 1 with lateral switch, W + 1 basic formation and W + 1 with wing setter, into an overall service receive system for a team with two setters

effectively. A system must enable a team to play to the limit of its present ability. It is no use trying to play penetration when a team cannot play the basic W + 1 system effectively. If a team cannot dig accurately enough or does not have high quality setters, it is pointless carrying on trying unsuccessfully to use penetration. It is better that they play the modified W + 1 system well and put up successful attacks than to try unsuccessfully to play a more advanced system. The system must fit the players and not the players fit the system.

As pointed out earlier, the coach can use several systems in his overall service receive system. There are six different front line combinations of players during a set. If the coach is using the system of pairs, this means that there are three setter situations for which he must decide formation; the setter in 4, 3, & 2, (Fig. 87) shows how the coach can combine the basic W + 1, the modified W + 1 (Type 1), and the modified W + 1 (Type 2), in his overall service receive system.

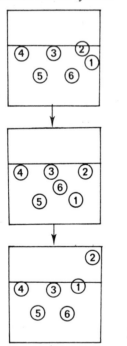 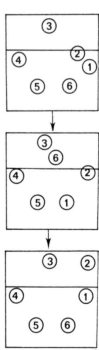

Fig. 88a Combining penetration from positions 1 and 6 with the W + 1 wing setter formation

Fig. 88b Combining penetration from position 1 and 6 with the wing setter formation, receiving on four players in each case

130

Fig. 88a shows how penetration from positions 1 and 6 can be combined with the W + 1 wing setter system. Fig. 88b shows how penetration can be combined with the W + 1 wing setter system using receiving on four players in each case.

Hints for players—service receive.

The most important thing is to be ready and waiting for the service. Too many players start discussing the last point or rally and do not give themselves time to get into position and to watch the server. As soon as the last rally has finished get yourself into position and look at the server.

It is difficult sometimes to remember which line-up your team is using and where on court you should be. If you look for the setter you will get an idea of the line up that is being adopted. Look for the player who is next to you in the rotational order and check that you are in the right position in relation to him. Also make sure that you are not overlapping with the player who is behind or in front of you in the rotational order.

As soon as you have found your right position and have confirmed where the setter wants to receive the ball, get into the ready position. Lock your arms in front of you with your hands above waist height. All you will have to do to dig the ball is to move the two locked arms together at the hands. This movement is very quick and means that you can concentrate on more important aspects of the game. Make sure that if you are in the wing position your outside leg is the forward leg. This will make it easier to play the ball into the centre of the court.

If you are setter, make sure that you tell the players before the ball is served where you want the first pass to be played. It is too late to give this information as they are playing the ball. There is so much to think about in a volleyball game that it is essential to remind players each time where the first pass is to go.

You must decide long before you actually play the ball that it is going to come to you. Look at the server and observe the angle of his body and his foot placement. Nearly all servers angle their feet and body towards the direction they wish to serve the ball. Obviously the server is aiming for maximum reliability. He is unlikely therefore to hit the ball across his body or out to the side of his body. Most serves are hit along the line of the shoulder. If you look at his positioning this will give you some clues about the possible direction of the serve. As soon as the ball has been hit you must start to predict exactly where it is going to go. Decide if it is going to pass over the net on your side of the court. If it is, then you must decide from the speed and trajectory of the serve whether it is going to land in the front or back half of the court. Using this method it is possible to make your call for the ball before it passes over the net.

131

If you have decided the ball is not going to come to you turn to face the receiver (Fig. 89). Ideally the remaining players should form a circle around the player so that if he makes a mistake and the ball flies off at an angle at least one of them will be able to play the ball. It is very demoralising if a player makes a bad dig and the others stand by and watch the ball fall to the floor.

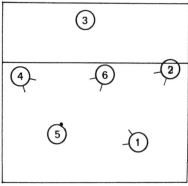

Fig. 89

You must make sure that you fully understand your role and position during each rotation. If the ball is not played sufficiently well during this phase of the game, a team will stand little chance of avoiding defeat. It is no use having great attacking or blocking strength if you cannot get the ball to the setter so that you can progress beyond service receive. Bad digs that result from bad positioning or players too slow getting into position are inexcusable.

Team formation when serving

When a team is serving it is essential that they make use of the opportunity to switch players into their best positions. The three front court players should all be at the net ready to block. If the blockers are going to switch their positions then they should stand close together to cut down the distance they have to move. When standing ready to switch, blockers must make sure that they do not form a screen and contravene Rule 13 Article. 7:-

The screen:

At the moment of service, it is illegal for players of the serving side to wave their arms, jump or form groups of two or more players with the aim of forming a screen to mask the server's action.

If the switching players stand one yard apart and keep their arms still they will not be breaking this rule.

When switching it is best if the players decide who is going to pass in front and who behind. The switch must be carried out as quickly as possible so that the blockers can get into position to watch their opponents' attack build up. If they waste time pushing each other out of the way they are reducing their chances of making a good block. If one player decides to pass in front of the other all mix-ups will be avoided.

Back court players who are also making a switch should get as close together as possible. They must make the switch quickly and watch their opponents while they are doing so. If they are too casual in their switching, the opponents may play the ball over the net on the first touch and catch them out of position.

As soon as possible the back court players should be preparing for defence. If the team is playing a system which involves the No. 6 player covering behind the block he should get up to the attack line straight away. The two other back court players must resist the temptation to come too far forward. They should keep about one yard in from the side line and a yard from the base line. They should keep as low as possible with their arms out in front of them. In this position they are ready to receive the smash. They will know that any ball passing over their head is going out of court and they are in a position to let the ball go. If they are standing up they will find it difficult to get out of the path of the ball in time. By starting at the back of the court they have only two ways to go to play the ball—forwards or sideways. If the players are too far forward they will find it very difficult to move backwards and play a deep smash.

Just as the team receiving the service must be prepared before the ball is served, so must the serving team. If they are in position early they will have more time to concentrate on predicting the course of the smashed ball. This extra time may make all the difference between scoring a point and losing service.

Covering the smash
Once the setter has set the ball, the team must start to move to cover the smasher. The block is the counter to the smash. If the block is successful the attacking team must prevent the blocked ball from hitting the ground. If the team stand and watch the smasher hit the ball they will have no chance of playing the blocked ball.

Around the smasher three players form an arc (Figs. 90, 91, 92). These players must be as low as possible with their arms clear of their bodies. The ball that comes off the block is usually travelling quite fast. The lower the players play the rebound, the more time they have to judge its direction and position. The extra two feet that can be gained by getting as low as possible can make all the difference between a successful pick-up and a unsuccessful one.

133

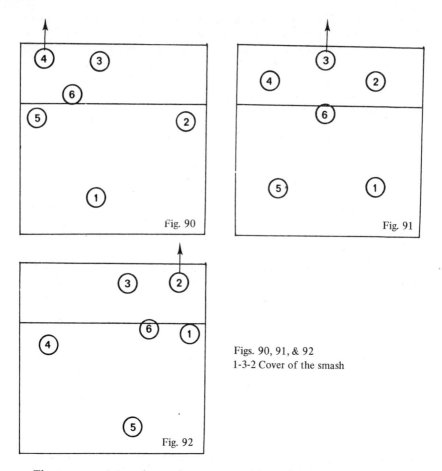

Fig. 90

Fig. 91

Figs. 90, 91, & 92
1-3-2 Cover of the smash

Fig. 92

The two remaining players form a second line of defence. Their job is to pick up the rebound that is directed into the back court. Skilful blockers are able in certain circumstances to direct the rebound. For this reason the two back players must be ready to move quickly in any direction to play the ball.

Some coaches feel that with three players around the block the movement of each player is restricted. In consequence they only use two players to form the first line and the remaining three the second (Figs. 93, 94, 95).

When deciding where to place his players, the coach must take into account several factors. He should consider the defensive system he is using to cover behind the block. The players from the back court should be able to move quickly—if the smash passes the block—from covering the smash to

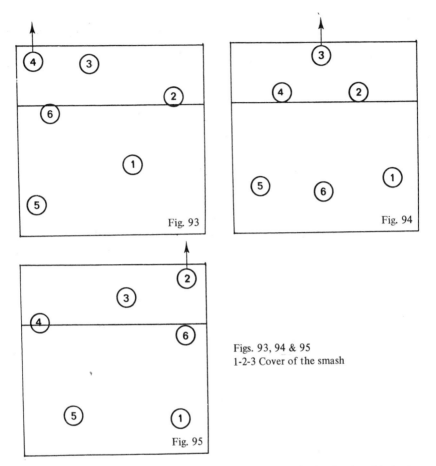

Fig. 93

Fig. 94

Fig. 95

Figs. 93, 94 & 95
1-2-3 Cover of the smash

covering the block. If a penetrating setter is used what does he do after he has set the ball? Coaches are divided about this. On one hand it is argued that if the ball is picked up successfully from the block he should be in the centre front court waiting for it. In this way a very quick counter attack can be made. Other coaches argue that the number of times the ball is picked up from the rebound does not warrant keeping him at the net during the covering of the smash. Instead they bring him back to the attack line so that he has less distance to travel back to his back court position, once the ball has passed into the other court. It is up to the individual coach to make his own mind up on this point after taking into account the ability of his team.

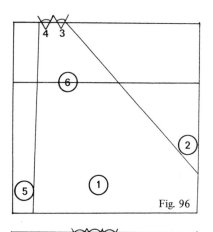

Fig. 96

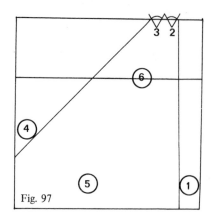

Fig. 97

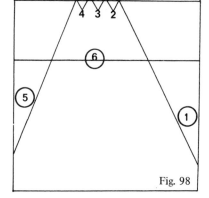

Fig. 98

Figs. 96, 97 & 98
2-1-3 (No. 6 cover behind the block)

Cover behind the block

So far, the positions of the team on receiving service and as they smash the ball have been considered. While one team is smashing the ball the other must be defending the other court. The block as has been shown is the first line of defence. If the ball passes over, through or round the block the other players must be in position to play the ball.

When there are two or three players participating in the block, the number of players remaining is few compared with the area of court that must be defended. In deciding where to place the player, it is generally assumed that the block is not only defending the air space above the net but a large proportion of the court immediately behind it. Figs. 96, 97, & 98 show the area of the court that is within the shadow of the block in several situations. Providing the block is well formed and timed, the court in this area is safe from attack.

136

unless the player manages to hit over the top of the block. As a result it is usual to place one player to cover the area of court shadowed by the block. This now reduces the amount of court that must be covered to a manageable amount, bearing in mind the number of players available for defence. The positioning of these remaining players varies considerably depending on the defensive system employed.

The 2 - 1 - 3, No.6 cover system.
This is the simplest of all the defensive systems. It is recommended for teams just starting to play and club teams of a reasonable standard. If a team is playing this system with success there is little point adopting one of the more advanced systems unless the team is obviously playing below its potential.

The basic formation and distribution for covering against a smash from the left is shown in Fig. 96 and from the right in Fig. 97. The two lines projected back from the blockers indicate the area covered by the block.

When teaching any defensive formation, it is important to give the player some reference points with which to align himself. Too many coaches draw the positions on a blackboard, stand the players in those positions on court and then hope for the best. This process may work in the long run as the players learn from experience where to position themselves. However, it is the job of the coach to give them this information and help them to achieve success earlier.

If the players are distributed as in Fig. 96, the reference points would be as follows:

Player 5 should line up his inside shoulder with the outside shoulder of player No. 4. In this way any ball passing outside the block will come to him.

Player 1 should line himself up with the middle of the block i.e. where the two blockers hands meet. This is the most likely weakness in the block. If any ball comes through the block, he will be in a good position to play it.

Player 2 should line up his inside shoulder with the right shoulder of player No. 3. In this way any ball passing inside the block will easily be covered by this player.

The two wing players should try to see the smasher. If they can see the smasher then they have a chance of looking at his movements to predict where the ball is going to be hit.

The No. 6 player must cover the area in the immediate vicinity of the block. Many smashes just touch the block and fall just over, or, to the side of it. These and the dump shots must be picked up by No. 6. If he starts on the attack line then most of the balls will drop in front of him giving him room to play them. He should keep as low as possible so that he has as much time as possible to prepare for the shot.

When the smash is made through the centre, the formation is given in Fig.

137

98. As there are three players participating in the block, a gap will be left in back court. This means that the two wing players 1 & 5 will have to be prepared to move into the centre to play the ball that comes over or through the block. Once again it is essential that the players call if they intend to play the ball.

Advantages of the No. 6 cover system

1)   Its main advantage is its simplicity. When players are in position 6 they know that they must cover behind the block. When they are in the other two positions they know they stay back.

2)   The division of responsibilities is clear cut. The short balls are the responsibility of No. 6, the long ones the responsibility of the nearest back court player.

3)   For teams that are just learning the game it is very effective. It does not require a great deal of ability to play.

Disadvantages

1)   It assumes that the player in position 6 is agile or mobile enough to be able to play the ball that is dumped or touches the block. Very often the player in this position is a tall smasher who is perhaps too slow or not so agile.

2)   There is a potential weakness in the back of the court. Player number 1 very often does not bother to swing round into the middle of the court when the smash is from the left. This means that a ball hit over the top of the block is likely to score points.

3)   There are only three players defending the back of the court. Against a team that smashes hard and with a great deal of control this system is not as effective as other alternative systems. The speed of the smash means that the players must be in or very near the right position when the ball is hit.

The 2 - 1 - 3 back line cover system

With this system the centre back player, No. 6, stays back to defend the back court. The player covering the dump shot or the ball that touches the block and falls close by, is the back court player immediately behind the block. The distribution of players in this system is shown in Figs. 99, 100, 101.

The wing player behind the block in position 4, that is player number 5, must come up to the attack line to cover. Players number 6 and number 1 cover the area within the shadow of the block. Player number 6 must be prepared to cover line shots.

Advantages of 2 - 1 - 3 back line cover system

1)   If the wing player does not have time to get right up to cover behind the

138

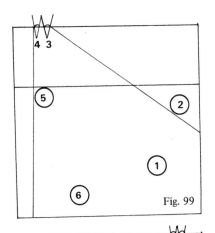

Fig. 99

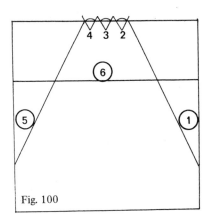

Fig. 100

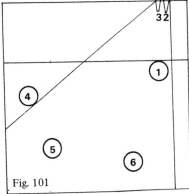

Fig. 101

Figs. 99, 100 & 101   2-1-3 (Wing cover)

block he is at least in a position to cover a smash. There is also less chance of a smash succeeding because the most likely areas for the smash to land, along the diagonal and centre, are covered by players already. With the number 6 system, there is a large gap in back court until the free smasher and back court players move across.

2)   During rallies the absence of a permanent cover player enables the setter to have more room to move.

3)   At all times during the game, all the players will have a clear view of the game. With the No. 6 system the forward player tends to obscure the view of several players.

4)   The tendency for the forward covering player to attempt to play a smash which could be best played by a back court player is considerably less with this system than with the No. 6 cover.

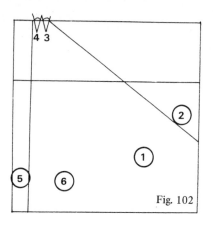

Fig. 102

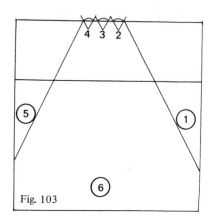

Fig. 103

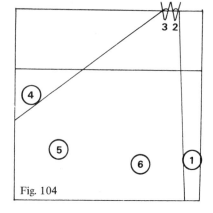

Fig. 104

Figs. 102, 103 & 104   2-0-4 Cover

2 - 0 - 4 cover system

This is the system played by all the top teams in the world today. It is more suited to the demands of top-class play and reflects the higher ability of the top players. As its name suggests the four non-blocking players are all defending the back court against a smash. Unlike the other systems, no other player is in mid-court waiting for the dump. The players are distributed as in Figs. 102, 103, 104.

Each player has responsibility for a channel of court (Fig. 105). If the ball drops in that court, front, centre or back he must play it. This means that the players must be mobile, agile and able to dive for a ball if necessary. Very often however they do not have to dive because they have read the smasher's actions well in advance and have had time to move in for the short ball.

140

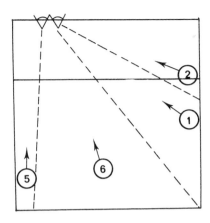

Fig. 105

Advantages of the 2 - 0 - 4 system
1)   It enables a team to have four players covering the back court.
2)   The free blocker is able to cover for the smash that is angled very sharply inside the block. This is a shot used quite often by top-class smashers.
3)   The free blocker is ready in position for a quick smash.
4)   The centre of the court is relatively free for a penetrating setter to come through as soon as he is sure he will not have to play the ball.

Disadvantages
1)   The main disadvantage is the high level of ability required of the players. If they cannot read the game, or are not very mobile, it is pointless playing this system.
2)   There is a large area behind the block which is vulnerable to the dump or soft smash.

The system that the coach chooses for his team must be one that is suited to their ability. If the team is inexperienced or has only been playing for a season or so, then it is best that they use the No. 6 cover system. The ability to read the game comes only after many matches and training sessions. Without this ability, and the ability quickly to make the necessary movements, it is pointless trying to be 'with it' and play a more advanced system. When a team has plenty of experience and the players are able to move quickly, then is the time to start learning a new system.

Hints to players in the defensive situations
Correct positioning is the key to good defensive play. Very often you will hear a smasher say that he seemed to be hitting the ball straight at the defensive player. This appears to be so because the defender has first picked

the most likely spot the ball will go and then made other adjustments to his position on the basis of what he has observed about the smasher's position, action etc.

The reference points that are given earlier in this chapter will help you to pick your *starting* postition. Once you have this position don't assume that all you have to do is wait for the ball to come to you—more than likely it will not. Having picked the correct spot in relation to the block—or if the block is badly formed or incomplete, where you think the block ought to be positioned—look at the smasher. Supposing for example he is smashing from position 4, and you are in back court position 5 in the 2 - 1 - 3 wing system (Fig. 106). You can see that his line of approach indicates that the ball is most likely to be smashed to your side of the court. If you are in the position shown in the diagram you are to the right of the probable line of the smash. This line is the line of the smasher's hitting arm. First of all you must move into the line of the smash.

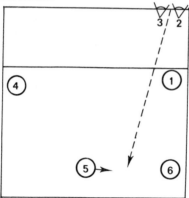

Fig. 106

Although you are now in the line of the smash this is not necessarily the position in which the ball will land. It could land anywhere in front of you. You can gain some idea of where the ball will land by looking at the distance the set is from the net and the height at which the smasher contacts the ball.

When the ball is set close to the net and is being hit from a position two feet above the net, it is likely to be a strong shot and to land about fifteen feet in court. When the ball is hit from higher it will be a slower ball because the player cannot use the full extension of his shoulder and elbow when he hits the ball. The ball is likely to travel a greater distance as well because the player is unable to get "on top of the ball".

If the set is further from the net the smasher must hit it from higher up to clear both the blockers and net. As a result the ball will travel further (see Fig. 107).

142

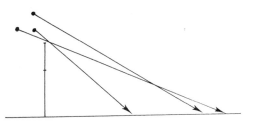

Fig. 107   The further the set is from the net the higher the point at which it must be hit so that it passes over the net and lands in court

It can be seen how it is possible to get some idea of the direction and the length of the smash before the ball has been hit. Obviously, there is a little more to it than this. The smasher uses his wrist to try and vary the direction of the smash. You must watch each smasher, try and spot his particular movements and preferences so that you are able to predict where he is going to hit the ball with more certainty.

Not every ball is smashed, some are dumped over or around the block. Whenever possible try and get a view of the smasher as he prepares to hit the ball. Watch particularly the action of his hitting arm. If it comes to a halt and straightens, he is going to dump the ball. If you have watched his arm movement you will be able to move forward as he plays the ball, thus destroying the element of surprise he had been hoping for.

Even if you cannot see the smasher you should be able to assess the likelihood of a dump. If the set is well into court the smasher will have little court to hit into (Fig. 108). He is likely to try and dump the ball between the outside blocker and the sideline. If the block is very well lined up, timed and formed in the air, the smasher will see that he has little chance of smashing

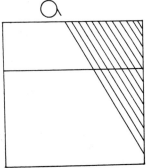

Fig. 108   When the set is well in court the smasher has less court to smash into unless he turns the ball over the block. In this instance the shaded area is the only area not covered by the block

143

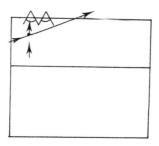

Fig. 109

past and will try to dump the ball. This is most likely to occur when the ball has been set close to the net on the outside of the court. Unless the player has made an approach to the net at an acute angle he is likely to be blocked out (Fig. 109).

When you are waiting for the smash, you must be doing the thinking for two people. You must try and think like the smasher and on the basis of that thinking and your own experience make movements that will enable you to dig the smash successfully. All the time the opponents are building up their attack you must be adjusting your position in relation to the ball and the changing circumstances. Your opponents will not always attack on the third touch. If you are playing against a team that thinks, they will be looking to see if you are out of position or not paying full attention. In these instances they will play the ball over on the first or second touch to catch you by surprise.

When you are in the back court you must keep low. If you are standing up you will have to lower yourself before you can play the ball at the best height. This all takes time, which is in short supply in this phase of the game. Spread your feet fore and aft to give yourself a good base which will enable you to move quickly in any direction to play the ball. Keep lifting your feet slightly while you are waiting for the smash. This will make it easier and quicker for you to move into position. Make sure that you do not move forward to cover your own smasher and fail to move all the way back to your defensive position. It is very easy to get engrossed in the game and forget to move back after the smash.

If you see that a ball is going to go out of court, give a loud call of "OUT". It is very dispiriting to let a ball go past you out of court only to see another player come across to play it, losing your team the rally or point. Give the player near you some help as well when you see that the ball that he is going to play will land out of court. Often this player is concentrating on playing his shot and cannot see that the ball will fall just out of court. If you give him an early call he will have time to move out of the way.

144

The phases of volleyball

So far the line-ups used for service receive, service, covering a smasher and covering the block have been considered. Although looked at as seperate units, they must merge together to enable the game to flow. It is useful to think of volleyball as a series of phases when a team is defending, attacking or preparing for either.

Many coaches teach each of these phases seperately and do not attempt to link them together. This is most unhelpful for the player. Each player must be moving continuously during the game. He should be moving into position for a phase of the game, participate in that phase, prepare for the next phase and so on. This linking of the phases will not come by mere chance. It must be taught. Whenever one of these phases is taught, make sure that it is related to the phase prior to it and the phase following it. The players do not suddenly arrive in the positions for covering the block, they have come from particular court positions. Start from these positions so that the whole situation is more relevant for the learners.

The following examples will help to show the positions players will pass through in a rally:

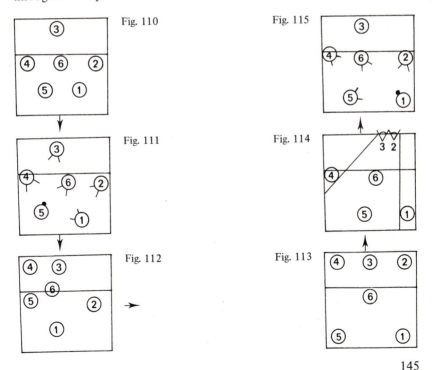

Fig. 110

Fig. 111

Fig. 112

Fig. 115

Fig. 114

Fig. 113

145

Example 1.

A team employs a W + 1 service receive formation with the setter at position 3 (Fig. 110). Player number 5 receives the ball and the other players turn to face him in case he fails to play the ball straight to the setter at position 3. Notice how player number 1 moves across as 5 digs the ball, to cover in case the ball rebounds backwards (Fig. 111).

The ball is set to player 4 for a smash and the rest of the team move in to cover in case the ball is blocked out. For cover of smash the team employs a 3 - 2 system (Fig. 112).

The ball has successfully passed over the net so the players move into position ready to block and defend. As the team is using a number 6 cover system, player 6 waits by the attack line (Fig. 113).

The opponents smash from position 4, so players two and three on the defending side move to block the smash (Fig. 114).

However, the block does not stop the ball and it goes to player number 1. The block splits and 3 goes in to the centre front court to set. Player 2 moves back to the attack line ready to make an approach for the smash (Fig. 115).

Example 2

This team is penetrating from position 1 and receiving on four players with number 3 at the net (Fig. 116).

The ball is received by player 6 and the rest of the team turn to face him. The penetrating setter has now entered the front court and the centre smasher returned to the attack line (Fig. 117).

Player number 4 smashes the ball from the left of the court. Player number 3 having made a fake attack through the centre now covers on the inside. The penetrating setter, player 1, moves to cover by the attack line. Player number 5 comes up to cover behind the smasher (Fig. 118).

The ball has now passed over the net and player 1, the setter, moves into position 1 in the back court. From this position it is easy for him to penetrate into the front court during a rally. (Fig. 119).

The opponents smash from 2 and a block is made by players 4 and 3. Behind the block the team play the 2 - 0 - 4 system (Fig. 120). The smash comes to player 6. Realising the ball is not coming to him, player number 1 now penetrates to the front court calling for the first pass. Both players 4 and 3 come back to the attack line ready to smash and all players turn to face the receiver of the smash, player 6 (Fig. 121).

Teaching tactics.

The importance of relating new formations to the positions of the players immediately prior to and after the particular formation has already been mentioned. It is also important to make sure that each player understands

146

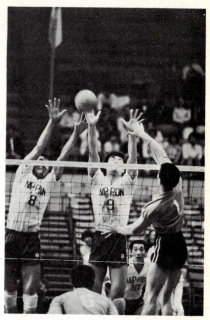

After the block has been made the arms must be brought back, clear of the net, as soon as possible

An excellent block by two members of the Japanese team. The height top players can reach and the way the centre blocker closes the gap between himself and the outside blocker are clearly shown

Although the ball is on its way overhead the centre blocker has not moved. The chances of a successful smash are therefore increased

A well angled and positioned block gives the smasher little chance. Notice how the back court players on the inside of the block are alert having anticipated the direction of the smash

The smasher starts his approach from the attack line

The Japanese centre blocker shows quite clearly that a blocker must be able to vary the position of his arms in the air in order to close the gap

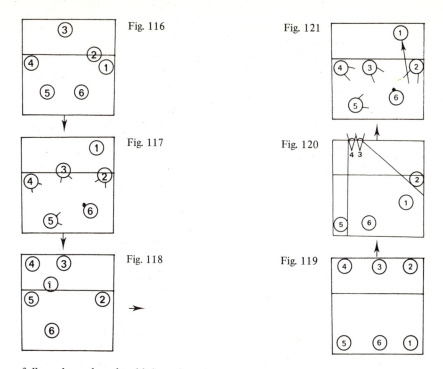

Fig. 116   Fig. 117   Fig. 118

Fig. 121   Fig. 120   Fig. 119

fully where he should be when he is in each of the six positions of a formation.

Having explained the system with the aid of diagrams, positioning players on court and explaining reference points, the players experience the system in practice. If it is a service receive formation, throw balls across the net to a team and let them play it through to a smash. If it is block and cover, provide a setter and smasher on the other side of the court.

Play each player in each position about twenty times before rotating the team. Check to see that each player is lining himself up correctly. Make sure that the setters also play the other positions and any players who might play as a setter in a game, play the setter's positions. It is important that all players are able to adapt to the system since the regular setter may be injured, fail to turn up for a match etc. In these instances players will be playing different roles to those they usually play. With some previous experience they are more likely to adapt to their new role with some measure of success.

If it is intended to adopt a new system it must be practiced thoroughly before it is used in a match. It is no use suddenly deciding half way through a game to experiment.

147

When first introducing tactics it is best to concentrate only on service receive and cover behind the block. If cover of the smash is introduced in the early stages, players easily get confused and fail to move back to the back court defensive positions. The W + 1 service receive pattern and the No. 6 cover system are the most suitable for beginners. As the players progress and the setter system changes, the receive line-up can also be developed (Fig. 122).

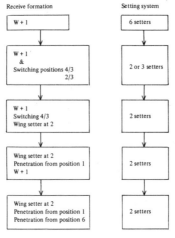

Fig. 122

It is better gradually to develop the service receive formation to include penetration. First of all penetration at 1 can be included instead of the lateral switch at 4 and 3. When this is mastered, penetration from 6 to full receive on four players can be introduced.

There are two important things for the coach to remember when planning and teaching tactics. Firstly, the system should not be so rigidly adhered to during a game that the players become robots. The coach must allow a certain amount of flexibility. Secondly, he must continually emphasise to the players that they are not defending a position but an area of court. Any ball coming into that area is their responsibility. However, this does not mean that a player may not go out of his area to play a ball should the need arise.

The tactics of serving

The serve is the first chance a team has to attack. A well placed serve can win a point outright, or affect the opponents' play so much that their attack is very weak.

It is important to remember that each serve has a potential value of two

148

points. The point the team can gain from that service or the following rally, and the point that the opponents can gain if they win the right to serve as a result of an illegal serve by the other team.

The server can score points as a result of serving to a particular point in the opponents' court or to a particular player.

The server should look at the service receive formation to see where he can place his serve so that the receiver will have to move to play the ball. This increases the likelihood of a mistake. With the W + 1 formation the area just behind the forward centre player is always vulnerable. There are three players in that area and it is very common for them all to leave it to another player to take the ball or all to try and play it.

No matter which service receive formation is used the corners are always weak spots (Fig. 123). The receiver will have to move diagonally back to play the ball. There is always the possibility that he will let the ball go past him and hope that it will go out of court. At the same time there is the danger that the server may hit the ball out of court.

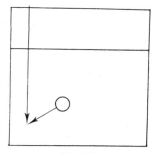

Fig. 123

When a team receives service on four players it leaves a large gap in the centre of the court. A ball served to this area may force the retreating centre player—3—to play it. This will upset his timing and very often is so much of a surprise to him that his pass is poor. Alternatively, the wing players may not come across to take the ball and it will drop in front of the two back players.

Fig. 124 and Fig. 125 show the weak spots for the W + 1 and receiving on four service formations.

If a team is lining up too far forward or too far back, then obviously the serve should land deep or short so that the players have to move to play the ball.

When two players are switching it is often effective to serve the ball to the middle of the switch. Even if it does not score an ace the serve will upset the rhythm of the switch enough to reduce the effectiveness of the resulting attack.

149

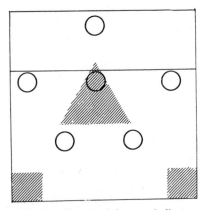

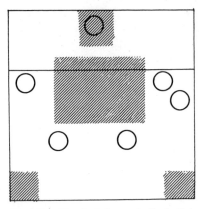

Fig. 124 The shaded areas indicate the weak spots in the W + 1 service receive formation

Fig. 125 The shaded areas indicate the weak spots in the Receiving on four line up

In a similar way a ball served at a penetrating setter can cause confusion. The player in front of the penetrating setter should take the ball. If the serve forces him to move out to the side of the court he will block the path of the penetrating setter.

The first pass can be made more difficult for the setter by serving down the line on the opposite side of the court. If the setter is penetrating from position 1, a serve down the line to player 5 will often result in the first pass failing to come back across court to the normal penetration position. Player 5 has to move back and across to play the ball. Unless he is very quick he will not have time to turn his body far enough towards the position he wants to send the ball. As a result the ball will probably be sent forwards between positions 3 and 4. This means that the setter has further to run, less time to get into position and less varieties of set are open to him. If the ball is served into the path of the penetrating setter he may be forced to play the first pass and one of the smashers will then have to set the ball.

It is quite natural for the setter to turn to face the side of the court to which the ball has been served. No setter is going to attempt to set a ball coming towards him that he cannot see! This fact has important bearing on the place to serve.

In Fig. 126 the player in position 4 is the best smasher and he is also in the strongest smashing position. If the ball is served to the opposite side of the court the setter will be forced to face that way. This will mean that he has to give an overhead set to reach the strong smasher. This is difficult enough when the first pass is really accurate. When the pass is not so accurate, the set he will give overhead, will greatly reduce the effectiveness of the smash. The

150

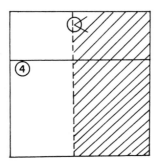

Fig. 126   If the ball is served into the shaded area the setter will turn to face it, with the result that a set to 4, the strong smasher, will have to be overhead

advice to servers, therefore, is to serve to the opposite side of the court to the best smasher.

In the same way it is possible to force the opponents to smash into the strongest block. The ball should be served to the side of the court where the best block is.

If the ball is served so that one of the smashers has to play it, this will upset his timing and preparation for the smash.

In addition to certain positions on court where it is advantageous to serve, there are certain players who should be served at.

If a player has been substituted into the game he will be hoping to settle gently into the game. If he is served at, he is immediately put under pressure. If he makes a bad shot this will not only upset him but the rest of the team for a few points. When a team has been losing points on receive and they have substituted their worst receiver, the new player will be very conscious of the fact that he has come on court to remedy the poor receive. If the first ball is served at him and he makes a mistake the harmony and spirit of his team will be severely shaken.

Volleyball is a game where calmness under pressure and even tempers can make the difference between winning and losing. Many points are lost because a team is worried, arguing amongst itself, or unable to get into a rhythm because their opponents are putting pressure on a particular part of the court or player. As tension increases, tempers rise and players will often be seen arguing amongst themselves. In this case the ball should be served on these players to increase the tension and to take advantage of the effect this tension has on their performance.

Usually the captain is checking to see that all his players are in the correct position, urging them on, or planning the next move, just before the serve is received. This leaves him with less time to prepare himself for the serve. If the ball is served at him he may not be fully prepared for it and may as a result make a poor first pass.

If there is a player who is particularly weak on service receive the serve should go as often as possible to that player. If he is slow to move serve the ball a few feet from him. If he is weak receiving a ball to one side serve on that side.

At the end of a rally the team should get the ball back to the server as soon as possible. The quicker the ball can be put back into play the less time the opponents have to regain their composure or to correct their line up etc.

Each server must perfect a reliable and accurate serve. He should be able to vary the speed of the serve and be able to hit specific parts of the court with 100% accuracy.

Three touch volleyball
It is generally accepted that it is best to use the three touches allowed on each side of the net before the ball passes back across the net. The first touch is usually a dig pass from the service or smash. From this point on, the team is on the attack. If the first pass goes straight back across the net then the team has not made any real attempt to attack.

The first pass therefore is directed to a front court player—the setter—who has to change the direction of the ball from a forward one to a horizontal one. The second touch is called the set pass and is aimed high above and near to the net. The third touch is then the attacking shot across the net. By using the three touches in this way the team can control the ball within its own court and finally position it for a player to play back across the net in such a way that it is difficult for the opponents to play. This three touch volleyball must be instilled in players and a team as early as possible. If teams play the ball back on the first or second touch each time, the game soon loses the character of volleyball and becomes what purists commonly call "beachball".

Already it has been shown how it is possible to position players at service receive and following a smash so that the most effective cover of the court area is obtained. The possible use of six, three or two setters in a team and how to position them in each of these situations has also been demonstrated. The concern now is with ways in which the attack can be made as strong as possible.

Attack points
When the setter is one of the front line players then only two attacking points can be used i.e. if the setter is at 2 then only 3 and 4 are attacking points. However, position 2 is also an attacking point on two occasions.

Firstly, if the first pass is particularly accurate to the setter he may be in a position to smash the ball. Secondly, if the first pass is not played to him, he should move back to the attack line so that he creates the second attack point.

Smashing the ball on the second touch often catches the opponents completely by surprise and can win a valuable point or rally.

If the setter is at the side, then the centre becomes an attack point. This is a very effective point because it means that the opponents have to bring all three front court players together to make an effective block.

The smash through the centre most often follows a short set. This means that the opponents have very little time to form a three man block. It is up to the player in the centre position to keep making an approach to the net to ensure that the opposing team regard the centre position as a real threat to them.

When the first pass looks to be a good one the centre smasher should make an approach in time with the ball to the setter calling for a short set. This will naturally keep the centre blocker in position until he can decide whether a short set will be given or not.

Although the centre smasher has called for a short set it does not mean that the setter has to give him the ball. The setter can play the ball up and over the centre smasher as he is in the air. The set will then go across court to the other smasher. If the centre player and setter have timed this well, it will leave the smasher with only one blocker to beat.

The centre smasher has a most important and difficult job. He must act as a decoy for the other front row smasher. He must not be discouraged by the fact that he gets less sets than the other smasher, and he must make use of the sets he gets as well as he can. If his timing is wrong he will not be able to make a good shot nor will he be of much use as a decoy smasher.

When the first pass is not very good and it is obvious that the setter will not be able to give a short set then the centre player should wait for a normal high set in the centre. It is pointless him trying to make a fake attack through the centre when he can see that the setter will not be able to set the ball to him. The opponents will not be fooled by this move and the smasher will have left only one attack point for the setter to play the ball to.

The centre player must be looking for every opportunity to attack through the centre. When the opponents play the ball across the net with a volley or dig then the centre player should be looking for the short set through the middle.

When a penetrating setter is used, a team is able to use all three attack points. The setter normally positions himself between positions 3 and 2. From this position he is able to set a high pass or, parallel pass to 4, various short and parallel sets and a high set to position 3, and short or overhead sets to 2 (Fig. 127). The potential variety of a team's attack is therefore greatly increased by penetration.

153

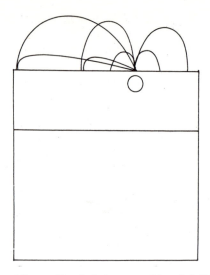

Fig. 127   From a setting position in between positions 2 & 3 the setter will be able to give the sets shown in this diagram

Where to play the attacking shot.

Each defensive formation has weaknesses. Each team has some players who are weaker than others. The attack should therefore be directed at either of these weak spots.

The No. 6 cover as we have seen is often vulnerable to a smash in back court position 6. If the wing player number 5 or 1 does not move across then there is no one covering deep behind the block.

The other defensive systems are vulnerable to a dump or soft smash as shown in Figs. 128, 129, 130, 131, 132.

The attack should where possible go through the weakest block. If there is a short blocker then the set should be directed to the smasher opposite this blocker. Where there is a weak receiver then the smash should be directed as often as possible to this player.

The attack must be varied for greatest success. If a team can predict with a high degree of certainty where the attack will be made then it will be able to prepare for defence with more confidence and greater accuracy.

The attack should be made as fast as possible. It is very noticeable that the sets of the Japanese are much lower and faster than those of East European teams. The dig pass to the setter is also much lower and faster. The result is that the Japanese attack is very fast. They have adopted this style of play because their players do not have the strength and build to play the orthodox

154

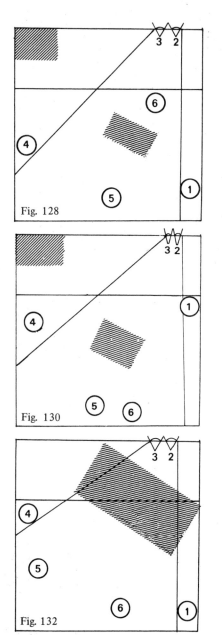

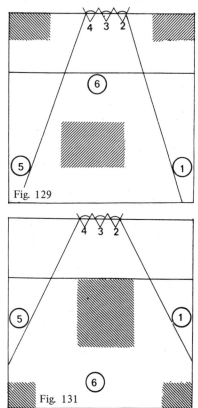

Fig. 128   The shaded areas indicate the court areas vulnerable to a dump or soft smash, in the 2-1-3 No. 6 cover system

Fig. 129   Areas vulnerable to a dump or soft smash in the No. 6 cover system when the smash is in the centre

Fig. 130   Areas of court vulnerable to a dump or soft smash in the 2-1-3 backline cover system

Fig. 131   Areas vulnerable to a dump or tactical ball when the smash is in the centre and No. 6 stays deep

Fig. 132   Areas of court vulnerable to a dump or soft smash, in the 2-0-4 system

155

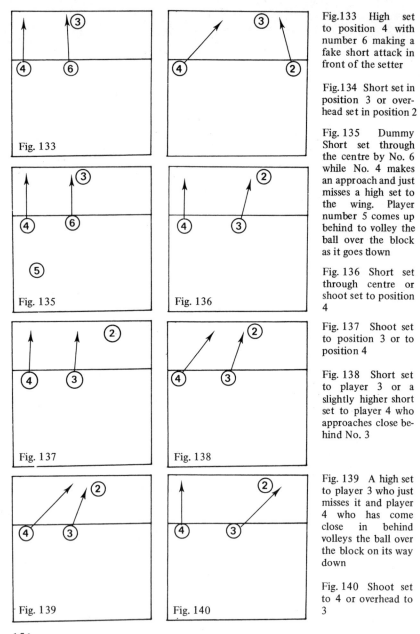

Fig.133 High set to position 4 with number 6 making a fake short attack in front of the setter

Fig.134 Short set in position 3 or over-head set in position 2

Fig. 135 Dummy Short set through the centre by No. 6 while No. 4 makes an approach and just misses a high set to the wing. Player number 5 comes up behind to volley the ball over the block as it goes down

Fig. 136 Short set through centre or shoot set to position 4

Fig. 137 Shoot set to position 3 or to position 4

Fig. 138 Short set to player 3 or a slightly higher short set to player 4 who approaches close be-hind No. 3

Fig. 139 A high set to player 3 who just misses it and player 4 who has come close in behind volleys the ball over the block on its way down

Fig. 140 Shoot set to 4 or overhead to 3

Fig. 133

Fig. 135

Fig. 136

Fig. 137

Fig. 138

Fig. 139

Fig. 140

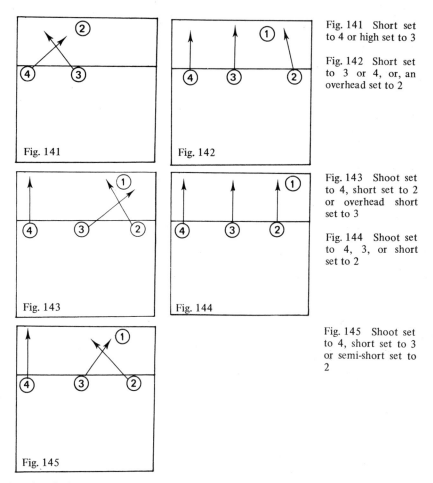

Fig. 141 Short set to 4 or high set to 3

Fig. 142 Short set to 3 or 4, or, an overhead set to 2

Fig. 143 Shoot set to 4, short set to 2 or overhead short set to 3

Fig. 144 Shoot set to 4, 3, or short set to 2

Fig. 145 Shoot set to 4, short set to 3 or semi-short set to 2

Fig. 141

Fig. 142

Fig. 143

Fig. 144

Fig. 145

style of play adopted by their major rivals the East Europeans. When a team is tall and strong then it is wise to take every advantage of this height and use high sets. The smashers will then be able to hit the ball over the top of the block. With the lower sets a team must rely on speed of take-off and the overall speed of the build-up to give them a good chance of passing the block.

Multiple attacks or wave attacks
The Japanese have developed their attacking pattern to include several players making an approach to the net at the same time. Players cross over and change positions, players come in front of and behind the setter. This

157

produces a spectacular and very effective attack. It does however require superb timing and an excellent setter.

Many other countries have copied the Japanese style of play with some success. Club teams in Europe have also adopted this style.

When using multiple attacks it is important that the setter is always left with one smasher to whom he can set an ordinary pass. If every attacking player is moving about and the ball that comes to the setter is poor, he has an almost impossible task.

Most often these multiple attacks are used at service receive. When the first pass is very good other multiple attacks are used during a rally.

Some examples of multiple attacks are shown in Figs. 133-145. Each coach will be able to devise many different multiple attacks himself. These can be tried in training and if successful used in a match. However, players must not try to play these regardless of the first pass. If the first pass is poor then they must attack accordingly. It is best if all the players know what move is going to be tried at service receive, before the ball is served. Usually it is the setter who tells the other players what move he will try and set up if the first pass is good enough.

There must be flexibility in attack. The coach should not insist on a rigid pattern of play. The team must improvise when necessary. A team of robots programmed for only one form of attacking play will not get very far in volleyball.

Attacking on the second touch

There will be many occasions when the opposing team have to play the ball across the net with a volley pass or dig, instead of a smash. When this becomes obvious the front court players should move back to the attack line to help in defence and also to position themselves for a quick attack.

When the volley comes into the front court the player who takes it can set it immediately for another player to smash. In this way the opponents have very little time to form a block.

The player taking the second pass may decide to fake as though he is going to smash and then jump set the ball across court. If the opponents have been quick enough to get into position to block the second touch they will have no chance of blocking the third touch on the other side of the court.

There are occasions when the ball comes across into the back court and the player can volley it across court for the smasher opposite him to smash.

To take advantage of the easy ball coming across the net, the receivers must be prepared to volley the first pass. If a dig is used, it is far less accurate and the chances of making a good attack on the second touch are reduced.

The front court players must move to and from the net very quickly. The movement of the smashers has been likened to the ebb and flow of the tide.

158

They are in at the net to block and quickly back to the attack line ready to smash and then back to the block.

Returning the ball on the third touch with a volley.

There are many occasions when the only way a team can get the ball back across the net is to volley or dig it. However, it is no use just sending the ball over the net and hoping for the best. This shot must also be an attacking shot.

Firstly, the ball should be sent as low over the net as possible. Naturally it must be high enough to pass over any block the opponents manage to put up. If it is sent over too high it will give the opponents time to get into position and to prepare for an attack.

Secondly, the volley or dig must be placed. It must be positioned so that it will make a player move to play it. Sometimes it is good to aim for the centre back court if a team plays with No. 6 covering. The corners are another good spot as this will make the back court players move to play the ball. If the centre player in the front court—3—moves back, it is often effective to volley the ball in front of him. He will be moving back and may not have enough time to check his backward movement and then move forward to the ball.

The third touch should always be an attacking shot.

Negative volleyball

Unfortunately for volleyball and the players concerned, some coaches of teams just beginning to play volleyball adopt what might be called negative volleyball. Instead of trying to use the three touches allowed and set up a proper attack, they play the ball back on the first or second touch with the hope that the other team will make mistakes. If the other team is playing three touch volleyball they will be playing the ball three times compared with one touch of their opponents, thus leaving more room for error. If they are used to blocking and covering they will also be caught by surprise. These tactics can win a few matches in the lower levels of volleyball but they do limit the development of the team and players. It is hoped that coaches would accept that in the early stages their teams will lose matches and resist the temptation to adopt this style of play for the sake of short term results.

6 TRAINING FOR VOLLEYBALL

Once the player has learnt the basic techniques of volleyball the coach must give him further training to develop these techniques to the high level required by the modern game. In this chapter advanced practices for all the techniques are given. In addition some practices suitable for developing aspects of team play are suggested. Once again it must be stressed that the practices given are examples and the coach must be thinking all the time of new practices or improvements to existing ones so that his coaching will be more effective.

It is not sufficient for the player to master merely the basics of a technique. He must be able to use the technique under varying match conditions. The position on court from which, and to which, he will have to play the ball will vary considerably during the game. He will have varying amounts of time in which to prepare for the shot. To enable the player to cope with these situations it is necessary to create similar conditions whenever possible in the training sessions. Having encountered these situations in training and practised the various techniques under these conditions, the player will be more likely to master them in the actual game. It follows therefore that the coach should not use exclusively the drills and practices in which players return the ball in exactly the same direction from which it has come. Players must be made to change the direction of the ball and to move into position for a shot. In the majority of situations in a game a player will have to move to play the ball. Wherever possible the practices for the volley and dig passes should involve movement so that the player can learn how to predict the best place to play the ball, from the speed, angle and height of the ball as it comes near him.

Setting

In chapter 4 a large number of practices for the volley pass were given. The setter must develop excellent volleying technique and the practices referred to will assist in this. He must also be able to move quickly into position to play the ball. While he is moving into position he must be making decisions about the type of set he can and should give in a particular situation. He must be able to judge distances and angles effectively. On many occasions he will find himself some distance from and at an angle to the net. He must be able to set the ball from that position so that the smasher will have a good chance of making a successful smash.

Training for the setter should develop the following;

    a) The ability to volley the ball legally and accurately in all directions, from varying heights and when the ball is low to the side.

    b) Positioning and decision making.

    c) Judgement of angles and distances.

a) Improving the volley

It is important for the setter to learn to control the ball well. He must be able to position himself very accurately in relation to the ball. He should know where it is and be able to control it in many positions. The following practices will help the player to improve his control.

1)   The ball is volleyed two feet above the head while the player walks across the gym.

2)   The ball is volleyed six feet into the air and the player turns through 360 degrees before volleying it again.

3)   The ball is volleyed six feet in the air. The player then touches his toes before volleying it again.

4)   The ball is volleyed forwards and the player runs into position to volley it again.

5)   The ball is thrown against the wall and the rebound is volleyed. The speed, height and angle that the ball is thrown should be varied.

6)   Standing in the corner of the gym the player volleys the ball first to one wall and then to the other, making sure he turns his body before he plays the ball.

7)   The ball is thrown low at the wall so that the player will have to do a rolling volley either to the side, or backwards.

8)   Volleying at the basketball ring. The rebounds should be controlled with a volley and another attempt made.

9)   Jump sets continuously above the head.

10)   The ball is thrown up and back over the head. The player must move back quickly to volley the ball.

Training in pairs

11)   Ten feet apart, one player feeding the ball low for the other to volley back, high.

12)   The ball is fed low and a little faster than (11) so that the player must roll back to volley.

13)   One player stands still and volleys the ball for the other player to move to. The angle of the first volley pass should vary, so that the receiver will have to take some balls from a low position.

14)   In pairs volleying the ball to and fro.The ball is first volleyed three feet above the head. While this is being done the second player changes his position. The first player has to look for this new position and then volley the ball to the other player.

15)   In pairs with one player moving to a point ten feet to his side to volley the ball. After playing the ball he must return to his original point before he can move back to play the ball again.

16)   Both players use the overhead volley. When the ball is received it is played three feet above the head, the player then pivots through 180° and returns it with the overhead volley.

17)   Ten feet apart, one player has his back to the other. As the first player volleys the ball he shouts "NOW". The second player can then turn round to play the ball.

18)   One player lies on the floor. The second stands 15 feet away and volleys the ball. As soon as he has volleyed it, the other player must quickly get to his feet to volley the ball.

19)   Sideways volleying in pairs.

20)   Players stand twenty feet apart facing each other. One player has to run forward ten feet to play the ball.

b) Positioning and decision making

21)   In threes on court. The setter must run forwards and set the ball to the wing player (Fig. 146).

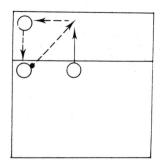

Fig. 146

162

22) As (21) but starting from position A, B, or C (Fig. 147).

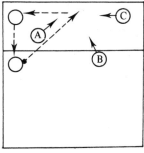

Fig. 147

23) See Fig. 148

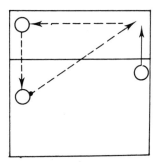

Fig. 148

24) See Fig. 149

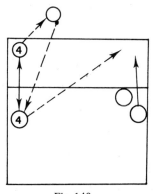

Fig. 149

25)   See Fig. 150. The ball is volleyed over the net to No. 4.

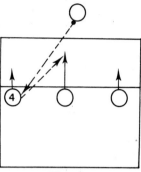

Fig. 150

26)   See Fig. 151. The ball is volleyed over the net to player 3.

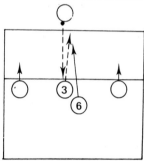

Fig. 151

27)   See Fig. 152. The ball is volleyed to player 5 who digs the ball to the right of the setter.

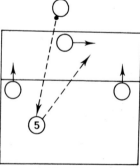

Fig. 152

28)   See Fig. 153

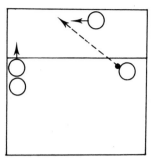

Fig. 153

29)   See Fig. 154. The ball is set high to the centre or wing positions.

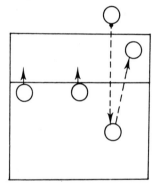

Fig. 154

30)   See Fig. 155

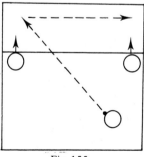

Fig. 155

31)   The ball is volleyed over the net for the setter to move back, and set the ball to the wings for a smash on the second touch. (Fig. 156).

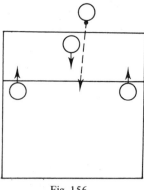

Fig. 156

32)   See Fig. 157

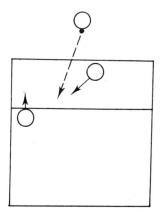

Fig. 157

33)   The setter should be fed balls by the smasher for a short or parallel set. As the setter begins to master these sets he should be volleyed the ball by another player instead of the smasher.

34)   The setter is thrown a ball which will make him set from a low position. As he becomes more proficient he can be made to set the ball using a rolling volley to the side or back.

35)   See Fig. 158. The ball is volleyed over the net to 5 or 6. The ball is then dug forward to the penetrating setter. The setter must now decide who he can set to, taking into account the quality of the first pass.

166

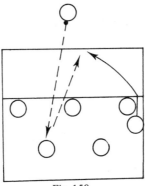

Fig. 158

36) The setter is fed a high ball so that he can give jump sets.

37) See Fig. 159. The setter can give an overhead short set, or high set.

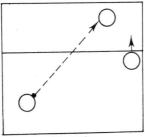

Fig. 159

38) See Fig. 160. This involves four setters and helps them to position themselves in relation to the net and to practice volleying the ball parallel to the net.

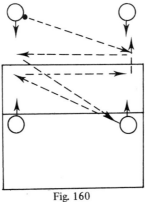

Fig. 160

c) Judgement of angles and distances

39)   See Fig. 161

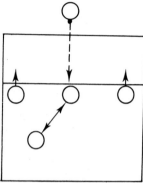

Fig. 161

40)   See Fig. 162

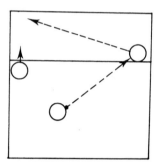

Fig. 162

41)   See Fig. 163. The setter moves back from the net towards the ball.

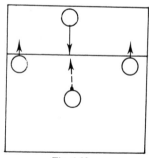

Fig. 163

42)   See Fig. 164

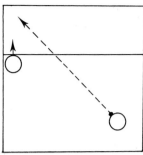

Fig. 164

43)   See Fig. 165

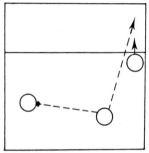

Fig. 165

44)   See Fig. 166

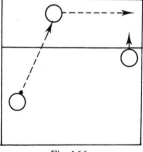

Fig. 166

45)   See Fig. 167. The setter moves towards the ball before setting it.

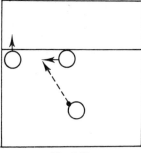

Fig. 167

46)   See Fig. 168

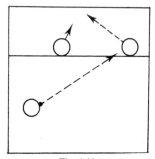

Fig. 168

The setter may be in a position to set the ball which comes off the block, net or is dumped over the block. These situations can be simulated and the setter given the opportunity to practise these sets.

The dig pass

Players must be able to control the dig pass they make with great accuracy if their team is to produce its most effective build up for an attack. When the serve or smash is hard the player must be able to reduce the speed of the ball to an acceptable level with his digging action. Controlling the speed is only one aspect of a good dig pass. The player must also be able to control the direction of the rebound ball.

Training for the dig pass must aim to develop the following:
a) Excellent technique.
b) Accuracy of length and direction.
c) Control of the speed of the dig pass.

a) Development of technique

The player should practice the drills given in the section on the dig pass in Chapter 4 until he has a sound basic technique. He should be able quickly to make a strong platform for the ball and to get a good flight path by use of the legs and the correct arm angle. Once he has obtained these abilities the player must concentrate on obtaining the fine control of length and direction that is so essential in the modern game.

b) Accuracy of length and direction

In a game a player must judge the distance he is from the net and limit the length of his dig pass accordingly. To help the player judge these distances it is best if most of the practices for the dig pass take place on court with the player facing the net.

1)   See Fig. 169. The dig pass must go to the player standing in the centre so that he does not have to move more than a pace to be able to set it. Initially the ball should be volleyed to the digger.

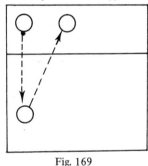

Fig. 169

2)   As (1) but the ball is served at the receiver.
3)   See Fig. 170

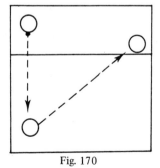

Fig. 170

171

4) As (3) but with the ball being served and not volleyed.
5) See Fig. 171. The receiver alternately digs the ball to 3 and 2.

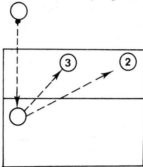

Fig. 171

6) See Fig. 172

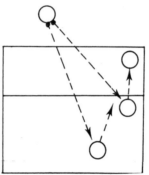

Fig. 172

7) The receiver stands in position 1 and digs a serve to 2.

8) See Fig. 173. The coach alternately plays the ball to the left and then the right. Each receiver plays the ball once on either side before rejoining the line.

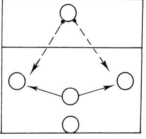

Fig. 173

9)   See Fig. 174. The coach feeds a ball which will force the player to run forward and take a very low ball, possibly with a rolling dig.

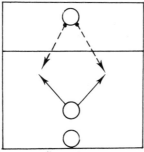

Fig. 174

10)   See Fig. 175. The player has to move very quickly across court to play the ball

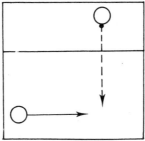

Fig. 175

11)   See Fig. 176. As soon as the ball is served the player may move into court. The ball should be served into the middle of the court. This practice helps players to decide quickly from where the ball can be played and also to get there and stop before playing the shot.

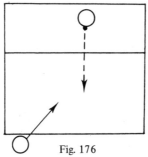

Fig. 176

12) See Fig. 177. The player in position 2 smashes the ball, which is set by 3, to the player in the opposite corner. The receiver must dig the ball to 3 who will set it again.

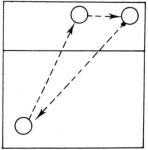

Fig. 177

13) See Fig. 178. The coach stands on a box or bench and smashes the ball to the three back court players who must play the ball to the setter.

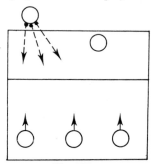

Fig. 178

14) See Fig. 179. The ball is smashed across the net either down the line or on the diagonal.

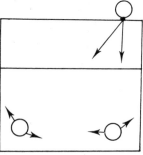

Fig. 178

174

15) See Fig. 180. The smasher either smashes the ball or plays a tactical ball into position 3. One of the receivers must be covering the smash and the other moving in to pick up the tactical ball.

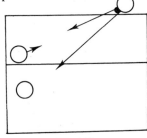

Fig. 180

16) The coach smashes the ball at the wall. The receiver who has his back to the coach must play the rebound. This is a good practice for making the player move quickly to play surprise shots (Fig. 181).

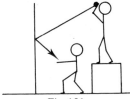

Fig. 181

17) The coach stands on a box behind the receiver who is facing the wall. The coach smashes the ball at the wall so that it will rebound low and to the side of the player.

18) See Fig. 182. This is a practice for diving dig recovery shots. The players zig-zag up the court diving for balls played close to the feeders. The aim should be to make this drill as continuous as possible.

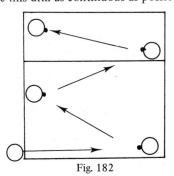

Fig. 182

19)   See Fig. 183. The two wing players must jump and then smash or dump the ball set by the centre player. The three back court players and the free smasher must play the ball to the setter. The setter sets each smasher alternately.

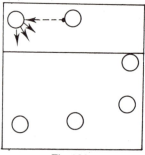

Fig. 183

20)   A pressure drill with one player receiving a large number of smashes from the coach who stands on a box top or bench. Some of the balls should be dumped instead of being smashed. The aim is to get the receiver to move quickly for every ball no matter where it is played on court.

Smashing

The smasher must be able to position himself accurately for every set. His approach should be accurate, smooth and well timed. He must be able to vary the direction of his shot by the use of a curved approach and the wrist action. When the ball is set back from the net, or at an angle to the net, he must be able to make the best of it. Whenever the ball is above net height he should aim to make his shot as difficult as possible for the opponents to play.

Training for smashing should aim to develop the following:

a) [A smooth, accurate approach.

b) The ability to vary the direction of the shot and to pass a block.

c) |The ability to hit all types of sets and sets which are badly positioned.

a) The approach and take-off

1)   Players run around in a circle making approaches and take-offs at the net.

2)   Players make an approach and take off at the net. They then come out to the attack line and make another approach to the net. In this way they move along the front court and round to the other side of the net.

3)   Instead of running in straight to the net the players make a curved approach.

176

4) The player makes an approach and twist in the air after take-off.
5) Consecutive approaches by following a figure of eight path.
6) Consecutive one-step approaches and take-offs. Take one step back after landing.
7) Consecutive jumps at the same spot.
8) The player makes a very acute approach to the net and alters the angle of his body to the net by adjusting his last step and feet position at take-off.
9) Player receives a ball volleyed to him over the net and then runs in and makes his smashing action.

b) Practices for improving the wrist action.
1) Players stand on the ten-feet line and smash the ball at the net.
2) Standing opposite the wall smashing the ball so that it bounces and rebounds off the wall. The aim should not be to hit the ball as hard as possible, but to control the ball so that the player can hit it alternately with the left and right hand.
3) Standing sideways on to the wall. The ball is thrown up and the player hits the ball at the wall by turning his wrist as he contacts the ball.
4) The players stand fifteen feet away from a mat. They throw the ball in the air and smash it so that the ball bounces on the mat. Vary the angle of the mat in relation to the shoulders so that the wrist must be used to change the direction of the smash.
5) In pairs ten feet apart one player smashes the ball and the other digs it. This practice calls for control of the speed of the smash and also for accurate positioning.

c) The full smash. Smashing all types of sets and from varying positions
1) Smashing the ball from the wing positions. After smashing either return to the end of the line or go across to smash from the opposite position (Fig. 184).

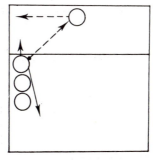

Fig. 184

2)   The setter receives a ball from position 6. The smasher starts as in (1). When the setter is in this situation there is some likelihood that he will not give a fully accurate set and this will put the smasher under pressure. In this and other situations which are described, both the setter and smasher are put under pressure (Fig. 185).

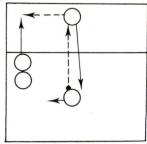

Fig. 185

3)   See Fig. 186

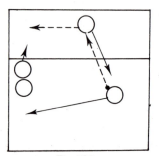

Fig. 186

4)   See Fig. 187. Setter at the side who sets a high pass to the centre or side. This can be varied and parallel sets given.

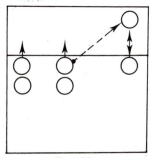

Fig. 187

A good example of the quick positioning of the Japanese players is shown by player No. 1. Low down, arms in front of him he stands a chance of playing the Rumanian smash

Boegayenkov of Russia is blocked out by a perfectly formed and timed Japanese block. Compare the state of readiness of the Japanese back court player, Minami, with the three Russian players!

Every player should be ready to play the ball at all times as this picture clearly shows.

A fast well disguised build up to the attack leaves this Rumanian player with only one blocker to beat.

5) The setter gives a forward or overhead set, from position three to the wing smashers.
6) Smashing for targets. Two mats are placed on the court, one on the diagonal and one straight down the line. The smasher must aim for these.
7) Short set and smash, in front and overhead. It is better if the setter is fed the ball by a player other than the smasher. This will help the smasher to learn the correct timing (Fig. 188).

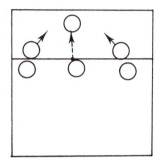

Fig. 188

8) See Fig. 189. Smashing the ball from a set at an angle to the net.

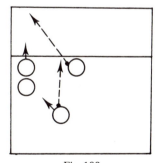

Fig. 189

9) Smashing a ball set six feet back from the net using a one-step approach.
10) Smasher digs a ball served over the net to him and then smashes the resulting set. When the dig is particularly accurate the smasher should go for a short set.
11) Smashing the ball after making a curved approach to the net. Start as in Fig. 190.

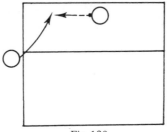

Fig. 190

12) Smashing a ball played over the net. Player stands at the net and smashes a ball volleyed low over the net.

13) Smashing after a block. The smasher blocks a ball hit out of the hand of a smasher on the other side of the net and then quickly returns to the attack line to smash a ball set to him.

14) Smashing the ball on the second touch from a dig pass from back court.

15) Making a dump shot after faking a smash. Place hoops on the court and get the smashers to aim to dump the ball in these. Put a block in as well to make sure that the smasher plays the ball from as high as possible.

16) Smasher jump sets the ball instead of smashing (See Fig. 191).

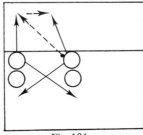

Fig. 191

17) See Fig. 192

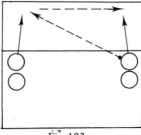

Fig. 192

18) Jump short sets (See Fig. 193)

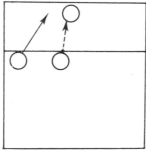

Fig. 193

19) Standing a yard from the net the smasher is fed sets very quickly. This simulates the situations which often occur during a game when players have no time to move out for an approach.

20) The player stands at the net and, as soon as a ball is sent to his setter, he runs back to the attack line and then makes an approach for the set.

21) The player stands in the back third of the court and smashes a ball which is set to him by a player to the side of him. This simulates the occasions when a player in back court is left to play the third touch.

Training for blocking

To block successfully with the frequency needed for a good level of play a team must possess good technique, timing and a great deal of experience. It is on the basis of previous experience that the blocker must predict where the smash is going to take place. When the team he is playing employs a very fast attack pattern the blocker must make the right prediction as early as possible, if he is to stand a chance of making a successful block.

Smashing should rarely take place in a training session without a block. The blockers will then be able to spend time on perfecting their technique as well as gaining the necessary experience.

Practices;

1) A line of smashers and one blocker. After smashing, the player takes the place of the blocker, who then goes to the end of the smashing line. The emphasis on this practice should be to develop positioning and timing. The smashers should hit along the diagonal or down the line for about twenty smashes each. In this way the blockers will know in advance where the ball is going and this will lessen the number of things they must think about, with, it is hoped, a consequent rise in their performance.

181

2)   As (1) but with two blockers. After blocking on the outside the player moves into the centre position. The centre blocker must wait in the middle until the set has been made.

3)   Three lines of smashers (so that the attack can come through all three attack points) and three blockers. Block first in position 2, then in the centre and then at 4. When the smash is at the wings the free blocker should not move from the net until the set has been made. He then retreats to the attack line to pick up any smashes passing on the inside of the block.

4)   The ball is set about five feet from the net so that the blockers must practice blocking higher with their hands than when the ball is set close to the net.

5)   The smashers try to hit the ball off the block out of court. The blockers must ensure that their outside hands are turned inwards.

6)   As (3) with the centre player always coming in for a short smash. The setter can give the ball to this player or to one of the other wing players. The blockers must learn to identify the type and direction of the set by the body attitude of the setter and the timing of the incoming smasher and the setter.

7)   Blocking against high sets in the centre position. The two wing players must not move in until the set has been made.

8)   Blocking against a tactical ball. The timing of the arm and hand movements is different for a tactical ball. The blockers must learn to delay their movements until the ball has been played.

9)   Consecutive blocking. A smash is blocked in position 4 and, as soon as the blockers land, another ball is set in position 3 for them to block.

10)   Blocking a ball played directly across the net from a bad dig or volley. The player should jump up and try to direct the ball by a slight sideways movement of one hand. When blocking a ball in this situation the player must be careful to see that he does not make it so vigorous that the referee decides that he has pushed the ball. It is safest to put the hands straight up in the air and provide a passive wall for the ball to rebound off. The slight sideways movement of the heel of one hand will direct the ball to a space.

11)   Playing the ball a second time after the block. One player stands on a bench and holds a ball above the net on his side. The blocker jumps up blocks the ball. As he starts to go down a second ball is dropped over the net. This ball must be played to a setter in the middle of the court.

12)   Playing the ball that comes down between the blocker and the net. The blocker jumps up to touch a ball held on his side of the net by a player on a bench on the other side of the net. After lightly touching the ball it is allowed to drop. The blocker must then play the ball on its way down or as it comes off the net.

13)   Breaking away from the block to prepare for a set or smash. A player hits the ball out of his hand into a two man block. After the ball is blocked

the two players must split so that one returns to the attack line to prepare for
a smash and the other moves into the centre to become the setter. As they do
this a second ball is played over the net to another player who digs the ball
forward for the setter to play to the smasher.
14)   As (13) but using a three man block and a penetrating setter (see Fig.
194).

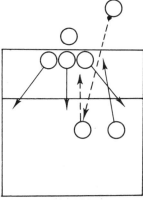

Fig. 194

Training for serving.
Training for serving should aim to develop accuracy and consistency. Each
player should perfect at least one type of serve which he can use with 100%
reliability. Every player should be able to perform the underarm serve with
this reliability. It is no use having players who can score one or two aces with
their serve but waste twice as many by serving out of court or in the net.

Practices:
1)   In pairs with one ball. One partner stands on court as a target for his
partner's serve.
2)   Mats are placed on court at the various weak points of service receive
systems, as a target for the servers.
3)   The court is divided into six squares and the players serve at each in
turn. As soon as they have got three balls into one square they move on to
the next one. A competition can be arranged to see who can complete the
circuit in the smallest number of serves.
4)   Two players stand in a circle, one in each half of the court. The rest of
the players are divided equally so that half serve from each end. The balls are
served from the serving position and the winning team is the first team to
serve twenty balls such that the player can catch them without moving out of
the circle.

Training for recovery of a ball played into the net.
There are many occasions in a game when the ball·is played into the net and another touch is still available to the team. These balls can be most difficult to play until a player has learnt the timing and technique needed.

The ball should be left to drop off the net before any attempt is made to play it. Beginners usually make the mistake of trying to play the ball when it is on or still close to the net. This means that it is almost impossible to play the ball so that it comes away from the net.

To play the ball the player should aim to get his arms or hand well under the ball and play it upwards and backwards.

Practices:
1) The ball is thrown into the net by the player, who then tries to play it back into the air clear of the net using the digging action.
2) One player throws the ball into the net at an angle to the player who is attempting to play it. This will give the receiver less time to play the ball and also make him have to move.
3) After the ball is played into the net the player must try to set it up using a rolling volley.

Training for playing the third pass back over the net from a difficult position.
Many points are lost in games because players fail to return the ball across the net on the third touch when the ball is out of court or the player cannot see the net. It is important that players develop the ability to play the ball safely over the net from all manner of angles and positions. It is silly to throw away points in this way.

Practices:
1) The player starts facing the net about five feet from it, in one of the wing positions. A ball is thrown across the net to a point about fifteen feet from the net and on the extreme edge of the court. The player must watch the ball as it comes across and move to play it with his back to the net. The ball should be played over with the dig pass. The position of the player and the position to which the ball is thrown should be varied.
2) Three back court players are waiting in position. The coach who is standing at the side of the court throws a ball near one of the players who must play it across the net with a dig pass or volley pass depending on the position of the ball.
3) A player stands at the net as though he was the setter. A ball is played to him, which he must play over the net.

Individual training.
There will be many occasions when a player has some time available for

training in the gymnasium but has nobody to practise with. There are many practices he can use to develop particular techniques on his own. A few are described here and others can be found in the sections on technique.

Practices:
1) Volleying at a point on the wall.
2) Volley the ball against the wall and turn to volley the rebound against another wall or, into the basketball ring.
3) As (2) but using an overhead volley.
4) The ball is thrown high against the wall so that a rolling volley is needed to play the ball.
5) Alternate forward and overhead volleys at the wall.
6) The ball is thrown high in the air for the player to jump and smash from the spot.
7) The ball is thrown up in front of the net and the player uses his wrist to smash the ball into various parts of the court.
8) The ball is volleyed high forwards by a player standing on the attack line. He then makes an approach and smashes the ball.
9) The ball is thrown hard and low at the wall. The player must move to play the ball with a dig pass. If the basketball ring is nearby he can utilise this as a target.
10) The ball is thrown low and at an angle to the wall so that the player has to dive to play the ball.

Multi-purpose drills.
There are many drills which can be used to practice at the same time: service receive, setting, smashing, blocking etc. These are most useful in a training session. Not only do they give players useful practice but they help to make their practice more realistic and meaningful. Some of these drills have been given earlier, a few others are given here.
1) See Fig. 195. This is a drill which involves accurate serving, a fairly difficult set and a smash.

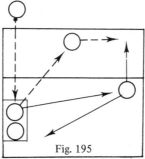

Fig. 195

2)   See Fig. 196. This drill also involves serving, receiving, serving and smashing.

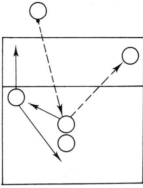

Fig. 196

3)   The court is split lengthways so, that two service receive and smash games can be played (Fig. 197).

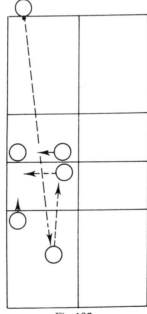

Fig. 197

4)   See Fig. 198. This drill sets a team a definite player who should smash the ball. In this case it is player 2 and he is to use a line shot to hit a mat deep in court. Many times during a game a team will want to exploit a weakness of their opponents and they must be able to set up their attack properly in order to exploit this weakness.

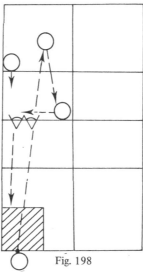

Fig. 198

5)   See Fig. 199. This drill involves use of a tactical ball, receiving this ball and an overhead set.

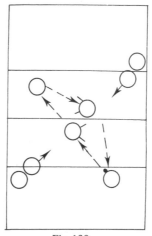

Fig. 199

187

6)   See Fig. 200. This drill is a continuous smash, receive, set smash drill calling for control and accurate smashing and receiving.

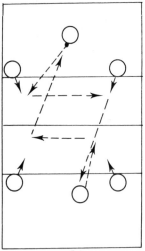

Fig. 200

7)   See Fig. 201. The ball is set and smashed without a block. The back court players must receive the ball and send the ball to the setter for a set to position 4.

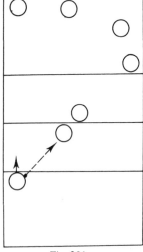

Fig. 201

8) A ball is thrown over for a team to receive, set up and smash. The players must cover the smasher and as soon as the ball is over the net a second ball is thrown over to simulate a rebounded ball.

9) Two teams each having thirty serves. One team always receives the ball. After each five serves it rotates one position. The team receiving the ball plays it right through to the smash and if it is returned off the block sets it up again. The serving team may not play the ball back across the net except when it is blocked. If the servers win the rally it is a point to them and vice versa. After 30 serves the teams change roles.

7 THE ROLE OF THE COACH IN VOLLEYBALL

Unlike some sports, it has been accepted in volleyball for many years that a coach is essential. The complexity of the techniques and tactics of volleyball means that the development of the full potential of a team can only be achieved by having someone off the field of play, not actually involved in the training sessions, planning the sessions and directing the pattern of play. Unlike other team games there is not the time in volleyball for a player to act as a coach during the game. In football and rugby there are long periods when certain players are not involved in the game and can watch the pattern of play. In volleyball the only place for spectators is off court. The rules of volleyball allow a person off court—a coach—to be involved in the game through the use of timeouts and substitutions. The coach is able to concentrate on viewing the individual and corporate performance of his players during training sessions and matches because he is not playing himself.

The coach is concerned with preparing his players for a match and also assisting them during the game itself.

Pre-match duties of the coach;
   a) Preparing training sessions which will develop individual skills and general team play in the various phases of the game.
   b) Analysing the next opponents and preparing tactics and formations to be used against these opponents.
   c) Preparing a team mentally and physically for volleyball.

Match duties.
   a) Planning the team line-up, informing the scorer and umpire of the first six players and the rotation order.
   b) Confirming tactics with players before the match starts.

c) Using times-out and substitutions where necessary.

d) Analysing the performance of his team and their opponents during the game with a view to giving the team information during time-outs and between sets which helps them to improve their performance.

e) Reviewing the team's performance at the conclusion of the match so that future training sessions can be planned to eradicate mistakes and weaknesses highlighted during the game.

The training session.

It is essential that the coach approaches each training session with a clear idea of what he hopes to achieve. Stringing together a few practices and a conditioned game without giving thought to the object of the session is not coaching.

The coach may decide to work on weaknesses that were shown up in recent games, either individual or collective, preparing for a particular match or to introduce and develop new patterns of play and techniques.

Before the session starts the coach should have decided on the order of the session, the drills to be used and the groups in which the players will work.

Ideally the training session should consist of the following sections;

a) Warm-up.

b) Practice of techniques which are weak, or relevant to the main part of the session.

c) Concentrated work on the technique or tactical aspect chosen as the main theme of the session.

d) Match practice with special emphasis on the quality of the particular technique or aspect covered in the previous part of the session.

e) Warming down exercises to reduce the likelihood of stiffness.

It is important that the coach adopts an active and not passive role in the training sessions. The sessions must be alive so that the players are kept working hard and meaningfully. Unless the coach obtains this good working atmosphere and relationship with his players, he will communicate little and the players will lose interest.

The players must feel that the coach is the source of knowledge not only about volleyball techniques and tactics generally, but about each player's strengths and weaknesses. This knowledge will come from a detailed study of volleyball literature, films of top players and teams, matches and training sessions and, discussions with other coaches and players. The coach must be an active seeker of information.

A good coach will be able to explain quickly and simply to players the elements of techniques and tactics. Long and complicated descriptions do not explain, merely confuse. The ability to give good explanations is the result of deep understanding of all aspects of the game.

191

It is important that the coach has an overall plan for the season's training. In the early part of the season the work will be mainly concerned with improving fitness and sharpening up all the techniques. As the season progresses more specific work is done to develop techniques needed to improve the overall standard of the team's play and to allow the introduction of more advanced tactics. If the coach does not have a plan the sessions will be disjointed and the players will become frustrated.

The phases of volleyball

The game of volleyball may be divided into the following consecutive phases;
Phase 1; Receipt of service and making the first attack
Phase 2; Preparing to block and the blocking action
Phase 3; Receiving an attacking shot that is not blocked.
Phase 4; The counter attack.

The coach should concentrate on developing the phases in the order given above. In this way the team will develop in a logical way and the players will be able to see the improvements in their team play. In the first few matches teams will be taking several receives each time in Phase 1 before they regain service. If they do not make an attack from Phase 1, which puts their opponent's under pressure then they have surrendered the initiative in the rally. When a team fails to return the ball over the net from Phase 1 play because of poor build-up rather than the opponent's good block, it is giving away points to the opponents. Every team must be proficient in Phase 1 play if it is to have a chance to play the other phases in the game. The coach should therefore make the development of Phase 1 play his first priority.

When working on Phase 1 play the coach should ensure that all players know their correct court positions and responsibilities in each of the six rotational positions. Applied technique work in realistic situations must be carried out by the smashers and setters on their specialist roles and by all players on the first pass. Great emphasis should be placed in this training on moving to the ball before it is played. Players must develop their ability to judge quickly the correct court position from which to play the ball. Smashers must be trained to play any ball above net height across the net with a smashing action and not wait for the ball to drop to the volley position. Every third touch should be played so that the opponents will be put under pressure.

Once team play in Phase 1 has reached a satisfactory level the coach should move on to the next phase and repeat the process. In this phase, the players must move from the positions they adopted when covering the smasher, to the starting position for the block at the net. The players must be ready quickly so that they will have as much time as possible to watch their opponent's attack build up. The coach should work on the movement of

192

players when forming a multiple block so that points are not lost by net touches during this stage. Blockers should practice blocking against all types of sets and be given the opportunity to learn to identify the different sets by the setter's body and hand positions.

Phase 3 play involves the correct positioning of the players not participating in the block. For maximum success in this phase, each player must know instantly where he should be covering when playing any position on court. Players must be trained to predict where the ball is likely to go from the position of the set and the actions of the smasher. Their digging and diving techniques in particular must be perfected.

The counter attack, Phase 4, involves a great deal of court movement by all players before it can be successfully started. Setters must either penetrate or split from the block. Smashers should position themselves on the attack line ready to make an approach as soon as possible. All players should be prepared to set the ball if it does not go direct to the specialist setter. When this happens the remaining players should know how to adjust their court positions to ensure that the best attack can be made.

Success in each of these phases is a result of good technique and positioning. It is these factors that the coach must develop in realistic situations if a team is to develop fully.

The drills that are selected for each session must be carefully chosen. The coach should examine each drill he proposes to use, to see if it satisfies the following conditions:

a) it gives practice in the particular aspect to be developed

b) the players have sufficient ability to be able to carry out the drill in such a way that they will gain some benefit.

c) sufficient equipment and players are available to make the drill effective.

Once a drill has been chosen it should be carefully explained and demonstrated to the players. They should know what the object of the drill is and exactly what they are supposed to do. In this way the players will be able to get down to hard and productive work immediately, instead of the coach having to explain the drill to each player individually.

If a player is obviously showing bad technique the coach must closely observe him to identify the cause of the poor technique. It is no use telling the player he has a fault if he is not also given the cause of this fault and some information on how he can eradicate it.

Most faults in technique result from failure of the player to:

a) pick the right court position to play the ball

b) adopt the right body position

c) time his movements correctly.

The coach should look at the players movements to see which of the above reasons is at the root of the trouble. Once this has been identified the coach should design a practice which will help the player to improve that particular aspect.

Players need to be encouraged if they are to achieve their full potential. The coach should try to watch each player at work in training and discuss his performance with him. Not only does this foster a good working relationship between the coach and player it helps the player to maintain interest and direct his work correctly.

At all times the players must feel that the coach is present. If the coach stands and watches the players at work then he is wasting his time. No team is so good that there are no flaws in technique or team play for the coach to identify and correct. It is human nature for players to try and relax during some training sessions. They may feel a bit tired or bored. If the coach is constantly on the move encouraging players, talking to them about their performances and involving himself in the training, these players will soon forget their lethargy.

The psychological basis of skill development

In recent years a more scientific approach to sport has been taken by coaches and performers with the result that standards today are far higher than many ever considered possible. Research into human performance by physiologists and psychologists has produced much of importance to coaches. As a result, coaching is becoming more of a science and less of an art. Coaches now accept that it is necessary to have some knowledge and understanding of the mechanisms contributing to human performance.

Of particular interest and value to the coach is the work of Whiting (1970)* of Leeds University Physical Education Dept. His systems analysis of perceptual motor skill performance (Fig. 202) illustrates very simply many important concepts. Whiting elaborates this model as follows:

Information about the *display* (immediate external environment in which the skill is to be carried out) or about the internal environment (proprioceptive information) is relayed to the central mechanisms of the brain via the sense organs. Since the performer of a skill cannot utilise all the information available in the display at any one instant, *selective attention* determines both the area of the display which is scanned and the particular information which is abstracted. Sensory data from the external and internal environment is interpreted (the process of perception) in the central perceptual mechanisms. On the basis of such perceptions, decisions are made with regard to new responses or adjustments to ongoing responses. If a response is to be made, the translatory mechansism selects

* Whiting, H.T.A. (1970). *Acquiring ball skill : a psychological interpretation.* London: Bell

194

the appropriate response pattern and the effector system gives the executive command to appropriate muscular response systems. The carrying out of an effector response brings about a change in the display giving rise to 'feedback' information about the effectiveness of the response. Such information, together with other information from the display and the internal environment, can then be monitored by the sensory systems and used in the control of ongoing responses or utilised in initiating future responses.

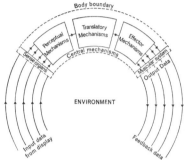

Fig. 202   Systems analysis of perceptual-motor performance (from Whiting H.T.A. (1970) **Aquiring Ball Skill;** a psychological interpretation. London, Bell)

It can be seen that the movements a player makes are determined by the commands given to the muscles, which are in turn determined by the preceding analysis of the information selected from the display. Therefore, a breakdown in skilled performance can result from a failure to select the right information from the display as well as from badly carried out movements. It is therefore essential for the coach to assist the player in his early stages of learning, to focus his attention on those aspects of the display which will yield the correct information.

Poulton (1965)* has suggested that the player needs to make the following precise predictions in order to play a moving ball successfully:

a) the technique to be used to play the ball

b) the timing to use in order to contact the ball with the correct amount of force needed to play the ball to a required point.

c) the direction in which to play the ball.

To make these predictions the player must select from the display, information which will enable him to determine the speed of the ball, the angle of the ball, the course of the ball and, the relative positions of his team mates.

The earlier the player can make these predictions, the more time he will have to make his movements and therefore the greater potential for making

* Poulton, E.C. (1965). Skill in fast ball games. *Biology and Human Affairs*, 31, 1-5.

195

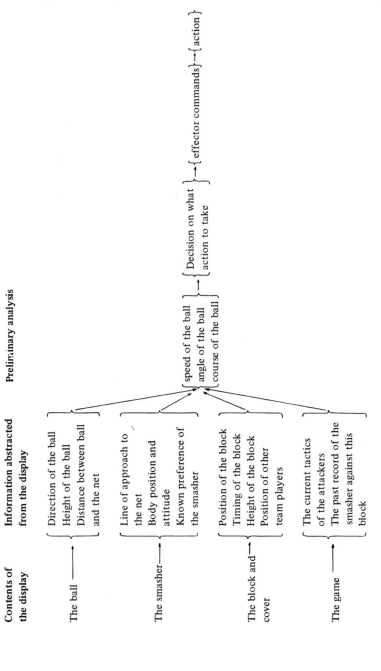

Fig. 203   Process of predicting the course of the smash and taking the appropriate action

successful movements. The amount of time the player has to obtain this information and to initiate his response is very small, due to the speed of the game and the rules which prevent him from allowing the ball to bounce, come to rest or to play the ball twice in succession. The time taken for a smashed ball to travel from the net to the baseline is only marginally longer than the average human reaction time of 0.2 secs! This means that most of the decision making must be completed before the ball is actually hit! The player will then be able to start moving into the predicted course of the ball before or as it is being hit. He can confirm the correctness of his decision by watching the flight of the ball over the first few feet. On the basis of further information received at this stage he will be able to make any minor adjustments to his court or body position that are necessary. Fig. 203 illustrates the process of predicting the course of the smashed ball.

The information that has to be handled in this situation is enormous but somewhat less than that confronting a beginner who has received no guidance. By now it should be clear to the coach that he must direct the player's attention to the correct aspects of the display during training sessions. Some players will learn this without the help of a coach and others will not. All players will progress faster if this information is given to them early in their training. Throughout the chapter on Technique this sort of information has been included and more especially in the sections giving 'hints to players'. In the tactical sections reference points have been given for players which will help them to select the best starting positions and ones which will give them a clear view of the most important aspects of the display.

At all times the coach should aim to make his drills as near to the game situation as possible. An essential part of being a good volleyball player is the ability to decide which shot to play in a particular situation, exactly when to inititate the movements and, where to play the shot. This decision-making originates from the identification and analysis of certain cues concerning the ball, players and court position etc. Unless the players have practice during training sessions in decision-making in game-like situations, they cannot be expected to make the correct decisions in a real game. There are many players with exceptional techniques in the confines of certain training drills who, when they are in a game situation show a much lower level of ability. This is because they have become skilled in identifying the cues relevant in that training situation only. Players in a game must be skilled in thousands of situations.

The coach should introduce variety into training sessions by devising and introducing new drills and not relying on a small number of multipurpose drills. If the same drills are used each week, or session, then players will quickly get bored and the level of performance will decrease. Performance

197

will also suffer if the same drill is used for too long at a time. After a while players will cease to be interested as the drill is no longer novel. Research has indicated that short practice periods with short rest periods in between, are superior to continuous practice.

While players are practising, the coach should be watching their performance to see that they are doing the drill correctly. Sloppily performed drills are of no benefit to the players concerned or the team. The coach should also tell players how well they are performing. When a player is learning a new technique, or trying to remedy a fault in technique, the coach should tell him how his performance measures up to the required standard after each attempt or series of attempts. The player must try and remember the pattern of movement which resulted in the achievement of the required standard. This is more likely to result when the coach helps him in this way.

For a long while coaching has been an art and not a science. Players have learned despite bad coaches and with the aid of good coaches. The increasing demand for higher performances has coincided with an upsurge in academic interest in the psychological aspects of human performance. As a result a greater understanding of the factors underlying human motor performance has come about and many promising lines of research developed. Coaches should aim to keep themselves up to date with current ideas in this area. The following books summarize in an easily readable way much of the present knowledge and are essential reading for the dedicated coach and teacher:

Whiting, H.T.A. (1970) *Acquiring ball skill: a psychological interpretation.* London: Bell

Fitts, P.M. & Posner, M.I. (1969) *Human performance.* California: Brooks Cole.

Singer, R.N. (1968) *Motor learning and human performance.* New York: Macmillan.

Holding, D.H. (1965) *Principles of training.* London: Pergammon

Match analysis in volleyball
The coach must be able to give his team information on the tactics (both individual and team) and individual technical ability of the opposing team. In addition he must be able critically to observe his own team's performance so that weak points can be corrected in forthcoming training sessions.

The opponents
If the coach is to prepare his team effectively for a match he will need to know the following about the opponents:

Serving
   i) Who is their best server.
   ii) What type of serve each player uses.
   iii) How reliable are their serves.
   iv) Which areas each individual serves to most often.
   v) Who is the most accurate server.

Receiving
   i) Which formation is used in each of the setter positions.
   ii) The weakest receiver and his weak point.
   iii) The weakest area of the formation.
   iv) The path of the setter in penetration and switching.

Setting
   i) How many setters are used and who they are.
   ii) Which sets are their favourite.
   iii) Which sets they are poor at giving.
   iv) Which attacking positions they use most.
   v) The set distribution pattern.
   vi) Which setters penetrate and from which positions.
   vii) Any mannerisms that the setters have which will help identify the type and direction of set they intend using.
   viii) When they use multiple attacks and which ones they use.

Smashers
   i) The specialist smashers.
   ii) The most effective smashers.
   iii) The left-handers if any.
   iv) If the smashers like the sets near or far from the net. Also, the speed and heights they prefer.
   v) Which shots they use most.
   vi) Which attackers like to use the tactical ball and hitting off the block.

Back court play
   i) The defensive system they use.
   ii) Which players are particularly mobile/immobile.
   iii) The weak spots in their defence which can be exploited with a tactical ball.
   iv) Any players who are often badly positioned in back court.

Blocking
   i) Who is their best blocker. Which blocking combination is best.

ii) If they get their hands round the outside thus preventing the smasher hitting the ball off them out of court.
iii) How many blockers they usually get to the wings/centre.
iv) How well they block against short sets, high sets, wave attacks.

Tactical play
i) Their usual rotation order.
ii) Who they substitute most often and why. The strengths/weaknesses of this substitute.
iii) The overall pattern and tempo of their attacking play.
iv) From where their setter usually sets.
v) Any players who get irritated when the pressure is on.
vi) Who is the captain. How his play stands up under pressure.
vii) What circumstance cause their coach to call a time-out.
viii) How strong is the team spirit. Do they give up when a few points down?

With this information, the coach can plan the tactics to be employed by his team, the rotational order he is going to use and give his players much essential information. With this information the players will be able to get straight into the game and not have to learn about their opponents' style of play as they go along.

The coach will also be able to understand what the opposing coach is likely to do in various game situations. When times out are called he can ensure that his players know with reasonable certainty what their opponents are likely to do when play resumes.

Obtaining this information.
To get this information, the coach must take every opportunity he can to watch other teams in his league and likely cup opponents. There are several ways in which this information can be recorded. The simplest way is to make a chart of the main headings dealt with and rate the opponents on a five-point scale. Under each heading brief notes can be made on each of the points. The rotational order and the usual shirt numbers must be recorded. Other features which help to identify players in case they are wearing different numbers when they next play, should also be recorded.

More detailed information can be obtained by using a notation system to record the pattern of various aspects of play. The system used must be simple and quick to record. It is no use using a system that takes several minutes to write down each little point. The coach should be able to record the game as it happens and not have to take his eyes off for a long while, or he will miss most of what he is trying to record!

A notation system must be objective, not subjective, i.e. it must be clear whether a particular shot was successful or unsuccessful.

The notation system described here is one the author has employed on many occasions and found quite successful. Other coaches have developed their own systems and the reader will no doubt soon evolve a system suited to his own needs.

The volleyball court is already divided into six areas by the rotation system and these areas can be utilised to locate the position of the ball and players during the movements under analysis. Each player wears a number on his shirt and this can also be used in the notation system.

When the movements under analysis result in a point being scored either as a direct result or a consequence, then it is recorded with a plus (+) sign e.g. if a serve lands in court or the team fails to return the ball across the net then a plus is given.

If the serve hits the net or goes out of court then a point is lost directly and a minus is recorded. When play successfully continues i.e. an attack results from the receive of service then a nought (0) is recorded.

To distinguish between the various techniques of volleyball each is given a distinguishing letter or sign. The major techniques and suggested symbols are:-

Serve	X
Dig	D (includes dives and rolls)
Volley	V (includes the set pass)
Smash	S
Block	B

Where possible in the system described, the first letter of the technique has been used as this makes it easier to remember them during the game.

However, these symbols only give limited information. By adding a second letter a particular style can be identified in each of these overall techniques e.g.

Serve = X

Floating Serve	=	Xf
Tennis Serve	=	Xt
Hook Serve	=	Xh
Underarm Serve	=	Xu

Smash = S

Tactical Smash	=	St
Dump	=	Sd

Volley = V

Set pass	= Vs
Shoot set	= Vsp
(Parallel)	
Overhead set	= Vso
Short set ·	= Vss

Dig = D

Dive = Dd	
Roll = Dr	

A sequence could be recorded as follows;

$$Xf\ D\ Vso\ S\ +$$

Interpreted this means that a floating service was received with a dig pass and an overhead set was successfully smashed.

.Situations and aspects which need to be analysed are:-

1) Mistakes

If a team is to win a game it must not only have a successful attack and defence, it must not throw points and serves away by silly mistakes. Very often games are lost because the simple things are not done well enough. Analysis will show the coach how many points are lost through mistakes, what they are and who makes them.

Mistakes can be classified as illegal plays of the ball, passes so bad that other players cannot successfully play them and balls missed through bad positioning and lack of calling.

These can be recorded on the following chart;

Set	Service	Setting	Smash	Block	Volley	Digging	Positioning	Total
1	536	21	333	33	5561	511	6	18

By putting the number of the player under each heading it is easy to see who made the mistake. The results of this analysis will help the coach to plan future technique sessions tailored to individual needs.

2) Position of the smash/variety of the attack.

A successful team uses as wide and varied attack as possible. It does not limit its attack to one of the attacking positions in the front line, but spreads them out through all three positions. Analysis shows how well this distribution is carried out, how successful each player is in each position and what sort of shot is used.

The position of the smash, the effectiveness of the smash and, the direction of the smash can all be recorded in the following way;

Set	Position 4		Position 3			Position 2	
	Line	Diag	Left	Centre	Right	Diag	Line
1	5 5 5 4 + − − + dd	5 5 5 4 2 + + + − + d	3 + d	3 5 − −	5 3 3 4 + + − + dd	65 − −	65 − +

Again the number of the player is recorded and the sign underneath indicates its success in relation to the block. It can be used to signify the end result of the smash if preferred. A further line underneath identifies dump shots and their direction.

3) Blocking
The proportion of successful blocks made by the team as a whole and by each blocking combination can be easily recorded on a similar chart to that above;

Set	Position 4	Position 3	Position 2
1	43, 43, 24, 52, + + − o	321, 321, + o	21, 21, 21, + − −

Each blocking combination is recorded and the result of the block shown by the usual notation system. If the block does not touch the ball and it passes into court then a nought is recorded. On the occasions when the block touches the ball and it is not played back into the opponents court a minus is recorded.

If the coach wishes to see if the block is positioning itself accurately some idea of this can be obtained by plotting the direction of the smashes which pass the block. The chart recommended for this is the chart used for the smash with the sub-divisions, line and diagonal. If a block consistently lets shots past on the diagonal then this is an indication that it is not positioning itself correctly.

203

Service receive.

The effectiveness of the receive line up chosen and the performance of individual players needs to be examined. The simplest way to record this information is to use the notation system as follows:-

e.g. 5,4. + ; 5,4-

This can be interpreted as player 5 receiving the ball in position 4 and making a first pass which went straight to, or in the immediate vicinity of, the setter. The same player playing his second receive in the same court position made a pass which was not accurate in length height, or direction.

The total number of receives needed before side-out is gained in each rotation position will yield information concerning the effectiveness of the line-up. If a team takes, for example, three receives before it gains a side-out with one form of line-up, it could indicate that a substitution or change in formation would be advisable. To record this the coach should write out the six receive combinations for the team, with the first rotation order at the top of his sheet. Then working down the page he records the number of receives in each order before side-out. Additional information concerning the reason why service was not gained can also be recorded in note form. If a team is making a successful attack from receive and subsequently loses the rally this would not indicate a fault in service receive and this fact should be noted.

Serving

Analysis will pinpoint the most successful servers, the weak servers and the landing point of the serves. Unless the ball is legally served into play a team cannot stand a chance of winning a point. For this reason, players must develop a consistent serve and be aware of the actual consistency of their serve under match conditions. Many players remember the serves which score aces and forget the number of chances they waste by serving illegally. Analysis will give them the true facts.

The basic notation symbols will provide information quickly and efficiently e.g.

6Xf4 +

6Xt5-

This can be interpreted as a floating serve by player 6 aimed at position 4 and scoring a point as a direct result. The second serve by player 6 was a tennis serve aimed at position 5 which was illegal and lost his team the right to serve as a result.

Analysing the scoresheet

The new International pattern scoresheets give the coach a record of the pattern of the match. The coach can profitably use the scoresheet to provide the following information:-

a) The rotation order of both teams. The effectiveness of this order can be judged in part by the distribution of points scoring. The service record on the scoresheet shows how many points were scored in each rotation order. By reproducing the rotation order of both teams, checking the points scoring in all sets and his own analysis of the strengths of each individual player the coach can see which rotation order was the weakest and strongest in both teams. On the basis of this information he may decide that it is necessary to alter the line-up or starting order in future matches against the same team.

b) Which server was the most effective.

c) See the exact time when substitutions and times-out were taken and their effect on the pattern of scoring.

d) See the effect of changing line-ups and starting order in different sets.

e) See the length of each set, the number of side-outs. Very often the scoreline does not always reflect truly the pattern of play. A long set whatever the score indicates that the teams were relatively evenly matched and many side-outs resulted.

f) See when times-out were called by the opposing coach and which players were substituted and in what positions.

It is not sufficient for a coach to rely on his subjective impressions of a game. It is human nature to remember the outstanding and forget the bad parts of each game. In fairness to his team and to enable him to 'plan constructively and accurately for the future the coach must make use of analysis.

The rules affecting the coach

The coach and players should be familiar with the articles of Rule 4 — the rights and duties of Players., and Rule 6, Articles 1-3.

The main rules concerning the coach are those controlling times-out and substitutions.

Rule 12—Duration of the game and choice of ends.

Art. 6. Interruptions in play

Times-out:

(a) A time-out may be granted by the referee or the umpire only when the ball is dead.

When the captain or coach requests a stoppage, he must make it clear whether it is for a time-out or a substitution. If he makes no indication, the referee must presume that the stoppage required is a time-out.

(b) During a time-out, the players are not allowed to leave the court and may not speak to anyone except to receive advice from their coach, who, however, may not enter court.

(c) Each team may take two times-out per set. The length of such time-out is limited to thirty seconds.

Two consecutive times-out may be requested by either team, without resumption of play between them. A time-out may be followed immediately by a substitution requested by either team, and a substitution can be followed immediately by a time-out.

(d) If in error a third time-out is requested, it shall be refused and the captain or coach making the request shall be warned. If the offence is repeated during the same set, the offending team will be penalised with the loss of service, or, the opponents will be awarded a point.

Substitutions

(e) Following the substitution of a player, play will resume immediately, and no one, including the coach is allowed to advise the players during a substitution.

(f) IN THE CASE OF INJURY, an interuption of three minutes will be allowed and will not be counted as a time-out. This interuption for injury can only be allowed if the injured player cannot be replaced.

As soon as the referee notices an injury, he shall stop play. The point shall be replayed.

Interval between sets

(g) A maximum interval of two minutes is allowed between sets. This interval shall be five minutes between the fourth and fifth sets.

The interval includes time spent changing ends and recording rotational orders on the score sheet.

Captain of the team

The duties of the captain involve;

a) Acting as team representative at the toss up.

b) Acting as team representative during contacts with the referee during the game.

c) Calling for times-out and substitutions in the absence of a coach off court.

d) Signing the score sheet.

The role of the captain during the game is:-

206

1) To maintain morale in the team by encouragement and example. Ensuring that players concentrate on their personal performance and not on that of other people. Seeing that players do not comment verbally or otherwise on other players' performances as this can have a disastrous effect on the team's morale and play. When players make a good shot a quick word from the captain will be a tremendous boost to their morale.

2) Seeing that players play to the whistle and not to their own interpretation of the rules. Too many teams stop when they think a foul has been committed instead of stopping when the referee or umpire blows the whistle. The captain should see that players prepare to receive service in good time.

3) Seeing that the tactics and formations decided by the coach are implemented. When players are unsure of their position the captain should quickly give them the necessary guidance.

4) Taking decisions regarding a change of tactics if the pattern of play makes it necessary. Sometimes the coach is unwilling to use a time-out or, has no time-out left, in these circumstances the captain must take the decision. During training the coach should maintain close contact with the captain so that the latter will know what to do in certain game situations.

When choosing the captain the coach should exercise great care. It is very common for the best player to be made captain. This is not always a wise choice. This player's game may be adversly effected by the extra burden of the captaincy.

The captain must be respected by all the team. He must be able to inspire the team and hold it together when the pressure is on. He should not have a quick temper—comments made in haste are more disruptive than constructive.

Once the game has started the coach can only help the players by calling times-out or substitutions. A good captain is worth his weight in gold and can act as a second coach on court. For this reason the coach should choose the captain with great care.

The warm-up before the game

The pre-match warm-up must be thorough if the team is to produce its best standard of play immediately. If the team does not prepare fully it could find itself losing the first set unnecessarily.

All players should familiarise themselves with the floor markings, obstructions above the court and the general layout of the gym. It is important for the player to be able to orientate himself quickly during a game.

Setters should particularly look for markers above the net e.g. beams etc. and at the sides of the court which will help them to judge how far they are from the net while they are preparing to set the ball.

It is usual practice for players to warm-up on their own before the official warm-up starts. Initially players should warm-up without a ball, making sure that they loosen all joints. The official warm-up normally allows about ten minutes general court warm-up with a ball and six minutes smashing over the net. In the court warm-up the players should practice volleying, digging, recovery dives and smashing. Where possible work should be done in threes as well as in pairs. Volleyball techniques involve changing the direction of the ball. It is not sufficient to warm-up in pairs only. Partner work does not allow a player to practice moving to face the direction of his pass.

Teams usually have a choice of three minutes smashing on their own or six minutes with both teams smashing together. Three minutes does not really allow all the setters to have a good warm-up, nor the smashers to have more than a couple of smashes.

Smashers should take the first smash easy and not try to hit the cover off the ball. They should also make every attempt to hit the set they are given. A setter needs to get into a rhythm and players fussing about bad sets only make things more difficult for him and effect his concentration. Make sure that each setter has a chance to set and get his eye in. After the setter has set about a dozen balls the feed should not come from the side but some other part of the court so that he gets used to changing the direction of the ball. It is a source of amazement to see teams warming up with the smashers feeding the ball to the setter from the sides only! This means that both smashers and setters are only warming up for smashes which build up from that position, in that way! By all means start off the warm-up in this way so that the first few sets and smashes are made easier but, after a while let both smashers and setters warm-up in a more realistic way.

Setters should also practice a few short sets, shoot sets and overhead sets. Usually the first of each of these sets is inaccurate. However, it is better that this inaccuracy occurs in the warm-up and not in the match.

Once the umpire has ended the smashing warm-up the players should quickly practice a few serves. Although time is not officially allowed for this, most referees and umpires do allow a minute or two.

While the warm-up is taking place, the coach should write down his rotational order on the special slip and return it to the umpire.

Before the set or match starts the coach should go over the main tactical points that he wants the team to carry out. Any additional information concerning the opponents' line-up, players form etc. should be given to the players.

After the referee has blown his whistle for the teams to come on court the umpire will check to see that the rotational order of the players corresponds with the order the coach has put'ón the special slip.

It has been said that there are three stages in each set; from the beginning to the first four points, from 4 points to 9 points and from thirteen to fifteen

208

points. Once a team has reached these scores it has passed a pyschological barrier. The losing team must aim to catch up a team in each of the three stages. If they are more than two points adrift in any section it is very difficult for them to get back on terms. To slow down the advance of a team in any of these sections, or to help his team get back into the game the coach. should take advantage of the two times-out and six substitutions allowed in each set.

When to call for a time-out and/or substitution.

1)   When the opposing team gains three successive points through its serving, smashing or blocking.

2)   When the team is confused and players are out of position.

3)   When the opponents are employing new tactics, or tactics which are playing the chief smasher out of the game.

4)   When opponents have reached one of the stages i.e. 4, 9, or 13 points and your team is two or more points adrift.

5)   When a setter or smasher is going through a bad patch.

6)   When it is wished to alter the tactics of the team at a decisive point in the game.

7)   When it is wished to upset opponents. For example, if they have called a time-out at a decisive point in the game with the intention of upsetting players concentration, request a time-out for the team immediately following theirs. They will have got themselves keyed up ready to fight for the next point. The extra delay will upset them and at the same time allow your players time to relax and maintain their composure.

8)   When a player is playing badly and the opponents are playing on him.

9)   When it is wished to bring on a new attacker to upset opposing blockers.

10)   When it is wished to bring on a strong server at a crucial point in the game.

11)   When smashers are tiring and it is wished to rest them in back court.

12)   When one of the players in back court or front court is weaker than another player on the bench, substitute the bench player and play him in each of the three front court or back court positions.

13)   When all times-out have been used and it is necessary to break the concentration of the opponents at a vital point in the game a substitution can be used.

Times-out must be requested from the umpire who will inform the coach how many times-out he has had that set. The coach must be careful that he does not request more than the permitted two times-out per set.

When the coach wishes to substitute a player he should send the substitute to the scorer's table and then request a substitution from the umpire. The

209

umpire will supervise the changeover so that both players report to the scorer's table.

If a coach is expecting to use a substitute during a set he should send the substitute down to the end of the court to keep moving and warm. If the player has been sitting on the bench with his tracksuit on he will not be fully prepared to go on court and play his best immediately.

Using times-out

There are only two times-out of thirty seconds each, for each team in each set. If both teams call both times-out then a coach has two minutes in the set when he can give his team advice. It is important that these two minutes are not wasted. As soon as a time-out is called by either side the players should run across to the sideline. It must be remembered that neither the players nor, the coach may cross the sideline.

The coach should be constructive and not destructive during the time-out. If a team is playing badly it doesn't need the coach to tell it during a time-out. What it needs is thirty seconds of advice on what to do to improve play. Instead of telling a player his defects in technique the coach should briefly give him hints on what to do to improve it. The player needs advice that he can use then and not at a later training session.

If the formation of a team is incorrect or needs adjustment as a result of the pattern of play adopted by the opponents then the players should be told the new positions as quickly and briefly as possible.

Advice on where to serve, which players to set to, which part of the court to smash at etc. should also be given if possible. The coach should aim to improve his team's performance by giving advice on how to tighten up its play and how to weaken the opponent's.

During the thirty seconds the coach should not tolerate arguing between players or discussion. Time is too valuable to waste. A coach who gives advice is reassuring to a team, a coach who complains and loses his temper is demoralising. The way in which advice is given will communicate quite quickly and painlessly to a team what the coach thinks of their play. Depending on the condition of the game the coach should try to relax his players or put some fight in them.

While the game is being played the coach should not gesticulate wildly or, overexpress his feelings about the way his team is playing. If a team sees its coach acting out a major Greek tragedy by the side of the court each time they lose a point or make a mistake their team spirit is weakened and the relationship between coach and players endangered.

The interval between sets

The rules allow an interval of two minutes between sets and five minutes

210

The ball is not dead until it touches the ground!

It is important that team members cover their own smasher during an attack. The Italian players demonstrate clearly the low ready position of the covering players

The blockers should, as the picture clearly shows, watch the smasher throughout the smashing action so that they can make last minute adjustments to the position or angle of their arms

Ambroziak of Poland dives to recover a ball placed inside the block. Notice how the blockers and the back court men are all ready to play the ball once it has been picked up

between the fourth and fifth sets. During this time the coach and players should review the previous set and discuss the tactics to be used during the next set. The coach should consider whether the rotational order he used last time was effective, whether it needs to be varied in view of the opponents' line-up, whether it needs to be changed because the team has service or will be receiving service.

The winning team of a set very often relax after the struggle and therefore are liable to slip into a low level of play. The coach should make sure that even if his team has no chance of winning a set the opponents have no opportunity to let-up. At the end of each set the winning team should feel relieved to have won. If they are they will be easier to defeat in the next set because there is a certain anti-climax about it for them. If however, they won the set easily they will not be so easy to beat.

The coach of the team that won the last set must ensure that his team get back into top gear as soon as possible. It is often valuable to take one or two players off for the beginning of the set and rest them on the bench. They will then be very keen to get back on court and into the game once it has started and they see the others playing. If the opponents get a two or three point lead in the first stage of the game they will be pleased. However, the bringing back of the substituted players who are really keen for action will demoralise the opponents and enable the team to get back the two points deficit and to again exert their superiority.

After the game
The coach should record his impressions of the game, how individuals performed in various situations, the effectiveness of the various tactical situations and weaknesses that were highlighted during the game.

As soon as possible the team should meet to discuss the game. The players should be given the opportunity to talk about aspects of their play and the team play in general. These team meetings will help to clear the air after a defeat and to focus the players attention on the work to be done in coming training sessions.

8 OFFICIATING VOLLEYBALL

There will come a time when every teacher, coach or player will be asked to referee a game. Ideally everyone should be a fully qualified official. For a variety of reasons this is not always the case.

Volleyball is a subjective game, difficult to referee well. For this reason the referee and umpire in volleyball often feel as though they are on trial before the players, coaches and spectators all of whom see every foul missed by the officials and many more besides. It is only when these people actually attempt to officiate a game that they realise in fact just how difficult it is. Teachers and coaches should encourage their players to referee practice sessions so that they will have a greater understanding of the difficulties of the officials during a match.

There are five officials in volleyball, a referee, umpire, scorer and two linesmen. The referee stands or sits on a special stand so that he has a good view of the court and the top of the net. The umpire is on the opposite side of the court and moves along the sideline, on his side of the court.

The referee is the senior official and his duties are laid down in RULE 8;

THE REFEREE—(Located above one end of the net)

The referee controls the game and his decisions are final. He has authority over all players and officials from the beginning to the end of the match, including any periods during which the match may be temporarily interrupted for whatever reason.

The referee has the power to settle all questions, including those not specified in the Rules, and can over-rule decisions by other officials when he considers that they have made a mistake. He must be located approximately 50cm (20") above one end of the net, in order that he can clearly see the play. In accordance with Rule 4, the referee penalises bad behaviour of players, coaches and managers.

The umpire shall place himself on the other side of the court facing the referee.

1. He blows his whistle when a player has crossed the centre line or has illegally played the ball within the attack zone.
2. He points out any contact of the ball with the vertical side markers (flexible sticks) and whenever the ball passes outside them.
3. He times the duration of time-out.
4. He supervises the conduct of coaches and substitutes on the bench.
5. He authorises substitutions if requested by team captains or coaches.
6. He judges contacts with the net, except those over or near to the top of the net.
7. He checks that the rotational order and positions of the receiving team are correct at the time of each service.
8. He calls the attention of the referee to any unsporting actions.
9. He verifies at the beginning of each set that the initial positions of each team correspond exactly to the order of rotation as shown on the score sheet.
10. He watches for contact of the ball with any foreign objects.
11. He gives his opinion to the referee in all matters when so requested.

NOTE—the ball is considered to be 'dead' when either official blows his whistle.

Official I.V.B.F. Commentary on rules 8 & 9.

His responsibilities during the game are:

The referee is responsible for the correct conduct of the match. He must blow his whistle whenever he judges it to be necessary and at the beginning and end of each point. Each rally is considered to be finished when the referee blows his whistle. Generally speaking, the referee should only interrupt play when he is sure that a fault has been commited. He should not blow his whistle if there is any doubt.

Should the referee need to deal with anything outside the field of play, he should ask the organisers and players to help.

If the referee is sure that one of the other officials is not fulfilling his functions as defined by the rules, he may over-rule the decisions of that official and even dismiss him.

RULE 9—THE UMPIRE

Whenever a time-out is asked for, the umpire takes possession of the ball and then signals to the referee the number of times-out already claimed by each team. He then tells the captain and coach of each team the number of times-out they have had.

The umpire will only allow a substitution when the player who is to go on court is standing ready near to the scorer's table.

Should the referee suddenly be indisposed, the umpire must take charge of the game in his place.

The game

The referee summons the captains of both teams before the match and tosses a coin, in the prescence of the umpire, to determine which team has the choice of ends or service. The winner of the toss may choose either the end he prefers, or the right to serve first. Before the start of the deciding set, the referee makes a new toss of the coin to decide the choice of ends or service.

The umpire ensures that the teams submit lists and the numbers of players to the scorer. He also sees that the captains or coaches sign the scoresheet before the match to signify that the sheet used is the official one for the match.

The official warm-up for the match usually consists of a five minute general court warm-up followed by smashing practice over the net. Smashing practice may be of three minutes duration if each team smashes separately or, six minutes when they smash together. When the teams smash together, the umpire blows his whistle after three minutes and signals the teams to move to the other side of their court so that the teams practice smashing from positions 4 and 2.

The referee selects a match ball and presents it to the two captains for confirmation. The pressure of the ball is checked. The umpire and referee should be watching the warm-up to prepare their eyes for the game. They should familiarise themselves with the speed of the ball and the court markings.

At the conclusion of the warm-up, the umpire checks the height of the net at the centre and sides and the positioning of the net markers over the sidelines.

As soon as the umpire has confirmed that the net is correct, the referee takes his place on the stand and calls the first six players of each team to the end line.

The referee calls the players on court and the umpire checks the rotational order of the players with the slip given him by the coach of each team. The slip must correspond with the rotational order on court and on the scoresheet.

The referee then confirms the captains of both teams. If one of the captains is not on court the player who is acting as captain on court should be identified.

When the umpire has checked that the scoresheet is correct, the scorer is ready, and the players on court are in the correct rotational order he informs the referee. The referee then blows his whistle for the start of the game. The umpire then rolls the ball to the server.

Service

The referee blows his whistle for service as soon as both teams are on court in their respective positions and the server is holding the ball. If a team is very slow in getting ready for service the referee should warn the team. If a team is slow in returning the ball to the other side of the court for the opponents to serve he should warn that team.

It is important that the referee remembers which team is serving so that at the conclusion of a rally he is able to give the correct decision of point or side out. Some posts have a special device fitted to them which the referee can click onto the side of the serving team. Some referees have an elastic band around the hand on the side of the serving team. Still other referees place the hand on the side of the serving team on the headwire of the net. This serves two purposes. Not only does it identify the serving team it helps the referee to tell whether the ball touches the net on service.

After the referee has blown for service he should allow the server five seconds in which to make his serve. Should the server make an error in the throw-up and request a second attempt a further five seconds is allowed. However, the referee should warn a player who is deliberately delaying service in this way in order to try and gain some advantage for his team.

The server may not strike the ball until the whistle is blown. If he does the serve is invalid, the referee warns the player and the serve is retaken.

If the serve is not made within five seconds, if it is made with the feet in contact with the base line or, from outside the serving area the referee should blow the whistle and indicate side out.

At the time of service the umpire should be watching to see that players are not overlapping or in the wrong rotational order. The usual position for the umpire is on the receiving side of the court level with the front court players. The umpire should be able to tell that the ball has been served by the sound of the whistle and the sound of the contact of player and ball that follows. If players are overlapping or out of position at the time of service the umpire should blow his whistle, point out the offending players and make the correct hand signals.

215

The umpire should try to identify the two setters, the star smashers in a team and their respective "diagonals". This will help him to see whether players are in their correct positions at the time of service. Apart from the start of each set or after the changing of ends in the final set, errors in serving order discovered by the referee or umpire must not be pointed out.

After the serve has been made successfully the referee should watch each player as he plays the ball. When the dig pass is used there is little likelihood of a fault occuring. Although the player may appear to be in an unstable position, especially when receiving a ball near the net or extremes of the court the referee should only blow the whistle if he is certain that a fault has occurred. At receive, the most likely fault is a double touch. The ball may hit both arms independently, hit both the arms and body or, roll up the arms.

Very often the referee's view of the setter is obstructed by other players especially when the first pass is low. The referee should move his body to see around the players or through the net in order to have a good view of the player.

Volleyball is a very subjective game and the referee is often called upon to make very difficult distinctions between a ball that is carried or held and the ball that is played legally by a player who has extreme flexibility of the wrists. The referee should ideally be a player or former player so that he has has experience of the techniques he must judge. He should be present at as many training sessions as possible so that he becomes fully conversant with the techniques of the game. At these training sessions he should offer to referee so that he keeps in training as well.

It is essential that the referee is consistent throughout the game. If he is not the players and coaches will become irritated and the game will suffer. Even if the players and coaches disagree with decisions the referee must be firm, otherwise his authority will suffer.

When the attack is made the referee should be watching the attacking players and the umpire the blockers. The umpire must be looking for touches of the net below the headline, touches by the block and crossing of the centre line by both attackers and blockers.

Very often disputes arise over touches by the block. Many times the block will only just touch the ball when it is on its way out of court, or the other players will play three further touches. If the captain of a team appeals for a touch the referee should consult with the umpire and linesmen if he did not see it himself. The umpire should as a matter of course signal to the referee, with the appropriate sign, if he sees a touch by the block during the course of a rally.

The referee must also watch for blockers touching the net with their hands or arms, and for 'held' balls. He must watch the action of the smasher to make sure that he does not pull or throw the ball. The dump

216

pass or tactical smash causes a lot of controversy. The amount of force the smasher is allowed to give the ball without being penalised for throwing the ball varies from country to country. It is impossible to lay down precise distinctions between a valid dump and a thrown ball. Each referee should watch closely the interpretation of the leading referees in his country.

Although the linesmen are in the best position to judge whether a ball is in or out of court the referee has the final judgement. The umpire should signal to the referee if the ball is out or in court on his sideline. If he is not sure whether the ball is in or out he should refer to the linesman on his side of the court. Remember that a ball landing on the line is in court. To signal that a ball was in court the linesman should point his flag down towards the ground in front of him. To signal ball out of court he points the flag behind his head.

Times-out and substitutions are controlled by the umpire. Each team is allowed two times-out of thirty seconds duration and six substitutions in each set.

The substitute must report to the scorer's table before the substitution is called. He should have his tracksuit off and be ready to go straight on court. As soon as the ball is dead the coach can request a substitution from the umpire. The umpire then blows his whistle and signals to the referee by rotating his clenched fists that a substitution has been called. He then goes to the scorer to check which player is coming on court and which player is coming off. The umpire must ensure that the player coming off court reports to the scorer immediately. Before signalling to the referee that the substitution is complete the umpire must check that it has been correctly recorded by the scorer, check to see how many substitutions have been made that set by that team and that the players are still in their correct rotation order. He then signals to the referee how many substitutions have been made by the team and that the game can be restarted.

If the substitute is not ready to go on court then the umpire can refuse the substitution. If the player delays getting onto court then a time-out should be charged to the team. If the team have used all their times-out for that set they should be penalised by loss of service or their opponents are awarded a point.

When the captain is substituted, the referee should find out who is acting as captain on court.

Times-out are requested from the umpire when the ball is dead. The umpire making a 'T' shape with his hands and, indicating which team has asked for the time-out. Whenever a time-out or substitution is requested, the umpire must collect the ball and keep hold of it until play is resumed.

During a time-out or substitution, the coach is not allowed on court. In the case of a substitution the coach is not allowed to communicate with the team. The players may not leave the court during times-out or the substitution of other players.

Two consecutive times-out may be requested by either team, without resumption of play between them. A substitution may follow a time-out or precede a time-out.

If a team requests a third time-out it must be refused and the offending coach or captain warned. In the event of him asking yet again during the same set his team will be penalised with loss of service or point.

At the end of the set the referee makes the crossed arm signal and waves both teams back to the base line on the serving side. On his whistle the teams then walk around the edge of the court to the other end. As each team walks along a different sideline they will not meet.

An interval of two minutes is allowed between each set and five minutes in the deciding set. Before play resumes the umpire must collect the new rotation order for each team and communicate this to the scorer.

The scorer

The scorer must be opposite the referee so that he can see his signal regarding point or loss of service.

The rules lay down the following duties for the scorer;

1. Before the beginning of each match, he records on the score sheet the names and numbers of the players and substitutes, and obtains the signatures of the captains and coaches who are authorised to make substitutions.

2. He records the score as the match progresses, carefully noting substitutions and the number of times-out requested during each set.

3. At each new request for a time-out, he shall announce the number of times-out that have been requested during each set.

4. After the toss and before each set, he records on the score sheet the position of the players on the court (i.e. rotation order). The position of the team serving first is recorded first on the score sheet.

He shall not give the respective formations of the teams to anyone, except to the officials when requested.

5. During the set, he shall see that the rotation order is observed.

6. He announces the changing of ends after the end of each set, and after the eighth point made by one of the teams in the deciding set.

7. During the stoppages of play, he points out to officials the number of requests for times-out.

8. At the end of the match, he presents the scoresheet to the referee and umpire for signature.

Official I.V.B.F. commentary on rule 10.

The scorer, when asked, must tell either of the coaches or captains the number of substitutions and times-out they have already been given. At the beginning of each set the coaches must give the scorer a piece of paper on which the line-up of their players is marked. The scorer must control the order of service. He must score each point and make sure that the score on the scoreboard corresponds with the score sheet.

The scorer must write down all remarks and incidents that lead to a player being disqualified.

N.B. Should there be a dispute about the correct score, the score on the scoresheet is regarded as the official score. The scoreboard is there for information purposes.

The scoresheet
In recent years, most countries have adopted, with a few minor differences, a scoresheet as shown in Fig. 204. Although it looks rather complex completing the sheet is not very difficult. This type of sheet enables scorers to control service orders and substitutions very effectively and the coach can glean much useful information from it following a match.

The names, numbers of the players are entered at the bottom of the sheet. In the top left hand box the starting time of the 1st set is recorded. The first six players on court for each team are recorded as per rotational order. Their numbers are written in the top half of the box. In between the two sections in the first box is the running total.

As soon as a player loses his service and side out is called, the scorer should put the number of points scored by the team that has just lost service, in the columns numbered 1-6. The score is placed in the square opposite the former server. When completed correctly the scores recorded at the conclusion of one complete rotation will have filled column 1. The seven columns allowed for seven complete rotations in the set, a number that will very rarely be exceeded.

As each point is scored it is crossed off on the respective running total.

When a player is substituted, the scorer records not only which player takes his place but the score at the time of substitution. The number of the substitute is recorded in the square below the original player. The score is written in the next column next to the number of the original player. When the second and final substitution of that player takes place the score is written in the remaining space. In this way it is impossible for the scorer not to notice when a player is substituting illegally.

Each team is allowed two times-out each set and the score at which these are called is written in the boxes below the running totals. There are two boxes, one for recording each time-out.

219

Amateur Volleyball Association

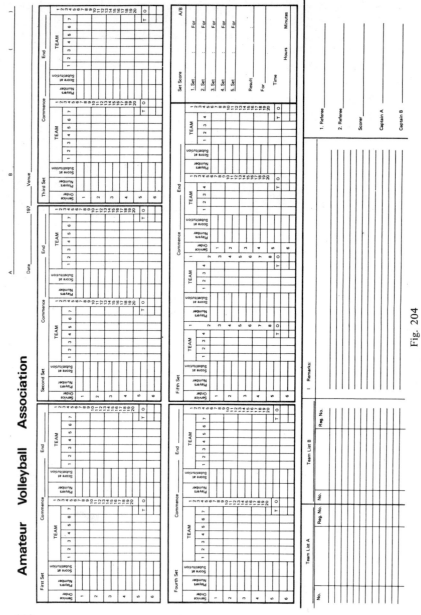

Fig. 204

At the conclusion of the set, the time is recorded at the top of the section. The score is also recorded in the right hand box in the second row.

In the fifth set in a five set match or the third in a three set, the special section is used. When one team reaches eight points in the deciding set, both teams must change ends and retake their positions. When this changeover occurs, all the details in the first two columns are transferred to the other side. If all the details are not transferred, then mistakes in rotation order, substitution etc. could occur.

The total time for the match and the result are completed in the box on the right hand side.

If a player or coach is sent off, the referee must record this fact and the matters leading to the situation in the Remarks section.

The linesman

Rule 11.

Where there is only the minimum of two linesmen, they should be at diagonally opposite corners of the court, (not the service corners), at a distance of one metre indoors and three metres outdoors.

Each linesman watches the side lines and the end line nearest to him. The linesmen signal to the referee. They raise their flag when the ball is 'out', and point it downwards when the ball is 'in'.

The referee can request the linesmen to signal with their flags when a ball which was out, was contacted by a player on the receiving team's side.

The linesmen also draw attention of the referee to errors made by players when serving or when a ball passes completely outside the vertical sidemarkers.

Official commentary on rule 11.

Whenever the linesmen want to attract the attention of the referee to a fault committed by a player or to rude remarks made by a player, they must raise their flag and wave it from right to left.

For important competitions it is better to use four linesmen than two.

Linesmen should be positioned on the extension of the lines.

Linesmen shall be standing.

The quality of the game is dependent to a large extent on the referee. If he allows sloppy handling in the first set, the game will easily degenerate. If a player has bad handling, the referee must blow every fault. It is no use feeling sorry for him and letting some fouls go. Apart from the fact that the opposing side is being penalised as a result, the player will not have the incentive to work on improving his handling.

221

The referee must refrain from indulging in conversations with the players. Decisions must be clear and prompt. If the appropriate hand signal is given, the players will know the reason why the referee blew the whistle. Once the referee starts giving verbal explanations, he is opening himself up to arguments and discusions on decisions.

If the captain queries a decision, the referee should briefly give the reason for blowing the whistle and prepare to restart play. As soon as the service whistle is blown, players will soon get back to the game.

Under no circumstances should the referee tolerate remarks made to him or the officials concerning their decisions. The referee should call the captain of the offending team to the stand and give him a warning that his team will be penalised if the offence is repeated. If the remark made was of a serious nature the referee can, under Rule 4 Article 4 (2), disqualify immediately the offending player.

It is essential that all coaches and teachers and as many players as possible obtain the referee's qualifications. To obtain this award, the person must make a detailed study of the rules and their interpretations. This knowledge will benefit coaches, teachers and players on numerous occasions other than when they are actually refereeing. Once the qualification has been obtained, the referee should ensure that he keeps up to date with rule changes and new interpretations.

9 FITNESS FOR VOLLEYBALL

Although volleyball was originally intended to be a leisurely recreation, it has developed into a highly competitive sport which requires a high level of fitness. The wide variety of techniques in the game each have their different physical requirements. As a consequence the player must work on a wide ranging programme designed to improve his strength, muscular endurance, cardiovascular efficiency, flexibility and agility. The player who relies entirely on the normal club training sessions for his fitness work will never achieve his maximum performance in a game.

It is well documented that the onset of fatigue is accompanied by a deterioration of the skills carried out. Naturally, the fitter the performer, the later in the game that this effect will be manifested.

All of the techniques have minimum physical requirements in order to carry them out e.g. volleying requires strength of fingers and wrists, blocking and smashing, the ability to jump high enough to contact the ball when it is above net height etc. Improvement in physical performance above this minimum in all cases, results in improved technical performance.

Volleyball is a game requiring quick, sudden movements and fast reactions. On many occasions the player will be forced to move very quickly to his side or forwards to play a ball. To do this he must be agile. The demands of everyday life are such that few individuals reach their optimum level of agility without specific training. The volleyball player will need to achieve his optimum level if he is to be an effective player. Volleyball matches have no time limit and some matches will last several hours or more when teams are evenly matched. To be able to play effectively for this period of time the player must have good muscular and circulo-respiratory endurance.

A great deal of research into the methods of improving human physical performance has been carried out in recent years and is being continued in

223

universities and colleges throughout the world. The results of this research are extensively reported in specialist texts and journals. However, the average coach will find these works too deep for his purposes. It is intended therefore to outline the basic concepts and general principles that the coach should know. Once these have been grasped the coach will find it easier to delve into the more detailed works.

The four performance factors which the coach is interested in developing are;
a) Strength
b) Endurance
c) Flexibility
d) Speed

The maximum development of all four aspects is essential if the player is to perform at his maximum.

Overload principle

Basic to the improvement of strength, endurance (muscular and circulo-respiratory) and flexibility, is the overload principle. Improvement in these performance factors is brought about only by subjecting the body to greater loads than normally encountered.

To improve strength, the resistance (i.e. weight used) should be such that the player is unable to carry out the exercise more than 12 times consecutively. If he can exceed twelve repetitions then gain in strength will be minimal but, gain in muscular endurance will result.

Improvement in circulo-respiratory endurance is obtained by imposing a work load such that in general the heart rate is raised to over 160 beats per minute. When the heart rate is less than this, no improvement in endurance occurs.

To improve flexibility, the overload point is that at which the tissues surrounding the joint offer resistance. Care must be taken to see that too much stress is not applied and damage to tissue results.

Working at or above the overload level will result in some improvement of the relevant performance factor under training. However, the intensity of the performance is also an important determinant of the rate of improvement. The aim should be to reduce the amount of time needed to perform a certain amount of work.

The improvement of these performance factors and the subsequent maintainence of the improvement is affected by the frequency of training.

Strength training should be carried out on alternate days. Daily training is not recommended unless the muscle groups receiving training are changed.

Training to develop other performance factors should be carried out at least five times a week.

224

As the training effect increases, the threshold which must be reached before improvement will result also increases. This means that the training programme must be increased either by increasing the amount of work carried out in the same time or, by carrying out the same amount of work in a shorter time.

The volleyball player must develop strength in his legs to aid jumping, in his wrists to aid volleying and his arms to aid smashing. He must also improve the endurance of each of these muscle groups and the speed at which they work. The faster he can take off, the more difficult the smasher is to block; the longer he maintains a high vertical jump, the longer he will be able to smash and block effectively.

Endurance

The ability to maintain physical activity for a considerable period of time is refered to as endurance. There are two kinds of endurance—muscular and circulo-respiratory.

The volleyball player needs local muscular endurance particularly in his legs to enable him to keep jumping throughout the game. He also needs general circulo-respiratory endurance to maintain whole body endurance over a long time.

Strength plays an important part in determining muscular endurance. The stronger a muscle is, the fewer muscle fibres it will have to use in a movement. This means that it is not having to work at full capacity and can therefore work for a longer period of time before it is fatigued.

The skilled player is able to carry out movements more economically than the unskilled. There is economy of movement. Muscular endurance can therefore be improved in conjunction with improvement in skill.

Methods of improving the performance factors

The following methods can be used to develop one or more of the performance factors;

    a) Weight training
    b) Circuit training
    c) Interval training
    d) Flexibility exercises.

Weight training

There are few top volleyball players, or sportsmen, who do not use weight training to improve their physical performance. The nature of the weight training programme for volleyball varies from country to country. The emphasis is usually on improving the vertical jump and the training may involve the use of heavy weights and low repetitions, medium weights and

225

maximum repetitions or, low weights with limited repetitions at maximum speed.

It is interesting to note that despite the different programmes employed by the major volleyball countries, each manages to produce players with vertical jumps of 1 metre or above. When the Japanese mens team visited London in 1969 their coach Yasutaka Matsudaira was asked what training his players did to enable them to jump as high as they did. He replied that he had asked the same question along with the coaches of Russia and Czechoslovakia to the Cuban coach at the World Cup that year. At this tournament several Cubans were jumping 108 cms! The Cuban coach replied that his players did no special weight training! This serves to illustrate how little we really know about muscular actions involved in the vertical jump and the methods of improving it.

It would appear that the Cuban players are the exception and that for most other players weight training can be of great value. The use of medium weights lifted at maximum speed are favoured for this purpose. This develops muscular endurance and strength with little loss in speed of movement.

The training schedule below, used by the England team, is based on one developed by the Belgian National Coach Nicolau. It is an excellent all round schedule suited to the demands of modern volleyball.

SCHEDULE 1

1. Arm movements holding dumbells (2-4 kg) in all directions to include throwing type movements, lateral movements, and circular movements. Two sets of one minute, with two minutes rest between.
2. Warming up of legs (flexion, skipping etc).
3. Work with a medicine ball weighing 3-6 kg.

a. Basketball chest pass against a wall 15 feet away, 20 times, then a two minute rest.

b. Soccer throw in against a wall 15 feet away. Ten times and one minute rest.

c. Throw with one arm—elbow leading the movement—against a wall. 15 feet away. Ten throws with each arm and 1 minute rest.

d. Back to wall throw the ball overhead from 20 feet away. Ten times followed by one minute rest.

4. Jumping on the spot holding weights in the hand (5-15 kg), as high as possible. Two sets of twenty with two-three minutes rest between.
5. Three sets of press-ups. Fifty per cent of maximum with two-three minutes rest between.
6. Holding a medicine ball (15-20 kg) standing with one foot on a bench and the other leg on the floor. Using the leg on the bench jump up as high as possible. The other leg is used to help in landing. The bench should be in line with the shoulders.

226

Four sets of ten, two sets with each leg. Two minutes rest between each set.
7.   Repeat the whole of section 3 without a rest.
8.   Smashing approach and jump.
Three sets of 15. All as high as possible. Three minutes rest between each set.

NOTES
All exercise must be done with maximum speed.
Rest periods must be used to ensure that speed is not lost.
Progress is made by increasing the speed and not weight.
This schedule should be used three times a week.

SCHEDULE 2
1.   Arm movements holding dumbells (2-4 kg) in all directions to include throwing type movements, lateral movements, and circular movements.
Two sets of one minute with two-three minutes rest between.
2.   Bench press with 40 kg.
Two sets of ten with two minutes rest between.
3.   Standing with legs apart, holding barbell behind the neck, raise and lower back over as wide as range as possible. Keep the back straight.
Three sets of ten with 25 kg. Three minutes rest between each set.
4.   Press-ups.
Three sets of seventy-five per cent maximum number possible. Three minutes rest between.
All the following exercises must be done with explosive action.
5.   Jumping on the spot holding a barbell across the shoulders (40 kg).
Three sets of seven-ten. Two-three minutes rest between each set.
6.   Pull over triceps with 30 kg.
Three sets of seven-ten with two-three minutes rest between.
7.   Squat jumps with weight on bar equivalent to own body weight, *the knees should not bend past ninety degrees*
Three sets of four. Two-three minutes rest between.
8.   Dead lift with weight on bar equivalent to own body weight.
One set of ten followed by two-three minutes rest.
9.   With a weight of 20 kg stand with one foot on a bench and jump as high as possible.
Two sets of ten (one set with each leg) with two-three minutes rest between.
10.   Smash approach and jump with weights in hands.
               1st set ; 2 kg-10 repetitions
               2nd set ; 3 kg-10 repetitions
               3rd set ; 10 repetitions without any weight.

227.

NOTES
This schedule should be used twice a week on days when the other schedule is not being used.

Other weight training exercises suitable for volleyball players.
For the wrists;
1)   Whilst sitting, a barbell is held just in front of the knees with the forearms resting on the thighs. The wrist is fully flexed downwards and then raised as far as possible upwards.
2)   A rope is tied to a ten pound weight. The end of the rope is attached to a short bar or stick. The weight is wound up by turning the stick in the hands.

For the triceps;
(These muscles situated at the back of the upper arm are used to extend the forearm in the smash and overhead serves).
1)   A barbell is held overhead with the arms straight. The upper arm (shoulder to elbow) is kept straight and the weight lowered behind the head and then raised to the vertical position.
2)   French-press—sitting on a bench with the back kept straight a dumbell is held with both hands above the head. The dumbell is then lowered as far as possible behind the head before being raised to the starting position again.

For the legs;
1)   Halting high dead lift—the feet are placed under the bar, back kept straight and head erect, which is then pulled to waist height. The legs should be extended vigorously and the arms contribute to the action by pulling upwards.
2)   Calf raises—with the bar resting across the shoulders the heels are raised as high as possible and then lowered. It is helpful if the lifter places a block of wood about two inches high under his heels during this exercise.

Safety;
To avoid injury through actually lifting weights, or whilst preparing to use them, it is essential that players are familiar with the basic safety consider-ations in weight training, the exercise they are doing and the correct way it should be carried out.
    Before lifting any weights the performer should check the following;
    a) That all weights are securely attached by collars to the bar.
    b) That any weight training machine (e.g. leg press) is securely anchored and that all adjusting pins are secure.
    c) That other weight trainers are ready to assist when a new exercise is being performed, or, a new weight lifted.

228

d) That he understands fully the movement to be carried out.
e) That the weight on the bar is within his capabilities. A bar should never be picked up and lifted to see how heavy it is.
f) That there is enough room around him to carry out the exercise.
g) That the floor area around the place he is going to work is clear of weights etc.
h) That any bench he is going to step on is safe.
i) That he is warmed up for activity. General stretching exercises and some running before any lifting takes place will minimise the risk of muscle injuries.

When lifting;
The weight trainer should breathe deeply and regularly throughout the exercise. In most exercise he should breath in as the weight is lifted and out as it is lowered. However, when squats or abdominal exercises are being carried out he should reverse this pattern.

The head should be kept up and the back straight during the lifting movements. The feet should be placed shoulder width apart under the bar when lifting if off the ground.

Circuit training;
This method of improving physical performance was developed by Morgan and Adamson of Leeds University Physical Education Dept.* and has been adopted throughout the world as a simple but effective method of improving the performance factors.

Circuit training simply involves a series of exercises which must be performed in a specific order until a specified number of circuits have been completed. Each exercise must be done a particular number of times depending on the maximum number the individual managed on his testing circuit. Once he has tried all the exercises, the time he takes to complete three circuits carrying out half the maximum repetitions at each exercise is recorded. The target time for future circuits is two-thirds of this time. Once the performer has attained the target time, the number of repetitions he can do at each exercise is measured and a new circuit and target time worked out. A full description of the method for those unacquainted with it can be found in the account by the originators.*

Circuit training exercises for volleyball.
1) Press-ups
2) Hopping shuttle runs with a dumbell in one hand.
3) Sit-ups.

* R.E. Morgan & G.T. Adamson (1956) *Circuit training*, London: Bell.

229

4) Successive blocks against the basketball backboard.
5) Back raises
6) Wrist swinging on the beams.
7) Triceps extensions with barbell.
8) Throwing a medicine ball at wall using one hand and elbow leading the movement.

Interval training

This form of training involving running, helps to improve circulo-respiratory endurance and speed of movement.

It involves working for a period of time (not more than one minute), at maximum capacity followed by a short break. For example, it could involve sprinting 50 yards as fast as possible and then slowly walking back to the starting point before sprinting again. The number of repetition runs depends on the fitness of the individual. The aim of interval running is to raise the heart rate to a level at which improvement will take place. This level is usually identified by a heart rate of around 160 beats per minute. The duration of the rest period should ideally be the length of time taken for the heart rate to drop to approximately 120 beats per minute. The individual can quickly gain an idea of his heart rate by measuring the pulse at the wrist for ten seconds and multiplying the count by six.

As the individual becomes fitter the work load can be increased accordingly. For example an advanced practice is for the athlete to sprint ten yards, walk back to the start, sprint 20 yards, walk back and so on until 100 yards has been reached in this fashion.

Flexibility exercises

It is important that this type of work is carried out regularly so that the player will have a wide range of movement when performing all the skills of the game. It is essential that it is only carried out after a thorough warm up.

To increase flexibility the muscles must be stretched to their maximum. Once they have reached their maximum, any movements made must be done carefully and slowly so that damage to the tissues is avoided.

Examples of exercises for improving flexibility

For the back:
1) Arch-ups—lying on the stomach with the arms extended, the arms, head and legs are raised as far as possible off the ground, thus arching the back.
2) Back to back—this exercise is done in pairs. Standing back to back the partners link arms and one leans forward thus pulling his partner off the ground so that he rests on his back. The procedure is then reversed and the player in the air becomes the supporter.

230

3) Cat stretches—the press-up position is adopted and the performer raises his hips as high as possible off the ground. The hips are then lowered as the arms are extended and chest lifted.

4) Lying on the back the legs are lifted up and back so that the knees touch the ground first on one side of the head and then on the next before returning to the starting position.

5) Back arches—the hands are placed on the floor in front of the feet and then raised quickly so that the back is arched.

For the legs:

1) Splits—one foot is placed in front of the other and the player lowers himself as far as possible. Once this position is reached, he should turn to face the opposite direction.

2) Touching the toes. The legs are kept together and straight at the knees while the player leans down and tries to place his palms on the floor.

3) Reach thrust—with the feet astride the hands are pushed between them and as far behind the body as possible.

4) In pairs, one player places his toes against his partner's spread thighs. Holding his partner's wrists he pulls him forward as far as possible.

For the trunk:

1) Trunk circling—the player stands three feet from a wall with his back to it. He then sweeps his arms round in a circle to touch the floor in front of him and the wall behind him.

2) Trunk twisting—with the feet shoulder width apart, the arms are stretched out to the side of the body parallel to the ground. The player then twists the arms as far as possible behind him on either side.

3) Side bends—standing with the feet apart and the arms above the head the player reaches as far as possible to each side. The trunk should not be bent forward.

For the shoulders:

1) The player stands opposite wall bars and grasps them at waist height by leaning forward keeping the back straight. The trunk is then forced down so that the shoulder muscles are stretched.

2) Arm circling—the arms are circled both around and across the body.

When preparing schedules for players the coach should take into account the weaknesses of the individual and the time of the season. Volleyball unlike other sports does not have a clear cut season. This means that the main bulk of the physical preparation, which is normally carried out in the close season, will probably have to take place during the summer. Once the League and championship programme have ceased and the tournament and festival season

231

commences, players can start to prepare physically for the coming season. It is essential that the coach devises a schedule for each individual and not one which all must use. Individual schedules will ensure that each player is carrying out work suited to his needs. A basic schedule, such as that outlined earlier, can be used with the weights varied according to the individual and supplementary exercises added where necessary. The players must be closely supervised to see that they work frequently and with sufficient intensity to make appreciable improvements in the performance factors.

10 TOURNAMENTS AND COMPETITIONS

Leagues

The normal league programme brings every team together twice in each season. Each team plays one match at home and one away. Organising the league programme can be very time consuming, unless a system is used to draw up the matches.

The total number of matches to be played can be calculated from the following formula, where n equals the number of teams;

$$n \times (n - 1)$$

e.g. with ten teams

$$10 \times (10 - 1)$$

$$= 10 \times 9$$

$$= 90 \text{ matches.}$$

To work out who plays who and in what order write the teams down in the following way;

```
1 - 10
2 -  9
3 -  8
4 -  7
5 -  6
```

This is the first round. To work out subsequent rounds move all the numbers (*except no. 1*) one place anti-clockwise;

1 − 9	1 − 8	1 − 7	1 − 6	1 − 5	1 − 4	1 − 3	1 − 2
10 − 8	9 −7	8 − 6	7 − 5	6 − 4	5 − 3	4 − 2	3 − 10
2 − 7	10 − 6	9 − 5	8 − 4	7 − 3	6 − 2	5 − 10	4 − 9
3 − 6	2 − 5	10 − 4	9 − 3	8 − 2	7 − 10	6 − 9	5 − 8
4 − 5	3 − 4	2 − 3	10 − 2	9 − 10	8 − 9	7 − 8	6 − 7

This now gives every team one match against each of the other teams in the league. For the second half of the programme the same order is used excepting that the first numbered team is the away team instead of the home team.

In a single match league the number of matches to be played can be computed from the formula:

$$\frac{n \times (n-1)}{2}$$

e.g. with ten teams—

$$\frac{10 \times (10-1)}{2}$$
$$= \frac{90}{2}$$
$$= 45$$

The two-pool system

The league entry is divided into two equal pools and all the teams in each pool play each other. At the conclusion of the leagues the top half of each pool join together and make a new league and the bottom halves make a second league.

There must be an even number of teams in each first round league. If there is an odd number, it is impossible to join the leagues together for the second round.

When the League is divided into two pools in this way, there are fewer matches to play.

League of 8 matches to be played $= n \times (n-1)$

$= 56$

League of 4 matches to be played $= n \times (n-1)$

$= 12$ matches

234

With two leagues there will be 24 matches in the first round and 24 matches in the second making a total of 48 in all.

Swiss system

This form of competition is derived from the Swiss ice-hockey leagues.

A full programme of one round is played so that each team plays once against all opponents. The league is then divided into two with the top teams playing each other and the bottom teams also playing each other. The points gained by teams in the first round still stand to their credit. This means that the top teams have a second half league programme against the better opponents. The teams in the lower half of this pool will have a real incentive to play as will the teams at the foot of the second half of the league. Very often, league programmes tend to die in the second half of the season as many teams know that they have little chance of winning certain matches (against the league leaders for example). By splitting the league in this way and retaining the first round points new life is injected into the league as teams play against others of the same standard.

Tournaments

It is very important when organising tournaments, to make sure that all the teams have enough games to make their visit worthwhile. Entries should be in early enough for the organisers to contact the teams with details of the order of matches and methods of qualifying for the final rounds. Nothing is more frustrating for a team than to turn up on the day not knowing when they are playing, who they are playing, which court they are playing on or, the competition rules.

The tournament organiser should aim to give teams as much written information before they arrive as possible. Courts should be clearly numbered and the rules of competition and order of play prominently displayed. Referees and scorers should also know their programme before the day of competition.

Types of tournament

The most common type of tournament is a knockout with the winners of the first round match going forward to meet other winners and the losers playing in a plate competition.

With eight teams the format would be as follows—

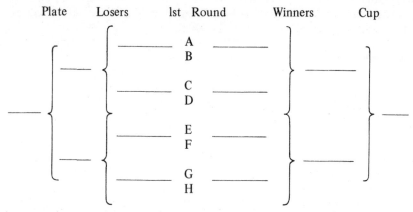

Another system is to bring the losing teams in at all stages of the tournament. This means that a team gets a second chance after it has been knocked out. This helps a good team that has been unluckily drawn against a strong team in the early rounds.

The format for this tournament with eight teams involving fourteen matches is—

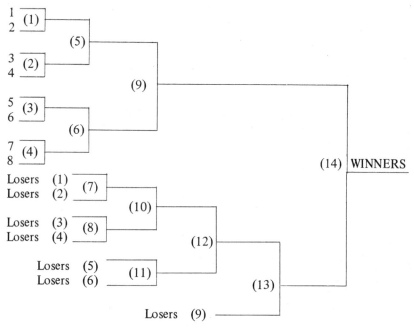

Sometimes tournaments are organised on a pool basis. Within each pool a league is organised. The winners and second team in each pool then go forward to the final rounds.

Winner Pool A   plays 2nd team in Pool B   Match (1)
Winner Pool B   plays 2nd team in Pool A   Match (2)
Final Winner of Match (1)   v   Winner Match (2)

Length of matches
Volleyball is a difficult game for which to plan a tournament. Some games will be over quickly and others take a couple of hours. This poses problems for the organiser in trying to fit all the games in the time schedule he has.

One way around this problem is to limit the early rounds to games of two sets. If a team wins both sets, then it is the automatic winner. If both teams have won a set, then a further half set can be played or the team which has scored the most points in the two sets is declared the winner. When pools are used, points can be awarded for each set a team wins i.e. two sets equals 2 points. If teams are still equal on points at the end, then it will depend firstly on the result of their match in the pool. If that match was drawn then on the total number of points scored by each team.

When the tournament is a knockout one in all rounds, the winning team must be decided on the basis of the number of points scored by a team.

A time limit can be placed on matches e.g. 30 minutes. If a match has been decided within 30 minutes then the result stands. If not the team that has scored most points wins.

The final and if there is time, the semi final, should always be the best of three or five sets. In this way the correct atmosphere is engendered.

1 RULES OF VOLLEYBALL

CHAPTER 1

Facilities, Playing Area and Equipment.

RULE 1–PLAYING AREA AND LINES

Art. 1. Playing Area:

The playing area shall be 18 metres (59 feet) long and 9 metres (29' 6") wide, and free from all obstructions up to a height of 7 metres (23') measured from the ground.

Art. 2. Boundary Lines:

The court shall be bounded by lines 5cm. (2") wide, which shall be drawn at least 2m. (6'6") from all obstructions. These lines are included in the playing area.

Art. 3. Centre Line:

A line drawn beneath the net, 5cm. (2") wide, divides the court into two equal halves.

Art. 4. Attack Area:

In each half of the court, a line of 9m. (29'6") by 5cm. (2") parallel to the centre line, is drawn 3m. (10') from it, the width of which is included in these three metres (ten feet). The attack area, as marked out by the centre line and the attack line, extends indefinitely beyond the side line.

Art. 5. Service Area:

Two lines 15cm. (6") long and 5cm. (2") wide, drawn 20cm. (8") behind and perpendicular to the end line, mark the service area of each court. One line is along the right hand side line, and the other 3m. (10') to the left of it. The service area shall have a minimum depth of 2 metres (6'6").

Art. 6. Minimum Temperature:

The temperature shall not be below 10 degrees Centigrade (50 degrees F).

RULE 2–THE NET

Art. 1. Size and Construction

The net shall be 1 metre (3'3") deep and 9.50 metres (32') long. It shall be made of 10cm. (4") square mesh. A double thickness of white canvas, 5cm. (2") wide shall be sewn along the top of the net. A flexible cable shall be stretched through the canvas.

Art. 2. Height

The height of the net, measured in the centre shall be 2.43 metres (7'11 $\frac{5}{8}$") for men and 2.24 metres (7'4 $\frac{1}{8}$") for women.

The two ends of the net must be an equal height from the ground and cannot exceed the regulation height by more than 2cm. (¾").

Art. 3. Vertical Side Markers

Two moveable tapes of 5cm. (2") wide white material, 1 metre (3'3") long, shall be fastened at each end of the net vertical to the side lines and the centre line.

Parallel to the tapes and just outside them, two flexible sticks shall be fastened to the net, at a distance of 9.40 metres from each other (i.e. 20cms beyond the outside edge of each vertical side marker).

These two sticks shall be 1.80 metres (6') long with a diameter of approximately 10mm. ($\frac{3}{8}$") and can be made of fibreglass or similar material and shall extend 80cm. (32") above the top of the net. The rods should be of contrasting colours, with sections 10cm. (4") wide.

The posts supporting the net must be at least 50cm. (20") from the side lines and shall not interfere with the duties of the referee or the umpire.

RULE 3—THE BALL

The ball shall be spherical, made of a supple leather case with the bladder made of rubber or similar material. The ball shall be uniform in colour; indoors this colour shall be light.

Circumference	..............................66cm. ± 1cm.
Weight	.... 270gr. ± 10gr.

CHAPTER II

The Players

RULE 4—RIGHTS AND DUTIES OF PLAYERS

Art. 1. All players must know the rules of the game and abide by them.

Art. 2. During the game, a player may address the referee only through the team captain.

Only the captain may address the referee and shall be the spokesman for his players. He may also address the umpire but only on matters concerning the umpire's duties.

Art. 3. Conduct of Players, Substitutes and Coaches

The following acts are punishable:

(a) Speaking persistently to officials concerning their decisions.
(b) Making uncivil remarks to officials.
(c) Acting in an uncivil manner with a view to influencing the decisions of officials.
(d) Making uncivil or personal remarks to opponents.
(e) The deliberate coaching during the game of a player or team by anyone in the out-court area.
(f) Leaving the court without permission of the referee (except between sets), during an interruption of play.
(g) At the instant of contact with the ball, particularly during

service reception, clapping, shouting or taking any action, the purpose of which is to distract the referee in his judgement concerning the handling of the ball.

Art. 4. Penalties:

1. For a minor offence, such as talking to opponents, spectators or officials, shouting or intentional delay of the game: a warning.

In the case of a repetition of the offence, a player receives a personal warning which is recorded on the score-sheet and his team loses the service or the opponents win a point.

2. For a serious offence, a penalty is recorded on the score-sheet and this automatically entails the loss of service by the offending team or the award of a point to the opponents. In the case of a repetition of the offence by the same player, the referee may disqualify him for the rest of the set or the match.

The referee shall disqualify, without any prior warning, any player making derogatory remarks to officials, opponents or spectators.

RULE 5—THE TEAMS

Art. 1. Players' Strip:

(a) The clothing of a player shall consist of a jersey, shorts and light and pliable shoes (rubber or leather soles without heels). It is forbidden to wear a head-gear or any article (jewels, pins, bracelets, etc.) which could cause injuries during the game. On request the referee may allow one or more players to play without shoes.

(b) Players' jerseys must be marked with numbers of between 8 to 15cm. (3" to 6") high on the chest and numbers of 15cm. (6") high on the back. The width of the material forming the number shall be 2cm. (¾").

In international matches, the captain shall wear a badge on the left side of his chest, measuring 8cm. by 1.5cm. (3" x ½") in a different colour to that of the jersey.

(c) Members of a team must appear on court dressed in clean, presentable strips of the same colour.

In cold weather, it is permissible to wear numbered training suits.

241

Art. 2.   Composition of Teams and Substitution:

(a) Number of players: A team shall consist of six players regardless of the circumstances. The composition of a complete team, including substitutes, may not exceed twelve players.

Before the start of a match, the names of all players, including substitutes, must be recorded on the score-sheet. Players not so listed may not play in the match.

(b) Substitutes: Substitutes and coaches must be on the side of the court opposite the referee.

Substitutes may warm up outside the playing area, providing they return to their designated place afterwards.

(c) Substitution of players: Substitution of players is made when the ball is dead, upon request from either the captain or coach of a team to the referee or umpire.

A team is allowed a maximum of six substitutions per set. Before entering the game, a substitute must report to the scorer in playing strip, and be ready to take his place as soon as authorization is given. If the substitution is not completed immediately, a time-out is charged to the team. In the case of a team having already exhausted the allowable number of times-out, the team is penalized by loss of service or the opponents are awarded a point.

The captain or coach, requesting substitutions shall indicate to the referee and to the scorer the number(s) of the player(s) involved in the substitution. When substitution has been completed, the team may not request a new substitution until play has resumed and the ball is dead again.

(d) Any player beginning the set, may, in that set be replaced only once by a substitute. The original player may go back on court during the same set. However, he must re-enter in the rotational position he previously occupied and must then stay on court for the rest of that set.

Furthermore, no other player except the one originally withdrawn may enter the set to take the place of the substitute. A substitute leaving the game may not re-enter it again in the same set. If a team becomes incomplete through injury to any player and if all other substitutes have been used, he can replace the injured player even if the substitute has already played in another position.

242

If the team becomes incomplete as a result of a player being sent off and all normal substitutions have been carried out, the team loses the set in progress but retains the points it has scored.

Art. 3. Position of Players.

At the time the ball is served:

Players of both teams must be within their courts in two lines of three players, taking positions as follows:

The three players at the net are front-line players, occupying from right to left, positions 2, 3 and 4, while the three players in the back are back-line players, occupying from right to left, positions 1, 6 and 5. The positions of the players on the court must conform to the rotational order recorded on the score-sheet; namely:

In the front line, 3 must be between 2 and 4, and in front of 6. In the back line, 6 must be between 1 and 5, and behind 3. Consequently, 2 must be in front of 1, and 4 must be in front of 5.

As soon as the ball is served:

Players are allowed to move anywhere within the playing area, except under the net into their opponent's court. The rotation order, as indicated on the official score-sheet, must remain the same until the end of the set.

Before the start of each set, the rotational order may be changed but such changes must be recorded on the score-sheet before the set begins.

Art. 4. Error in the Positioning of a Player:

When a team is found to be out of position, play must be stopped and the error corrected. All points made by the team whilst in the wrong position must be cancelled. If the team at fault is serving at the time of the discovery of the error a side-out (change of service) will be called. All points scored by opponents will be retained.

If it is not possible to determine when the error first occurred, the team in error shall resume its correct position and shall be penalized by loss of service or by the award of a point to their opponents.

RULE 6–TEAM COACHES, MANAGERS AND CAPTAINS

Art. 1. Team coaches, managers and captains are responsible for team discipline.

Art. 2. The coach or captain has the right to request a time-out or substitution. During a time-out, he has the right to speak to players, but may not enter the court.

Coaches and managers shall not, during play, contest the decisions of the referee.

Art. 3. The captain is the only player on the court who may speak to the officials.

CHAPTER III

Officials and their Duties

RULE 7–OFFICIALS OF THE MATCH

A match is conducted by the following officials:
one referee, one umpire, one scorer and two linesmen.

RULE 8–THE REFEREE (Located above one end of the net)

The referee controls the game and his decisions are final. He has authority over all players and officials from the beginning to the end of the match, including any periods during which the match may be temporarily interrupted for whatever reason.

The referee has the power to settle all questions, including those not specified in the Rules, and can over-rule decisions by other officials when he considers that they have made a mistake. He must be located approximately 50cm. (20") above one end of the net, in order that he can clearly see the play. In accordance with Rule 4, the referee penalizes bad behaviour of players, coaches and managers.

NOTE: Immediately after the whistle stops play, the referee shall indicate with the use of hand signals the nature of the fault committed and the team which has service.

RULE 9–THE UMPIRE (assisting the referee)

The umpire shall place himself on the other side of the court facing the referee.

244

1. He blows his whistle when a player has crossed the centre line or has illegally played the ball within the attack zone.

2. He points out any contact of the ball with the vertical side markers (flexible sticks) and whenever the ball passes outside them.

3. He times the duration of times-out.

4. He supervises the conduct of coaches and substitutes on the bench.

5. He authorizes substitutions if requested by team captains or coaches.

6. He judges contacts with the net, except those over or near to the top of the net.

7. He checks that the rotational order and positions of the receiving team are correct at the time of each service.

8. He calls the attention of the referee to any unsporting actions.

9. He verifies at the beginning of each set that the initial positions of each team correspond exactly to the order of rotation as shown on the score-sheet.

10. He watches for contact of the ball with any foreign objects.

11. He gives his opinion to the referee in all matters, when so requested.

NOTE: *The ball is considered to be 'dead' when either official blows his whistle.*

RULE 10—THE SCORER

The scorer's position is on the opposite side of the court to the referee and behind the umpire.

His duties are as follows:-

1. Before the beginning of each match, he records on the score-sheet the names and numbers of the players and substitutes, and obtains the signatures of the captains and coaches who are authorized to make substitutions.

2. He records the score as the match progresses, carefully noting substitutions and the number of times-out requested during each set.

245

3. At each new request for a time-out, he shall announce the number of times-out that have been requested during each set.

4. After the toss and before each set, he records on the score-sheet the position of the players on the court (i.e. rotation order). The position of the team serving first is recorded first on the score-sheet.

He shall not give the respective formations of the teams to anyone, except to the officials when so requested.

5. During the set, he shall see that the rotation order is observed.

6. He announces the changing of ends after the end of each set, and after the eighth point made by one of the teams in the deciding set.

7. During the stoppages of play, he points out to officials the number of requests for times-out.

8. At the end of the match, he presents the score-sheet to the referee and umpire for signature.

RULE 11–THE LINESMEN

Where there is only the minimum number of two linesmen, they should sit at diagonally opposite corners of the court, (not the service area corners), at a distance of one metre (three feet) indoors and three metres (ten feet) outdoors.

Each linesman watches the side lines and the end-line nearest to him. The linesmen signal to the referee. They raise their flag when the ball is 'out', and point it downwards when the ball is 'in'.

The referee can request the linesmen to signal with their flags when a ball which was out, was contacted by a player on the receiving team's side.

The linesmen also draw the attention of the referee to errors made by players when serving or when a ball passes completely outside the vertical side markers.

CHAPTER IV

Rules of the Game

RULE 12–DURATION OF THE GAME AND CHOICE OF ENDS

Art. 1. Number of Sets in a Match:

246

All international matches are to be played to the best of five sets.

Art. 2. Choice of Ends:

The captains toss a coin to decide ends and service. The winner may choose either the end he prefers or the right to serve first.

Art. 3. Choice of End for the Deciding Set:

Before the start of the deciding set, the referee makes a new toss of the coin to decide the choice of ends or service.

Art. 4. Change of Ends:

Teams must change ends after each set, except when the following set is the decider. Ends of the court in the deciding set are chosen after the second toss.

Art. 5. Change of Ends in the Middle of the Deciding Set.

When the teams have won the same number of sets and one team has eight points in the decider, the teams will change ends automatically, and the serving will continue by the player who served prior to the change of ends.

If the change of ends was not made at the correct time, it will take place as soon as the referee or one of the captains notices it. The score remains unchanged.

Art. 6. Interruption of Play:

Times-Out:

(a) A time-out may be granted by the referee or the umpire only when the ball is dead.

When the captain or coach requests a stoppage, he must make it clear whether it is for a time-out or a substitution. If he makes no indication, the referee must presume that the stoppage required is a time-out.

(b) During a time-out, the players are not allowed to leave the court and may not speak to anyone except to receive advice of their coach, who, however, may not enter the court.

(c) Each team may take two times-out per set. The length of such times-out is limited to thirty seconds.

Two consecutive times-out may be requested by either team, without resumption of play between them. A time-out may be

247

followed immediately by a substitution requested by either team, and a substitution can be followed immediately by a time-out.

(d) If, in error, a third time-out is requested, it shall be refused and the captain or coach making the request shall be warned. If the offence is repeated during the same set, the offending team will be penalized with the loss of service, or the opponents will be awarded a point.

SUBSTITUTIONS

(e) Following the substitution of a player, play will resume immediately, and no one, including the coach, is allowed to advise the players during a substitution.

(f) IN THE CASE OF INJURY, an interruption of three minutes will be allowed and will not be counted as a time-out. This interruption for injury can only be allowed if the injured player cannot be replaced.

As soon as the referee notices an injury, he shall stop play. The point shall be re-played.

INTERVAL BETWEEN SETS:

(g) A maximum interval of two minutes is allowed between sets. This interval shall be five minutes between the fourth and fifth sets.

The interval includes time spent changing ends and recording rotational orders on the score-sheet.

Art. 7. Interruption of the Match:

If any circumstances (such as bad weather, failure of equipment, etc.) prevent the completion of an international match, the following shall apply.

(a) If the game is resumed on the same court after one or more periods not exceeding four hours, the score in the interrupted set will remain the same, and the game begins where it left off.

(b) If the match is resumed on another court, the score of the interrupted set is anulled. However, the results of completed sets remain. The cancelled set will be re-played under the same conditions as before the interruption.

248

(c) If the delay exceeds four hours, the match shall be re-played completely, whatever court is chosen.

RULE 13—BEGINNING THE GAME AND SERVICE

Art. 1. The Service:

Service is the act of putting the ball into play. This is done by the right-hand back-line player, who hits the ball with his hand (open or closed), or any part of the arm, in order to send the ball over the net into the opponents' court.

The server stands in the service area and hits the ball. At this moment of contact the service is completed.

The ball is struck after having been thrown in the air or released from the hand. The server is not allowed to strike the ball, resting on his other hand.

After striking the ball, the player may land on the line or inside the court, so long as at the moment of impact he was behind the back line and within the service area.

If, after having been thrown or released from the hand, the ball falls to the ground without being hit or contacted the service is re-taken However, the referee will not allow the game to be delayed in this manner.

The service is considered good if the ball passes over the net without touching it, and between the vertical net bands. The service must be made immediately after the referee has whistled. If the service is made before the whistle, it must be taken again.

Art. 2. Duration of Service:

A player continues to serve until his team commits a fault.

Art. 3. Serving Faults:

The referee will blow his whistle and signal 'change of service' when one of the following serving faults occur:

(a) The ball touches the net.
(b) The ball passes under the net.
(c) The ball touches one of the aerials (supposed to be extended indefinitely), or crosses the net outside of them.
(d) The ball touches a player of the serving team or any object before entering the opponents' court.
(e) The ball lands outside the limits of the opponents' court.

249

Art. 4. Serving Out of Order:

If the service is made by the wrong player, the referee shall whistle 'change of service' and that side shall lose all the points scored whilst the wrong player was serving. The players of the team that was at fault shall revert to their correct positions.

Art. 5. Serving in Second and Subsequent Sets:

Serving in each new set is started by the team which did not serve in the preceding set, except in the deciding set, when the first serve is decided by the toss of a coin.

Art. 6. Delaying the Game:

Any act which in the opinion of the referee delays the game will be penalized.

Art. 7. The Screen:

At the moment of service, it is illegal for players of the serving side to wave their arms, jump or form groups of two or more players with the aim of forming a screen to mask the server's action.

RULE 14–CHANGE OF SERVICE

Art. 1. Change of Service:

Service is changed when the serving team commits a fault.

Art. 2. Side-out:

The service will change sides when a 'side-out' is called.

RULE 15–ROTATION

Art. 1. On change of service, the team to serve will rotate one position clockwise before serving.

Art. 2. Change of Position at the Beginning of a New Set:

At the beginning of a new set, the players may change their positions, providing the scorer has received the new line-up before the beginning of the set.

RULE 16–HITTING THE BALL DURING PLAY

During Play:

Art. 1. Each team is allowed a maximum of three successive contacts with the ball. The ball must cross the net on or before the third touch.

250

Art. 2. The ball may be hit with any part of the body above and including the waist.

Art. 3. The ball can contact any number of parts of the body down to the waist, providing that contacts are simultaneous and that the ball is not held but rebounds cleanly.

Art. 4. Contact with the Ball:

A player who contacts the ball or is contacted by the ball shall be considered as having played the ball.

Art. 5. Held Ball:

When a ball rests momentarily in the hands or arms of a player, it is considered as held. The ball must be cleanly hit. Scooping, lifting, pushing or carrying the ball shall be considered as holding.

A ball cleanly hit with both hands from below is considered as 'good'.

Art. 6. Double Hit:

A player contacting the ball more than once with whatever part of the body, without any other player having touched it between these contacts, will be considered as having committed a 'double hit' (exception: Blocking, Rule 17, Art. 4,b.)

RULE 17—SIMULTANEOUS TOUCH AND THE BLOCK

Art. 1. Simultaneous Touch by Opposing Players:

When opposing players hit the ball simultaneously above the net, the player of the team opposite to that receiving the ball is considered to have touched it last.

After such a simultaneous hit by opponents, the team whose side the ball enters, has the right to play the ball three times. If, after the simultaneous hit, the ball lands on the playing area, the team on whose court it lands is penalized; however, if the ball lands outside the court, the team on the opposite side of the net is at fault.

If the ball is held simultaneously by two opposing players, it is a double fault and the point is played again.

Art. 2. Ball Played by two Players of the Same Team:

If two or more players of the same team attempt to play the ball and the ball is touched only by one of them, this shall be considered as one touch only.

251

A player may play the ball whilst in contact with a player of his team. However, no player may be used as a means of support to reach the ball. It is allowed to hold back a player who is about to commit a fault.

When two players of the same team contact the ball simultaneously, this is considered as two hits (except in Blocking, Art.4. below).

Art. 3. Double Fault:

When two opponents commit a fault simultaneously, this is a double fault and the point is played again.

Art. 4. Blocking:

(a) The blocking action is made near the net and consists of attempting to stop the ball coming from the opposite side with any part of the player's body above the waist.
The block can be performed by any or all of the front-line players. Any player is considered as having the intention to block if he places one or both hands above the level of the top of the net, whilst in a position close to the net.

(b) Any player taking part in a blocking action in the course of which the ball is contacted, shall have the right to make a second play at the ball. Such a second shot, however, shall count as the second of the three hits allowed to the team.

(c) If the ball touches one or more players in the block, it will be counted as only one hit for the team, even if these contacts are not made simultaneously by the players in the block.

(d) The three back-line players may not block at the net, but may play the ball in any other position near or away from the block.

(e) The hands of the blockers may reach over the net. However, the blockers shall not contact the ball over the opponents' court until after the completion of the opponents' attack.

Art. 5. When the ball, after having touched the top of the net as well as the opponents' block, returns to the attackers' side, the players of this team have the right to three hits.

RULE 18—PLAY AT THE NET

Art. 1. When the ball touches the net between the vertical side-markers in the course of play (other than when served), it is considered to be good and play continues.

252

Art. 2. To be good, a ball must cross the net completely within the two vertical side-markers (sticks) or their indefinite extension.

Any ball crossing the net completely outside the vertical side-markers may not be played from within the opponents' court.

Art. 3. Ball in the Net Between the Vertical Side-Markers:

Providing the player does not touch the net, a ball hitting the net between the vertical side-markers may be played again (except on service).

If the ball was contacted three times by a team and then touches the net without crossing to the opponents' side the referee shall stop play, but only after the ball has been hit the fourth time or has hit the ground.

Art. 4. Net Touches Player:

If the ball is hit into the net so hard that the net contacts an opponent, such contact shall not be considered as a fault on the part of the latter.

Art. 5. Simultaneous Touch of the Net:

If two opponents touch the net simultaneously, this shall constitute a 'double fault'.

RULE 19–HANDS PASSING OVER THE NET

Art. 1. During the Block:

Touching the ball with the hands over the net in the opponents' court, before opponents' attack is completed, shall constitute a fault.

Art. 2. After the Spike:

Passing hands over the net after a spike is permitted.

RULE 20–CROSSING THE CENTRE LINE

Art. 1. Contact with the Opponents' Court:

Contact of any part of the body with the opponents' court during play constitutes a fault.

Touching the opponents court with one's foot (feet) is not a fault provided that some part of this foot (feet) still remains in contact with the centre line.

It is not a fault to enter the opponents' court after the referee has whistled to stop play.

Art. 2.   Crossing the Vertical Plane of the Net.

Crossing the vertical plane of the net with any part of the body with the purpose of interfering with or distracting an opponent while the ball is in play, is a fault.

Crossing the vertical plane of the net without touching an opponent or the opponents' court, is not a fault.

RULE 21—BACK LINE PLAYERS

Art. 1.   Back line players may not direct a ball from within the attack area into the opponents' court, unless the ball is below the height of the net.

From behind the attack line, they may, in any way permissible, hit the ball into the opponents' court.

A back line player, spiking from the back court, may land on or in front of the attack line, providing his take-off for the spike was clearly behind the attack line.

Art. 2.   Back line players may not take part in a block.

Art. 3.   As the attack line extends indefinitely, a back line player may not hit a ball into the opponents' court from above the height of the net if he finds himself to be outside of the court, but within such extended limits of the attack area.

RULE 22—BALL OUT OF PLAY

Art. 1.   Ball Touching the Net Outside Vertical Side-Markers:

A ball touching the net completely outside the vertical side-markers constitutes a fault.

Art. 2.   Ball Landing Outside:

The ball is considered to be out when it touches the ground or any object outside the playing area.

A ball touching any line is 'in'.

Art. 3.   Dead Ball:

The referee's whistle stops all play. The ball is then 'dead'.

RULE 23—POINT OR SIDE OUT

A team loses service or its opponents gain a point when:

1.   The ball touches the ground.
2.   A team has played the ball more than three times consecutively (Rule 16, Art. 1).
3.   The ball is held or pushed (Rule 16, Art. 3 and 5).
4.   The ball touches the player below the waist (Rule 16, Art. 2 and 3).
5.   A player touches the ball twice consecutively (Rule 16, Art. 6). Exception: Blocking (Rule 17, Art. 4,b.).
6.   Team is out of position at service (Rule 5, Art. 4).
7.   A player touches the net or the vertical side-markers (including the flexible sticks) (Exception: Rule 18, Art. 4 and 5).
8.   A player crosses completely the centre line (Rule 20. Art. 1).
9.   A player spikes the ball above the opponents' court (Rule 19, Art. 2. and clarification 19.2 and 18.4).
10.   A back-line player, whilst in the attack area, hits the ball into the opponents' court from above the height of the net (Rule 21).
11.   A ball does not pass over the net between the vertical rods or their assumed extension (cf. Rule 18, Art. 2–Rule 13, Art. 1 and 3).
12.   A ball touches the ground or an object outside the court, (Rule 22, Art. 2).
13.   A ball is played by a player who, in turn, is assisted by a player of his own team as a means of support.

After having touched the ball, a player can touch a post without committing a fault.

14.   A player receives a personal warning, (Rule 4, Art. 4).
15.   A team, after a warning, receives deliberate instructions from coach, manager or substitutes (Rule 4, Art. 3.e).
16.   When faults are committed on both sides of the net, only the first one will be penalized. If both faults are committed simultaneously, the point will be replayed (Rule 17, Art. 3 and Rule 18, Art. 5).
17.   A player reaches under the net and touches the ball or an opponent whilst the ball is on the opponents' side (exc Rule 20. Art. 1).

NOTE: *Crossing the vertical plane under the net is not a fault, providing the player does not touch either the court or an opponent and does not interfere with the opponents' play.*

18.   The game is delayed persistently (Rule 13, Art. 6).

19.   An illegal substitution is made (Rule 5, Art. 2.c and d).

20.   A team requests a third time-out after a warning (Rule 12, Art. 6.d).

21.   Extension of the second time-out beyond thirty seconds (Rule 12, Art. 6).

22.   Delaying of substitution after having used the two times-out (Rule 5, Art. 2.c).

23.   Player(s) leave the court during a time-out or an interruption of play without the permission of the referee (except between sets), (Rule 4, Art. 3.f).

24.   A player stamps his feet or makes gestures aimed at intimidating an opponent, (Rule 4, Art. 3.g).

25.   The block is made in an illegal manner, (Rule 17, Art. 4).

In addition to the above instances, the serving team loses service in the following cases:

26.   If the service is not made from the service area (Rule 13, Art. 1).

27.   If the player touches or crosses the back-line at the moment of serving (Rule 13, Art. 1).

28.   If the service crosses the net with the help of another player on the serving team's side, (Rule 13, Art. 3.d).

29.   If serving is performed out of the rotational order, (Rule 13, Art. 4).

30.   If the service is made incorrectly (Rule 13, Art. 1 and 3).

31.   If the players wave arms, jump or form groups of two or more the purpose of which is to form a screen to mask the server's action (Rule 13, Art. 7).

RULE 24–SCORING AND RESULTS OF THE GAME

Art. 1.   It is a fault when a team fails to return the ball over the net correctly.

This fault will be penalized by the opposition winning a point or services.

Art. 2.   A set is won when a team has scored 15 points and has at least a 2 points lead over their opponents.

If the score is tied at 14/14, the set continues until one team has a lead of 2 points, (e.g. 16/14, 17/15, 18/16, etc. . . .).

Art. 3.   Forfeits:

256

The game shall be forfeited by a team which refuses to play after the referee has asked for the game to be started. The score will be recorded as 15/0 for each set, and three sets to nil for the match.

This does not apply when the game is uncompleted due to injury, (Rule 5, Art. 3.d).

RULE 25–DECISIONS AND PROTESTS

Art. 1. The decision of the referee cannot be appealed against during the match.

Art. 2. Any dispute concerning an interpretation of the rules must be resolved on the spot by the referee. Only the captain of the disputing team may speak to the referee.

Art. 3. Protests:

If the explanation of the referee, following a protest of the captain, is not satisfactory, the captain may appeal to a higher authority. The referee shall continue to control the game and will later make out a report concerning the protest.

COMMENTARIES OF THE RULES OF VOLLEYBALL

RULE 1–PLAYING AREA AND LINES

1. Height of Ceiling:
For the Olympic Games, there must be a clear space of 12m. 50 above the court. For the final rounds of the World Championships or similar competitions, the same clear space is required unless a special concession is made.

2. Dimensions of Playing Area: variations

(a) A clear space of 3m. should surround an open air court.
(b) A clear space of 2m. should surround an indoor court.

For the Olympic Games there should be a clear space of 8m. behind the back-lines and of 5m. beyond the side lines. For the final round of the World Championships and similar competitions the same dimensions are required, unless a special concession is made by the FIVB.

(c) The line judges' chair and the referee's stand must be such that they present the least possible obstacle on court. If a chair or the stand obstructs a player, the referee can ask the point to be played again.

3. Other Factors:

(a) The court must be flat and horizontal. However, for outdoor courts a slope of 5mm. per metre is allowable for drainage.

(b) The ground: the game may be played indoors or out, on a hard surface, on beaten earth or on fine cinders. Indoors, the floor may be on natural ground or made out of wood. The court should not be on cement, sand or grass.

4. Courts that are Unsuitable:

The court must be approved by the special Referees' Commission in charge. Nevertheless the court must be under the referee's control before a match. He alone is responsible for deciding whether or not it is fit for play. The referee will declare the court unfit for play in the following cases:

(a) if snow or rain has made the court soft or slippery.

(b) when play could be dangerous (excessive cold can make the court so hard or uneven that there would be the risk of players being hurt.

(c) when fog or darkness make it impossible to officiate properly

5. If the weather is bad (thunderstorms, showers, high wind etc.), the referee can postpone the match or, if the match has already begun, interrupt it, (Rule 12, Art. 7).

6. Court lines made from wood, metal or other solid material are not allowed for outdoor courts: the ground might erode, causing the lines to stick out and become dangerous to the players. This ruling also applies to lines made from brick or other hard material and for the same reason hollowed-out lines are not recommended.

The court lines should be marked before the beginning of the match. On an outdoor court the lines must be made in some way—whether with whitewash, chalk or another substance—which does not make the ground uneven.

Indoors, the lines must be of a different colour to that of the floor. It is advisable to use light colours (white or yellow) which are the most visible. The lines, 5cms. wide are included in the area of the court. The home team is responsible for marking them correctly.

RULE 2—THE NET

1.   Round posts are preferable since they are convenient for the referee and present no danger to the players. They must be of a length that allows the net to be fixed at the correct height.

Fixing the posts to the floor by means of wires should be avoided.

2.   The height of the net must be measured before the match and at any other time that it might be necessary. The measurement should be made in the centre of the court but the referee must be sure to check that the height at each end of the net is within permitted variation.

3.   The referee must also check that the vertical side-markers and rods are perpendicular to the side and centre lines.

4.   The net must be tight throughout its length.

RULE 3—THE BALL

1.   Balls used for any international match must be those approved by FIVB.

2.   The referee must check before and during the match that the ball is in order.

3.   A ball that has become wet or slippery must be changed.

4.   Pressure: the pressure of the ball, measured with a special pressure gauge, must be between 0.48 and 0.52 kg/cm^2. However, the structure of the ball may affect the maximum variation of pressure allowed; for this reason, the judges of international competitions may reduce this margin of difference, within the above range.

The match organizers must provide the referee with a special pressure gauge.

Scoreboard

No special recommendations are made as to the size of the scoreboard. It should be divided into two parts. The names or initials of the two teams should be shown at the top.

Information shown on the scoreboard is for convenience only and may not be used as a basis of disagreement.

RULE 4–RIGHTS AND DUTIES OF THE PLAYERS

1.   The referee is responsible for the conduct of the players under his control. Under no circumstances may he allow incorrect or unsporting behaviour nor rude remarks from the players.

Only the referee is empowered to warn a player, or to warn him and mark this on the score-sheet. Only the referee may disqualify a player. If the captain asks, the referee must give his reasons for the decision and must not allow any further discussion. Should there be disagreement, team captains may state their case in writing on the score sheet, after the match.

2.   The other officials (the umpire, the scorer and the line judges) must immediately report to the referee any rude remark that is made by a player about the officials or about his opponents.

3.   All actions penalized by loss of service, by a point for the opposition, or by the loss of a point or of service, as well as the disqualification of a player must be recorded on the score-sheet. The reasons for the disqualification must also be noted.

A first warning involves no penalty.

RULE 5–PLAYERS' STRIP, COMPOSITION OF TEAMS AND SUBSTITUTIONS

1.   Numbering of Players:

Each player must wear a number on the front and back of his shirt. This number may be between 1 and 99. Numbers are obligatory, but they can be worn in any order.

2.   Colour of Strip:

When two opposing teams have strips of the same colour, the home team must change, if possible. If this happens when a match is played on neutral ground, the team entered first on the score-sheet must change if it has another strip.

If the temperature is low, the referee may allow players to wear tracksuits, provided that the tracksuits of a team are all the same and are numbered.

3.   Number of Players:

Under no circumstances may a team play with five players.

260

4. Substitutions:

Only the coach or captain of a team may ask the referee or the umpire for a substitution. When they do this, the player(s) going on court must already be standing beside the scorer's table so that the substitution can be made immediately.

The captain or coach must first announce the number of substitutions and then the numbers of the players concerned. It is preferable to indicate first the number of the player coming off court and then the number of his substitute. For example,

(a) one substitution, Number 6 is replaced by Number 8;
(b) three substitutions, Number 4 is replaced by Number 9, Number 3 is replaced by Number 12, Number 1 is replaced by Number 10.

If the substitutions are not made in this way and play is delayed, a time-out will be accorded to the offending team.

During substitution, the player or players leaving court, and their substitutes going on court, must raise one hand so as to be easily recognised by the scorer.

Referees are particularly reminded that the substitution must be immediate and that if two or more substitutions are to be made, they must be made in the same time that is allowed for a single substitution.

If a player is replaced this must be counted as a substitution. When more than one substitution is made, even if several are made at the same time, each substitution counts against the number allowed to the team.

5. Position of Players:

At the moment the ball is served, (i.e. the moment the ball is hit by the server), the back-line players must be at least a little behind their corresponding front-line players. It is a fault if a back-line player is the same distance from the net as his corresponding front-line player. The position of players is judged according to the positions of their feet.

It is at the moment the server hits the ball that the players must be in a correct position. Any positional fault must be signalled by the umpire or the referee, as soon as the ball has been hit. If one of the teams make a positional fault and the service is also incorrect, it is

261

the first fault which is counted. When the server hits the ball correctly, but there is a fault during the flight of the ball (touches team-mate, touches the net or goes out of court) and the receiving team is out of position, it is the fault of the receiving team that is counted.

RULE 6–TEAM MANAGERS, COACHES AND CAPTAINS

The team managers, coaches and captains must know the rules and abide by them strictly.

During the match, a player may not speak to the referee or the umpire on behalf of his team. In no case may the referee allow such an intervention.

To the left and right of the scoreboard, benches are to be placed. Only one or two trainers, a doctor or masseur and the reserve players can be seated on such benches.

The coach of each team marked on the score-sheet can only speak to the referee and the umpire in order to ask for a time-out or a substitution.

A coach may not give instructions to his players during the match (except in times-out and between sets) nor may he argue with or protest to the referee or umpire. The same applies, throughout the match, to all other persons on the team bench.

On the first occasion such a fault occurs in any one set, the referee must warn the team concerned. On the second occasion a further warning is made and noted on the score-sheet and the team in fault is penalized by loss of service or his opponent gains the point.

RULE 8–THE REFEREE

His responsibilities during the game:

The referee is responsible for the correct conduct of the match. He must blow his whistle whenever he judges it to be necessary and at the beginning and end of each point. Each rally is considered to be finished when the referee blows his whistle. Generally speaking, the referee should only interrupt play when he is sure that a fault has been committed. He should not blow his whistle if there is any doubt.

262

Should the referee need to deal with anything outside the field of play, he should ask the organisers and players to help.

If the referee is sure that one of the other officials is not fulfilling his functions as defined by the Rules, he may over-rule the decisions of that official and even dismiss him.

Should an interruption occur, particularly should spectators invade the court, the referee must suspend the match and ask the organisers and the captain of the home team to re-establish order within a set period of time. If the interruption continues beyond this period of time, or if one of the teams refuses to continue playing, the referee must instruct the other officials to leave the court with him. The referee must record the incident on the score-sheet and make out a report that he must send to the Commission concerned within 24 hours.

RULE 8—THE UMPIRE

Whenever a time-out is asked for, the umpire takes possession of the ball and signals to the referee the number of times-out already claimed by each team. He then tells the captain and coach of each team the number of times-out they have had.

The umpire will only allow a substitution when the player who is to go on court is standing ready near to the scorer's table.

Should the referee suddenly be indisposed, the umpire must take charge of the game in his place.

RULE 10—THE SCORER

The scorer, when asked, must tell either of the coaches or captains the number of substitutions and times-out they have already been given. At the beginning of each set the coaches must give the scorer a piece of paper on which the line-up of their players is marked. The scorer must control the order of service. He must score each point and make sure that the score on the scoreboard corresponds with the score-sheet.

The scorer must write down all remarks and incidents that lead to a player being disqualified.

RULE 11–LINESMEN

Whenever the linesmen want to attract the attention of the referee to a fault committed by a player or to rude remarks made by a player, they must raise their flag and wave it from right to left.

For important competitions, it is better to use four linesmen than two.

Linesmen should be positioned on the extension of the lines.

Linesmen shall be standing.

RULE 12–DURATION OF THE GAME, CHANGING ENDS, TIMES-OUT

1. Times-Out:

As soon as a time-out has been requested, the ball must be given to the umpire.

Times-out may be shortened if the captain or coach who asked for them wishes.

The extension of the first time-out is penalized by automatic accordance of the second time-out, whose entire length may then be used. The extension of the second time-out will be penalized by the referee as a serious offence and is recorded on the score-sheet (cf. Rule 4, Article 4, Paragraph 2).

If the captain or the coach of either team asks the umpire for a time-out or a substitution after the referee has blown his whistle, the umpire must refuse. If however, the umpire blows his whistle and play is stopped, the team asking for the time-out is not penalized; the point is restarted.

2. Changing Ends During the Final Set

Changing ends during the final set must be done without any interruption. No instructions can be given to the players as they change over. The players must adopt the same positions on court as they were in before the change.

As soon as the change has been made, the scorer must make sure that the players are in the correct positions.

RULE 13–BEGINNING THE GAME, SERVICE:

If the server throws the ball in the air but doesn't hit it and if it touches some part of his body as it falls, this counts as a fault and the ball is given to the other team.

Service cannot be made with two hands (e.g. with a dig).

At the moment he hits the ball, the server may not touch or step on the back line of the court. However, he may jump or move forward. As soon as the ball has been hit, the server may land on the end line or inside court, as he completes his serving action.

If the served ball touches the net at the moment the opposing team is whistled for a positional fault, the server's team scores a point.

The service is a fault when
(a)   the player serves from outside the service area,
(b)   the ball is thrown or pushed,
(c)   the player serves with two hands,
(d)   the wrong player serves,
(e)   the ball is not thrown or released before it is hit.

The referee must whistle for service as soon as he considers that all the players are in position and ready. The service must be made as soon as the referee blows his whistle. The referee will allow a delay of about five seconds after blowing his whistle.

The server may make a second and last attempt at service, for which he is allowed an additional five seconds. If the player does not serve within these time-limits he commits a serious offence which must be penalized by loss of service for his team.

The server is not allowed to delay his service after the referee's whistle, even if he considers that the players in his team are in the wrong positions or are not ready.

In order to clarify the interpretation of Rule 13, Article 6, it is necessary to explain that any attempt to delay the game must be penalized by the referee; after the first warning, the referee must penalize the team concerned by denoting it as a serious offence.

RULE 14—CHANGE OF SERVICE

At each change of service, the team winning service must rotate. Accordingly, at the beginning of a set, only the team serving the first ball remains in the same position. When this team makes a mistake, the opposition must rotate before serving.

RULE 15–ROTATION

Rotation must be clockwise. In the back row, the player in the right-hand corner moves to the centre and the player in the centre moves to the left-hand corner. This means that the player on the right in front moves to the right-hand corner in the back and serves. In this way each player occupies each of the six positions in succession.

Only as the server hits the ball must the players be standing in a particular position; at this moment they must be in the order noted on the score-sheet. As soon as the ball has been hit, the players can move wherever they like, switching within the front and back lines and between the two lines of players.

At the beginning of each set, the teams can change their line-up by putting on new players or by changing the order of the players already on court. However, the scorer must be notified before the set, of any changes that are to be made. The coaches or captains must give the scorer a piece of paper on which the line-up is marked.

If a team forgets to tell the scorer of any changes before the beginning of the set (i.e. before the referee blows his whistle for the first service), the players must line-up as for the preceding set.

RULE 16–HITTING THE BALL DURING PLAY

1.   The volley must be brief and instantaneous. When the ball has been hit hard (with a service or a spike) it sometimes stays very briefly in the hands of the player who receives it. In this case, a volley that· is played from below or a volley where the ball is received high in the air should not be penalized.

The following ways of volleying the ball should not be counted as faults:

(a)   When the sound made is different to the sound made by a finger-tip volley, but the shot is still played simultaneously with both hands, and the ball is not held.
(b)   When the ball touches the player's finger-tips and immediately rebounds behind him.
(c)   When the ball is volleyed correctly and the player's hands move backwards, either during or after the volley.

2.   Simultaneous Touch:

266

The ball may touch several parts of the body at the same time but if it does not do so simultaneously, this constitutes the fault of "double touch".

3. Double Touch:

The double touch fault is judged by sight: to judge it by sound is unreliable, especially if the match is played before a large number of spectators who intentionally make a noise to disguise what they think may be a fault.

It is the referee who must decide whether or not the ball has been played correctly.

4. If a player has accidental contact with any object beyond the ends of the net (e.g. a post, cables etc.) this should not be counted as a fault, provided that such contact has no effect on the sequence of play.

RULE 17–SIMULTANEOUS TOUCH AND THE BLOCK

1. Article 1 of this rule is designed to ensure the continuity of play. The referee must whistle only if the ball rests momentarily between the hands or arms of opposing players (two, or more players when the blocks are two–or three–man). The ball must then be replayed without a point or change of service being awarded.

2. The struggle and confusion that can occur between players in the same team, in an effort to play the ball, already constitutes a sufficient handicap to that team without there being any penalty awarded by the referee; the referee must therefore avoid calling a double touch whenever two players attempt to play the ball at the same time. The referee should only penalize a double touch when he has seen it clearly.

3. The referee must decide whether two or more faults, that have been made and each signalled by one of the officials, occurred at the same time. If they did not occur simultaneously he must state which occurred first.

4. The Block:

Each ball directed toward the opposing court can be blocked by one or a group of the opposing front line players, including the service. The members of a two- or three-man block must be placed close to each other and close to the net, if they are to be considered as a composite block and to benefit from the rule allowing any touch, even a touch that is not made simultaneously by the players involved, to be counted as a single touch. If the third front line player is separated from the other two players but also attempts a block and also touches the ball, this shall count as a second touch.

A player can only block above the opposing court after the opposition's first or second touch if, in doing so, he does not prevent any opposition player from playing the ball the second or third time. The arms and hands of the blockers may be in any position whatsoever. A player is considered to attempt a block whenever he tries to prevent the ball crossing the net.

The ball may be touched by one or more players taking part in the block, even if it can be seen that during the block the ball rapidly touched

(a)   the hands or arms of one player after another,
(b)   the hands or arms of several players, one after the other,
(c)   the hands of one or more players and then some other part of the body above the waist.

In all these cases, a single touch is counted.

On the other hand, if, after the ball has touched the block, one of the players plays the ball again with another action, this counts as his team's second touch.

When the ball touches the top of the net as well as the hands of an opposing blocker, the block is counted and the attacking team is allowed another three touches.

When a blocker touches the ball by putting his hands over the net, even over the side-bands or at a position completely outside these side-bands, his action is allowed and considered as a normal block.

Hence it is not a fault to make a block at a position outside the side-bands. Wherever such a block is effective,

(a)   The block outside antennae is allowed.
(b)   The touch by the blocker(s) of the cable supporting the net is not allowed.
(c)   Ball returned by the blocker(s) to the spiker's side remains in play normally.
       —if it lands out of court, it is the blocker(s) mistake
       —if it lands inside the opponents' court it is the opponents' mistake, since he was allowed to play three touches.

268

(d) After a block made outside the antenna, should the ball pass from outside or over the antenna into the blocker(s) court, the ball remains in play and the blocker(s)-team are allowed two more touches. (Exception to Rule 18 Point 4 of the Commentaries).

RULE 18—PLAY AT THE NET

1. If after the third touch the ball goes into the net, the referee must not blow his whistle until after the fault is committed (i.e. until the ball touches the ground or is played for the fourth time).

If the ball hits the net in such a manner that it subsequently rolls over the net, but the referee has stopped the play prematurely, the referee shall direct a play over.

2. If the ball goes into the net between side-bands, it can be played again (except on service) provided the player does not touch the net.

3. If the net is torn by the service, service is lost. If it is torn during a point, after the ball has crossed the net on service, the point must be played again.

4. If, during the play, the ball crosses the vertical plane of the net below the net or outside of the vertical rod (or its assumed extension), it may be returned to the playing team's side by a team-mate, providing the ball has not yet completely crossed the vertical plane when such contact is made.

RULE 19—HANDS PASSING OVER THE NET

1. When one or more of the blockers touch the ball on the opposite side of the net, after the opposing team has completed its action of directing the ball to their opponents, this does not constitute a fault. On the other hand, if they contact the ball above the opponents' court during the play (pass or set) or before the opponents have completed their action of directing the ball across the net, this constitutes a fault.

2. A player is not allowed to spike the ball on the opposition's side of the net but if he hits it in his own court and then follows through across the net, without touching the ball or an opposing player, such an action does not constitute a fault.

RULE 20—CROSSING THE CENTRE LINE

A player may put his hands under the net, in order to play a low ball near to the net, provided that he does not obstruct an opposing player.

Under no circumstances may a player move on to the opposing court before the referee or the umpire has whistled to denote the end of a point or an interruption.

RULE 21 – BACK-LINE PLAYERS

1.   A back-line player who is inside the attack zone may only play the ball directly into the opposition's court if, at the moment he plays it, the ball is not completely above the level of the top of the net.

2.   If a back-line player, along with blockers, lifts his arms towards the ball as it comes across the net, and the ball touches him or any of the players in that block, it is a fault: back-line players may not block. However, if the block containing the back-line player does not touch the ball, the attempt to block is not considered to be a fault.

GLOSSARY OF VOLLEYBALL TERMS

Attack line;
A line drawn across the width of the court parallel to the net in each half, 3 metres from the centre line.

Attack area;
The area between the attack line and the centre line. A back court player may not direct the ball from within the attack area, into the opponents' court, unless the ball is below net height when struck. If the player takes off behind the attack line he may hit the ball in any way and at any height before he lands in the attack area.

Back line player;
Players in positions 1, 6 or 5 at the time of service.

Block;
The block is the counter to the smash. The opposing players jump up and place a wall of hands in the path of the smashed ball with the intention of blocking its path across the net. Only front court players may block.

Covering the smash;
When a player is smashing the ball his team mates come closer to him in case the block sends the ball back into their court. They will then be in a good position to play the ball before it touches the ground.

Dead Ball;
After the official has blown his whistle, the ball is dead and substitutions and times-out may take place.

271

Dig pass;
The ball is played on the outstretched forearms. This pass is used when the ball is travelling fast or very low.

Double foul;
Players on opposite sides of the net simultaneously commit faults. The referee orders the point to be replayed.

Double touch;
One player touches the ball twice in succession or the ball touches two parts of his body at different times.

Dump;
Instead of smashing the ball the attacker plays the ball with his fingertips just over or, to the side of the block.

Fake attack:
An attacking player approaches the net, sometimes calling for the ball, with the intention of drawing the opponents' block so that the player who actually smashes the ball will have an easier shot.

Floating service:
The ball is hit in such a way that the serve moves through the air without any spin, thus giving it the appearance of floating in the air. The serve can dip or swerve suddenly when the speed drops.

Front court player:
One of the players in positions 4, 3 or 2 at the time of service.

Held ball:
A ball that is held simultaneously by two players above the net during the blocking action. The point is replayed.

Hook serve:
A style of serving the ball which involves making a circular arm movement starting from the thighs culminating in contact above the head.

Hook smash:
The same style of arm movement as used for the hook serve, but used to smash the ball.

Match:
A match is played the best of three or five sets.

Penetration:
The practice of bringing a back row setter into the front court to set. This means that the front court setter can act as a third smasher.

Rally:
The complete unit of play from the service until play is stopped by the referee and a point or side out is awarded.

Recovery dive:
A technique used to play balls well in front of or, to the side of players. By diving towards the ball and playing it on the back of the hand before landing, the point is saved.

Referee:
The chief official in the game. He sits at the side of the court so that he looks along the top of the net.

Rotation:
On regaining service teams rotate one position clockwise so that a new player comes to the serving position.

Service area:
A three metre channel of indefinite length is formed by the extension of the right sideline and the serving line which is marked three metres from this sideline. The server must be in this area when he contacts the ball.

Set pass:
This is the volley pass which is played near to and above the net for the smasher to hit.

Setter:
The player whose job it is to play the set pass. A specialist player is normally used because the job is demanding and requires a high level of skill.

Shoot set:
Sometimes known as the parallel set. It is played fast and low across the court for the smasher to hit. When timed effectively it results in a very fast attack.

273

Short set:
A set played near to the setter and only a short distance above the net. This also is a very fast method of attacking.

Smasher:
The more common name for the spiker. He is the player whose job it is to complete the attack by hitting the ball across the net on the third touch.

Spiker:
The American term for smasher.

Substitution:
Six players are on court at a time and a team may have a further six players off court. These players can be changed by the process of substitution when the ball is dead. A maximum of six substitutions may be made in each set by each team.

Switching:
The technique of changing the positions of players during the rally so that a more effective line up is obtained.

Time-out:
Each team may halt play for two periods of thirty seconds each, in each set. Times-out are used by the coach to give his team advice.

Umpire:
The second official in the game. He stands opposite the referee and moves up and down the sideline on his side of the court.

Volley pass:
The main pass in the game. It is played on the fingers of both hands simultaneously in such a way that the ball does not come to rest.

3 RESULTS

RESULTS OF MAJOR VOLLEYBALL TOURNAMENTS.

1st European Championships Rome 1948

1) Czechoslovakia
2) France
3) Italy

4) Portugal
5) Belgium
6) Holland

2nd European Championship Sofia 1950

1) Russia
2) Czechoslovakia
3) Hungary

4) Bulgaria
5) Poland
6) Rumania

3rd European Championships Paris 1951

1) Russia
2) Bulgaria
3) France
4) Rumania
5) Yugoslavia

6) Belgium
7) Portugal
8) Italy
9) Holland
10) Israel

4th European Championship Bucharest 1955

1) Czechoslovakia
2) Rumania
3) Bulgaria
4) Russia
5) Yugoslavia

8) France
9) Italy
10) Albania
11) Finland
12) Belgium

| 6) Poland | 13) Austria |
| 7) Hungary | 14) Egypt |

5th European Championship Prague 1958

1) Czechoslovakia	11) Albania
2) Rumania	12) Turkey
3) Russia	13) Holland
4) Bulgaria	14) Finland
5) Hungary	15) Egypt
6) Poland	16) Tunisia
7) Yugoslavia	17) Belgium
8) France	18) Austria
9) East Germany	19) West Germany
10) Italy	20) Denmark

6th European Championships Bucharest 1963

1) Rumania	10) Italy
2) Hungary	11) Turkey
3) Russia	12) Holland
4) Bulgaria	13) Belgium
5) Czechoslovakia	14) Finland
6) Poland	15) West Germany
7) Yugoslavia	16) Austria
8) France	17) Denmark
9) East Germany	

1st World Championships Prague 1949

1) Russia	6) France
2) Czechoslovakia	7) Hungary
3) Bulgaria	8) Italy
4) Poland	9) Belgium
5) Rumania	10) Holland

2nd World Championships Moscow 1952

1) Russia	7) Poland
2) Czechoslovakia	8) India
3) Bulgaria	9) Lebanon
4) Rumania	10) Israel
5) Hungary	11) Finland
6) France	

3rd World Championships Paris 1956

1)	Czechoslovakia	13)	Holland
2)	Rumania	14)	Italy
3)	Russia	15)	Portugal
4)	Poland	16)	Israel
5)	Bulgaria	17)	Belgium
6)	U.S.A.	18)	Korea
7)	France	19)	Cuba
8)	Hungary	20)	Austria
9)	China	21)	India
10)	Yugoslavia	22)	Turkey
11)	Brazil	23)	Luxembourg
12)	East Germany	24)	West Germany

4th World Championships Rio de Janerio 1960

1)	Russia	8)	Japan
2)	Czechoslovakia	9)	France
3)	Rumania	10)	Venezuela
4)	Poland	11)	Argentina
5)	Brazil	12)	Paraguay
6)	Hungary	13)	Uruguay
7)	U.S.A.	14)	Peru

5th World Championships Moscow 1962

1)	Russia	11)	East Germany
2)	Czechoslovakia	12)	Holland
3)	Rumania	13)	Korea
4)	Bulgaria	14)	Italy
5)	Japan	15)	Israel
6)	Poland	16)	Mongolia
7)	Yugoslavia	17)	Albania
8)	China	18)	Finland
9)	Hungary	19)	Austria
10)	Brazil	20)	Belgium

6th World Championships Prague 1966

1)	Czechoslovakia	12)	Holland
2)	Rumania	13)	Brazil
3)	Russia	14)	Belgium

4) East Germany
5) Japan
6) Poland
7) Bulgaria
8) Yugoslavia
9) China
10) Hungary
11) U.S.A.

15) Turkey
16) Italy
17) Cuba
18) France
19) Finland
20) Mongolia
21) West Germany
22) Denmark

7th World Championships Sofia 1970

1) East Germany
2) Bulgaria
3) Japan
4) Czechoslovakia
5) Poland
6) Russia
7) Rumania
8) Belgium
9) North Korea
10) Yugoslavia
11) Hungary
12) Brazil

13) Cuba
14) Holland
15) Italy
16) Mongolia
17) France
18) U.S.A.
19) Israel
20) Finland
21) Iran
22) Tunisia
23) Venezuela
24) Guinea

Olympic Games Tokio 1964

1) Russia
2) Czechoslovakia
3) Japan
4) Rumania
5) Bulgaria

6) Hungary
7) Brazil
8) Holland
9) U.S.A.
10) Korea

Olympic Games Mexico 1968

1) Russia
2) Japan
3) Czechoslovakia
4) East Germany
5) Poland

6) Bulgaria
7) U.S.A.
8) Belgium
9) Brazil
10) Mexico

WOMEN'S TOURNAMENTS

1st European Championships Prague 1949

1) Russia
2) Czechoslovakia
3) Poland
4) Rumania

5) France
6) Hungary
7) Holland

2nd European Championships Sofia 1950

1) Russia
2) Poland
3) Czechoslovakia

4) Rumania
5) France
6) Hungary

3rd European Championships Paris 1951

1) Russia
2) Poland
3) Yugoslavia

4) France
5) Holland
6) Italy

4th European Championships Bucharest 1955

1) Czechoslovakia
2) Russia
3) Poland

4) Rumania
5) Bulgaria
6) Hungary

5th European Championships Prague 1958

1) Russia
2) Czechoslovakia
3) Poland
4) Rumania
5) Bulgaria
6) Hungary

7) Yugoslavia
8) East Germany
9) France
10) Holland
11) West Germany
12) Austria

6th European Championships Bucharest 1963

1) Russia
2) Poland
3) Rumania
4) East Germany
5) Bulgaria
6) Czechoslovakia
7) Hungary

8) Yugoslavia
9) Holland
10) Turkey
11) West Germany
12) Austria
13) Denmark

279

1st World Championships Moscow 1952

1) Russia	5) Rumania
2) Poland	6) Hungary
3) Czechoslovakia	7) France
4) Bulgaria	8) India

2nd World Championships Paris 1956

1) Russia	10) Holland
2) Rumania	11) Brazil
3) Poland	12) France
4) Czechoslovakia	13) Belgium
5) Bulgaria	14) Israel
6) China	15) Austria
7) East Germany	16) West Germany
8) Korea	17) Luxembourg
9) U.S.A.	

3rd World Championships Rio de Janeiro 1960

1) Russia	6) U.S.A.
2) Japan	7) Argentina
3) Czechoslovakia	8) Peru
4) Poland	9) Uruguay
5) Brazil	10) West Germany

4th World Championships Moscow 1962

1) Japan	8) Brazil
2) Russia	9) China
3) Poland	10) Korea
4) Rumania	11) Hungary
5) Czechoslovakia	12) Holland
6) Bulgaria	13) West Germany
7) East Germany	14) Austria

5th World Championships Tokyo 1967

1) Japan	2) U.S.A.
3) North Korea	4) Peru

6th World Championships Sofia 1970

1) Russia	9) Poland

2) Japan
3) North Korea
4) Hungary
5) Czechoslovakia
6) Bulgaria
7) Rumania
8) Cuba

10) East Germany
11) U.S.A.
12) Mexico
13) Brazil
14) Peru
15) Holland
16) Mongolia

Olympic Games Tokyo 1964

1) Japan
2) Russia
3) Poland

4) Rumania
5) U.S.A.
6) North Korea

Olympic Games Mexico 1968

1) Russia
2) Japan
3) Poland
4) Peru

5) North Korea
6) Czechoslovakia
7) Mexico
8) U.S.A.